China and the Superpowers

China and the Superpowers

ROY MEDVEDEV

Translated by Harold Shukman

Basil Blackwell

© Roy Medvedev 1986

First published 1986

Basil Blackwell Ltd
108 Cowley Road, Oxford OX4 1JF, UK

Basil Blackwell Inc.
432 Park Avenue South, Suite 1505,
New York, NY 10016, USA

British Library Cataloguing in Publication Data

Medvedev, Roĭ A.
  China and the superpowers.
  1. Soviet Union – Foreign relations – China
  2. China – Foreign relations – Soviet Union
  3. Soviet Union – Foreign relations – 1945–
  4. China – Foreign relations – United States
  5. United States – Foreign relations – China
  6. United States – Foreign relations – 1945–
  I. Title
  327.47051   DK67.7.C6
  ISBN 0-631-13843-9

Library of Congress Cataloging in Publication Data

Medvedev, Roy Aleksandrovich, 1925–
  China and the superpowers.

  1. China – Foreign relations – Soviet Union.
  2. Soviet Union – Foreign relations – China.   3. China –
  Foreign relations – United States.   4. United States –
  Foreign relations – United States.   5. United States –
  Foreign relations – China.   I. Title.
  DS740.5.865M43 1986   327.51047   85-22337
  ISBN 0-631-13843-9

Typeset by Joshua Associates Limited, Oxford
Printed in Great Britain by
Billing and Sons Ltd, Worcester

Contents

Acknowledgements

The publisher is grateful to the following for permission to reproduce the plates: The BBC Hulton Picture Library for 'Women guerillas on parade' and 'Mao Zedong's fourth wife, Jiang Qing'; Camera Press for 'Soviet troops leaving Port Arthur', 'Khrushchev and Mao Zedong in Peking', 'Mao Zedong as The Rising Sun', 'Cast of the Shanghai–Peking Opera', 'Mao Zedong and President Nixon in 1976' and 'Alexei Kosygin and Zhou Enlai in 1969'; The Photo Source for 'Demonstrators in Peking'; Popperfoto for 'Poster proclaiming friendship', 'Poster showing caricature of the Gang of Four', 'Jiang Gai-shi aboard the USS *Wasp*' and 'Ronald Reagan and Li Xiannian in 1984'; and the Xinhua News Agency for 'Mao Zedong making a report to cadres in 1942', 'Chinese leaving for the Front' and 'Dr Henry Kissinger meets Mao Zedong in 1973'.

Introduction

In the complex world that has evolved since the end of the Second World War, only five states have been declared Great Powers. Two of them, France and China, although they were weak in 1945, were none the less given the power of veto in the United Nations Security Council by courtesy of the three members of the 1945 Yalta Conference, the USA, the USSR and Great Britain. Time, economic development and the logic of the arms race have put Great Britain in the same league as France, their influence no longer global in scope, but more or less limited to Western Europe and some of their former colonies. This has left only three countries as Great Powers, simply by virtue of their being the greatest in military power, in wealth and in population within the groups of nations they lead, one way or another, that is the industrial–capitalist, the industrial–Communist and the developing or Third World nations.

Among the Big Three, each has its own unique advantages: China, the oldest civilization and largest human potential; the Soviet Union the largest territory, richest natural resources and the first successful Communist revolution, which gave it an entirely new kind of political weapon; and the United States the richest and strongest economy in the world, and its democratic traditions. All three were close allies during the Second World War, and though the alliance survived the war, it has not survived the peace. Their interrelations – always as changeable and complex as the interactions of three planets in space, moving in relation to one another under the influence of mutual attraction and mutual repulsion alike – are similarly closely related to the internal developments of each of them.

The history of Russo-Chinese relations – contradictory and complicated – go back hundreds of years. Those between the

United States and China are also more than a hundred years old, and from studying both, we can see how illogical and artificial the Sino-Soviet conflict was during its sharpest phase in the 1960s, when mutual threats and confrontation were the order of the day, and how naïve and illusory was America's intention to try 'to play the China card' in order to advance American foreign policy, as well as America's attempts to use China as a surrogate or even substitute for American power in the Far East and Pacific.

Countries with global ambitions usually either have or have to create a chief adversary. The Soviet Union's global ambitions have mainly been ideological, while those of the United States are chiefly economic. The global ambitions of the Chinese People's Republic were closely connected with Maoism, which managed to thrive with *two* chief adversaries, one being Soviet 'revisionism', the other the imperialist policies of the United States. With the death of Maoism and the end of the global ambitions of China's brand of Communism, it was only natural that regional interests would render unnecessary China's desire to see the United States as a real adversary. Similarly, Chinese antagonism towards the Soviet Union has lost its ideological and political point, and only conflicts of a local character, such as Afghanistan and Kampuchea, remain as serious obstacles to the normalization of Sino-Soviet relations.

I do not believe that the United States policy which sees China as a counterweight to the Soviet Union shows a correct understanding of the Sino-Soviet conflict. Soviet policy towards China has similarly often been wrong and sometimes very dangerous. At the same time, the Chinese perception of both the Soviet Union and the United States, especially during the Maoist era, was false and did great damage to the economic and political development of China itself. Both the United States and the Soviet Union now want to help China, but for different and selfish reasons. The development of a strong China, however, is important for the rest of the world and for world peace only if this great country becomes more independent and more neutral. It is important as a potential counterweight to the two military superpowers.

There is a great amount of literature on the Sino-Soviet conflict at its different stages. This book is not intended as a comprehensive review or complete analysis of the subject, but is rather an attempt to discover a pattern in the complex picture of the past, and to trace possible tendencies for the future. My own interest in China goes back many years. On graduating from Leningrad University in 1950–2, I chose for my postgraduate thesis to analyse the history and characteristics of the Chinese revolution which, both in the forms it took and the nature of its driving forces, was so very different from the Russian revolution. My thesis adviser was Professor G. V. Yefimov, the noted sino-logist and Dean of the Oriental Studies Faculty of Leningrad University. I kept up my interest in China, and in subsequent years closely followed both events there and everything that was published on China in the Soviet Union, and at times I also followed what was being said about Sino-Soviet relations in the Western press.

There are many highly expert sinologists in the Soviet Union, and yet everything published here in the past 25 years on recent Chinese history or Sino-Soviet relations, as well as Sino-American relations, is stamped with tendentiousness and consti-tutes propaganda rather than academic research. Given the continuation of militant Chinese anti-Soviet agitation, it is hard for the time being to expect anything objective on Sino-Soviet relations to come out of China. Nor have Western China specialists succeeding in filling the gap satisfactorily. The German and American books on contemporary China that I have managed to get hold of contain interesting and important material, but they, too, are regrettably not free of tendentious-ness, especially when they deal with Sino-Soviet relations, and the main theme of many of them is the notorious 'China card'.

These circumstances have prompted me to try to draw together the results of my own reflections, my observations and the analysis that I have devoted to the subject for many years. I have tried as far as possible to be objective, and to avoid any propaganda clichés. To be sure, a Soviet historian who is an independent researcher to boot is invariably bound to suffer from a lack of sources and materials. Moreover, for an author living in Moscow, it is not easy to write a book on international problems. Many of the Western and Chinese sources that I have used in this book are not currently available in the Soviet Union, and I would therefore like to express my gratitude to my brother, Zhores, now living in London, and to many of my Western friends who, knowing that I intended to write on the subject, have supplied me for many years with books and papers published in the West, and with Western translations of Chinese publications. I am also grateful for the help I have received from friends here in Moscow who helped me by translating from French and Chinese. I am myself responsible for the translation of the German sources that I have used in my research.

Finally, I would be very grateful for any critical comments from my readers, as well as any offprints, clippings and other materials which might indicate errors in my judgement, and which would bring my knowledge of the problem up to date. When one lives in a country where the official policy of the government is both to limit and to shape in a particular way the information available to the general public and the academic community alike, all the help one can get from foreign colleagues is invaluable.

Nearly all the events I have here described took place before my eyes. Many of them I felt deeply, and I related to them not only as a historian, but as an interested witness. I have written my book with a feeling of immutable respect for China and for the great Chinese nation, and for the American nation, but also with a feeling of love for my own country and its people. I feel a deep sense of hope and a desire for the peoples of the Soviet Union, the United States and China to share a future of peace and benevolent co-operation, despite all the differences, which regrettably – or maybe for the good of all mankind – will separate our countries and our peoples for a very long time.

Roy A. Medvedev
Moscow May 1985

1

The USSR and China:
relevant historical events

The Soviet Union and the national-democratic
revolution in China

As early as 1911, countless armed mass actions in various
regions of China had led to the successful Wuchang uprising,
from which ensued the Shanghai revolution under the leadership of Sun Yat-sen. Despite the overthrow of the Manchu
Imperial dynasty which followed, Sun Yat-sen was compelled to
decline power as the first president of the Republic of China.
Even so, the revolutionary struggle continued with varied
success, led by the army of the Kuomintang which Sun Yat-sen
had created. By 1917, the influence of this party was limited to
only a few regions of Southern China, chiefly in the province of
Canton (Guangdong). On 25 August 1917 in the capital city of
Canton (Guangzhou) the decision was taken to create a Military
Government of Southern China to be led by Sun Yat-sen. In the
rest of China, the warlords were locked in fierce struggle to
capture the capital of the country in the hope of securing for
themselves recognition as the central government.

While the 1917 October Revolution was taking place in
Russia, the Anhwei group of warlords, led by Duan Qirui, held
power in Peking and the northern provinces of China. This
government, which declared war on Germany, and was recognized by virtually all capitalist countries as the 'legal' government of the whole of China, refused to conduct any talks
whatsoever with the government of Soviet Russia, and after the
onset of the Intervention by the Western powers and Japan, it
sent small detachments of Chinese troops into Siberian territory
and the Far East with the main object of giving support to the
Japanese.

The Civil War in Russia, however, resulted in the defeat of the White armies and the Interventionists. In the summer of 1919, the Red Army began a major offensive against the forces of Admiral Kolchak, 'Supreme Ruler of Siberia', and all his allies. The Soviet government published its famous declaration of 25 July 1919, addressed 'To the Chinese people and the governments of Southern and Northern China', in which the RSFSR repudiated all the unequal treaties and privileges by which tsarist Russia had bound China, and it offered to begin talks with a view to working out a new treaty, based on the recognition of China's full equality and independence. This important document declared:

> After two years of war and unbelievable effort, Soviet Russia and the Red Army are crossing the Urals to the East not in order to do violence, not in order to enslave anyone, and not in search of victories. ... We bring freedom from the yoke of the foreign bayonet and foreign gold which together have been stifling the enslaved peoples of the East, first and foremost among them the people of China. We bring help not only to our own toiling masses, but also to the Chinese people, and we repeat once more what we said to the Chinese people at the time of the Great October Revolution of 1917, and what no doubt the venal American–European–Japanese press kept from them.

The government of the RSFSR announced its repudiation of the indemnities imposed upon China at the time of the Boxer Rebellion of 1900, as well as all agreements with Japan which concerned China and which had been concluded between 1907 and 1916. It expressed readiness to enter talks with China over the cancellation of the 1896 treaty and the Peking Protocol of 1901. The declaration went on: 'The Soviet government repudiates all the conquests by the tsarist regime which seized Manchuria and other provinces from China. Let the nations inhabiting those areas decide for themselves within which state borders they wish to live.'[1]

The Chinese government in Peking did not respond to the declaration, but the first diplomatic contacts between the RSFSR and China were established after the defeat of Kolchak, and even trade relations were renewed, albeit on a very modest scale.[2]

Relations of a more intensive nature were carried on between the RSFSR – renamed the USSR in 1923 – and Sun Yat-sen's revolutionary government of South China, where there was for a time a group of Soviet diplomats, led by A. A. Yoffe, while a military delegation from Sun Yat-sen, under the leadership of Jiang Gai-shi (Chiang Kai-shek), was sent to Moscow. In 1923 the Soviet government provided financial aid to the government of Sun Yat-sen and despatched a team of military and political advisers to South China, led by M. M. Borodin, P. A. Pavlov and B. K. Blyukher. The reorganization of the Kuomintang and the revolutionary Chinese army was carried out by these military and political advisers, and a special military academy was established at Whampoa. Meanwhile, numerous military personnel from the Kuomintang and the Chinese Communist Party – which had been formed in 1921 – were undergoing training in Soviet military academies and schools. At various times, Lin Biao, Deng Xiaoping, Wang Ming and others all studied in Moscow. Jiang Gai-shi, who had been through Japanese military school, spent several months in the USSR studying Red Army war experience. The Chinese Communist Party (CCP) formed a political and military union with the Kuomintang, which at that time was considered to be the most influential revolutionary party in China, while Jiang Gai-shi was regarded as Sun Yat-sen's closest deputy and successor.

By the autumn of 1924, the complicated conflicts among the warlords of northern China had resulted in the growth of influence and power of the nationalist generals who, wishing to exploit Sun Yat-sen's popularity to their own advantage, invited him to visit Peking and take part in a proposed national conference on the country's military and political problems. Sun Yat-sen set sail from Guangzhou (Canton) to Shanghai in November 1924 accompanied by both his own Chinese as well as a number of Soviet advisers. Among the convoy escorting the party out of the harbour was the Soviet warship *Vorovsky*. The trip had enormous propaganda value, but unfortunately Sun Yat-sen, already seriously ill, was unable to return to Guangzhou, and died in Peking on 12 March 1925. The day before he died, and in the presence of the party leaders, he signed two political documents, one his 'Testament to the Kuomintang' and the other a 'Message to the Soviet Union', which read:

Dear Comrades! In parting from you, I want to express my ardent hope that the dawn will soon break. The time will come when the Soviet Union, as a good friend and ally, will welcome a powerful and free China, when in the great struggle for the freedom of the downtrodden nations of the world, both countries will go forward hand in hand and achieve victory.[3]

The history of relations between the Soviet Union and China, however, turned out to be much more complex and dramatic. The new dawn for which Sun Yat-sen had hoped came only a quarter of a century later, and soon the sky above our two countries was once again darkened by clouds of misunderstanding and hostility.

I do not propose to discuss here the events which took place in China in 1925–7: they were merely the initial phase of the national-democratic revolution. The problems connected with those events were under constant discussion, both in Comintern and within the Communist Party of the Soviet Union – at that time still called the All-Russian Communist Party (Bolsheviks) – indeed, the issues of the internal forces and policies of the Chinese revolution became the cause of a fierce factional struggle within the Chinese Communist Party itself, as well as within the Russian Communist Party and Comintern. The revolution brought the Kuomintang (KMT) to power in China, partly thanks to the revolutionary armies' victories over the warlords of the North, but also partly thanks to the compromise made by the most powerful of the warlords with the new leaders of the KMT who had destroyed the union with the Chinese Communist Party and unleashed mass terror against its members.

Diplomatic relations were established between the Soviet Union and China with the signing in Peking on 31 May 1924 of an 'Agreement on general principles for regularizing issues between the Union of Soviet Socialist Republics and the Republic of China'. The new Chinese government, headed by Jiang Gai-shi and based by its own choice in the city of Nanjing, conducted an anti-Soviet policy and had to contend with an equally hostile attitude on the part of the Soviet Union. Matters went as far as a short but sharp armed skirmish between the two sides over the seizure of the Chinese Eastern Railway by Chinese troops. The Chinese forces were defeated by the Special Far Eastern Red

Army under the command of B. K. Blyukher, former adviser to the KMT. The matter was settled with the signing of an agreement at Khabarovsk on 29 December 1929, according to which the question of the railway was restored to the previous position. Diplomatic relations with the central KMT government were, however, broken off and were not restored until 1932.

After the treachery of the KMT, the Chinese Communist Party tried to carry on under the old slogans, but it suffered a number of painful defeats in the largest cities of South China. The CCP in particular took upon itself the role of sole leadership of the revolutionary movement of the peasants, workers and lower middle classes. But a new strategy and tactics of revolutionary struggle needed to be worked out.

The discussions over past events as well as the outlook for the Chinese revolution had given rise to a series of conflicts between Soviet and Chinese Communist leaders even before the end of the 1920s. The Soviet party was the dominant force in Comintern and Stalin regarded himself as entitled to interfere in all important matters affecting other communist parties, including even the selection of their leading cadres. The heightened factional struggle within the CCP only facilitated this interference. Events in China, however, were moving along a different path from that imagined by both many Soviet and many Chinese leaders.

It was precisely at the time when the revolutionary movement in the big cities went into decline that a mass revolutionary movement in the remote countryside began to grow. Mao Zedong (Mao Tse-tung) was not the only Chinese Communist leader who recognized the highly important role to be played in the revolution by an armed peasant movement. The most prominent organizer and theoretician of the peasant movement in China was Peng Pai, a member of the Central Committee of the CCP who died in a KMT prison in 1929. Peng Dehuai, He Long and Zhang Guotao all became organizers of Communist power bases in the villages. An authentic, new 'alternative' party leadership began forming in the remote countryside with the group led by Mao Zedong and Zhou Enlai (Chou En-lai) playing the most important role.

The main centres of the CCP at the end of the 1920s were located in Moscow, where in 1928 the party's Sixth Congress took place, and in Shang-hai. Mao's plans to transfer the centre of the revolutionary struggle in China from the large cities to remote rural districts were viewed with reservation, not to say outright hostility, by many Soviet and Comintern leaders. And as the influence of Mao Zedong's group increased, so the ability of Moscow and Comintern to exercise influence over the formation of CCP policy diminished. Nevertheless, Moscow had to face facts. The remarkable successes of the Soviet movement in the rural districts, the formation there of a peasant Red Army, the proliferation of revolutionary support bases, and then the formation of the Central Workers' and Peasants' Government, all brought about a change in Comintern's attitude to the partisan movement of the Chinese peasantry. At the beginning of the 1930s, the journal *Communist International* carried a number of articles praising the successes of the Soviet regions in China, the chairman of the Workers' and Peasants' Government, Mao Zedong, as well as the commander of the Red Army, Zhu De. In due course, Comintern recommended that the CCP's governing institutions be transferred from the underground in Shanghai to one of the support regions of Soviet China.

The period 1931 to 1937 was a time of extraordinarily complicated military and political struggle between, on the one hand, the CCP and the Chinese Red Army, and, on the other, the troops of the KMT and groupings of local warlords. It was a time of victories and defeats, of the Long March and the continuing factional struggle within the leadership of the CCP. In the final outcome, it was Mao Zedong and his closest comrades-in-arms who concentrated the leadership of both party and army in their hands.

An extremely contradictory picture of the factional struggle in the CCP, as well as of the attitude of the Soviet Communist Party and Comintern towards the various factions of the Chinese leadership, emerges from the sources, whether from Soviet accounts published at different times, or Chinese official publications, memoirs of *émigrés*, such as the former CCP Politburo members Zhang Guotao and Wang Ming, or the books and memoirs of foreign participants in the events, for example Otto Braun,[4] or the research of Western sinologists and specialists on the history of Communism. Soviet books and articles published in the 1970s contain a great deal of criticism of Mao Zedong, who is accused of every kind of error and even criminality.[5] It is impossible to judge the validity of these accusations, especially as so many of these publications display a blatant political bias. What is beyond doubt, however, is that the victory of Mao Zedong and his group was due to something more than ambition, cunning and craftiness. Undeniably, it was precisely Mao Zedong who during those years was able to formulate the strategic aims that best conformed to the new phase of the Chinese revolution, aims that made it possible for the CCP and its armed forces to gain several important victories over the armies of the KMT, and that gave Mao Zedong authority as the most powerful political and military strategist, with the greater part of his political capital in the party guaranteed.

After decades of internal wars, in 1937 the Chinese people found themselves faced by new ordeals. Having earlier occupied Manchuria, the Japanese now launched a broad offensive against other regions of China. The Japanese army defeated the KMT troops and took Peking, Tianjin, Nanjing, Zhangjiaokou, Baoding and, by the end of the year, Shanghai. Japan had set out rapidly to subjugate the whole of China and to install a pro-Japanese puppet government. The KMT was compelled to offer armed resistance, and all over the country mobilization began in order to raise an anti-Japanese patriotic movement and repel Japanese aggression.

By 1937 the Chinese Communist Party still controlled only a few spacious, but sparsely populated, regions in the north-west of the country. The size of both the party and the Red Army had been severely diminished, and it was very difficult to maintain contact with the underground organizations in the cities. The war with Japan, however, decisively altered the internal political circumstances in the country. The KMT could not now decline the CCP's offer to co-operate. Jiang Gai-shi had to recognize the legality of the CCP and the Red Army, whose main forces were now renamed the Eighth National-Revolutionary Army. In the autumn of 1937, the central executive committee of the KMT published a manifesto on collaboration between the KMT and the CCP, and the Soviet Union welcomed the announcement.

Counting on a speedy victory in China, Japan had prepared herself for the capture of many other countries in Asia and also for an attack on the Soviet Union, and Japanese troops began to concentrate systematically along the Soviet border. Serious clashes between Soviet and Japanese forces in the Far East occurred in 1937 in the region of Lake Hasan and two years later on Mongolian territory in the region of the River Khalkin Gol. Naturally, the Soviet Union looked to China as an ally. To help the KMT army command, the Soviet Union sent a team of military advisers, and units of the Soviet Air Force were despatched to various fronts in China.[6] The Soviet Union also provided a certain amount of help to the Eighth Army and to the Special Zone which was the chief support base of the CCP. Apart from a number of doctors, some political representatives were also sent to the Special Zone and served there chiefly as observers. But under the circumstances, this help was barely significant.

During the years of the war with Japan, the Chinese Communists slowly but surely strengthened their positions and increased their influence in the country. It was precisely under the leadership of the CCP that the partisan movement developed in the regions under Japanese occupation. New support bases were created there and new armed forces which were soon combined to form the Fourth National Revolutionary Army. All this increased friction between the Chinese central government, now located in Chongqing under Jiang Gai-shi, and the CCP. A sudden assault by the KMT on the Fourth Army's headquarters, and an ensuing order from the KMT War Council announcing the disbandment and division of the Fourth Army between the Chinese Communist Party and the KMT, provoked the outbreak of undeclared war which, while helping the Japanese to increase the territory under their occupation, did not arrest the growth of the CCP's influence and the spread of anti-Japanese support bases under its control. The Fourth Army was reinstated and strengthened.

The German invasion of the Soviet Union, and the Red Army's failures during the first phase of the war, resulted in a reduction of immediate Soviet military aid to China, but in global terms the two countries remained allies. The war in China was one of the factors restraining the Japanese from invading the Soviet Union, while the concentration of the large and well-armed Guangdong Army on the Soviet frontier made the war on other fronts more difficult for Japan.

Relations between the central committee of the CCP and the Soviet leaders in the years 1941 to 1945 were far from untroubled. Serving as Comintern's liaison with the CCP, and also as Tass war correspondent in the Special Zone, was P. P. Vladimirov. His diaries, published many years after his death, bear such blatant signs of 'editing', however, that they cannot be taken as a reliable source, but nor can they be totally disregarded.[7] Works published before 1960 in the Soviet Union and China do not deal with the differences between the CCP and the CPSU at all, while in later works they are undoubtedly greatly exaggerated.

The history of the Second World War is sufficiently well known. The USSR and Japan were not formally in a state of war at the beginning of 1945, nor was the outlook very clear. The United States did not yet have the atomic bomb and it was in general still hard to predict whether such a weapon was feasible. England and the USA were afraid that after the total defeat of Germany, which was imminent, they would be dragged into an exhausting war in the Far East and this somewhat inhibited them from taking a sufficiently active part in the solution of Europe's problems. Therefore, at the Yalta Conference of February 1945, a secret agreement was reached on the entry of the USSR into the war against Japan three months after the defeat of Germany.

Only a few months later, however, the situation had changed. The atomic bomb had been made, and American troops had scored impressive victories over the Japanese fleet. The United States and Great Britain, apprehensive of the growth of Soviet influence in the Far East, were now no longer enthusiastic about the Soviet Union's participation in the war with Japan. The Soviet Union, however, had already completed its preparations, and on 8 August 1945 the Soviet government announced that from the next day it would consider itself in a state of war with Japan.

The movement of Soviet troops in Manchuria was swift and after only a few days the main force of the Guangdong army had been destroyed. On 14 August 1945 the Soviet Union and the Chinese republic signed a treaty of friendship and alliance, although the KMT government was in no position to fulfil many of its provisions.

As early as the end of April 1945, the CCP had under its

control territory amounting to almost one million square kilometres with a population of some 95 million. The People's Army
had more than 900,000 men under arms, while the People's
Militia amounted to a further 2,200,000, and self-defence units
accounted for up to another 10 million men. By the middle of
September, the Peoples' Armies, in an offensive launched by
Zhu De on only 10 August, had liberated 315 square kilometres
of territory with a population of 20 million.[8] Japan's unconditional surrender was not especially welcome to the KMT, as in
many regions of China its armies were in no condition to receive
the capitulation of Japanese troops. In many large cities the
Japanese garrisons handed their arms over to the People's
Liberation Army. In the Manchurian territories liberated by the
Soviet Army, a new Chinese administration was created in which
organizations of the CCP had overwhelming influence. The
Soviet Union did not think the advance into Manchuria of units
of the Eighth and Fourth Armies was advisable. However, in
Manchurian territory under the control of the CCP, a United
Democratic Army began forming and the weapons which Soviet
troops had seized as booty from the Guangdong army were
handed over to it.

At the beginning of 1946, the Soviet Union was obliged under
the terms of its treaty with the Chinese Republic to withdraw its
troops from Manchuria. Only a few large cities passed under the
control of the KMT as a result, however, and the Chinese
Communist Party retained control over most of the regions of
Manchuria, Inner Mongolia and north-eastern China. It was precisely this part of the country that became the main political,
economic and territorial base for the development of the
Chinese revolution, although CCP bases in other regions of
China were also strengthened. Speaking at the Eighth Congress
of the Chinese Communist Party, the Defence Minister of the
Chinese People's Republic, Peng Dehuai, said that in September
1945 the armies of the CCP numbered 1.3 million fighters, and
the population of the anti-Japanese bases amounted to 160
million men, creating, in his words, 'a mighty revolutionary force
such as had never been seen in the history of the Chinese
people.'[9]

Stalin and Mao Zedong: the Soviet Union and Communist China, 1946–50

Throughout the entire period from 1935 to 1945, Mao Zedong headed the Central Committee of the Chinese Communist Party, and all fundamental political and military directives issued from him. While the majority of Communists accepted Mao's leadership, he had his opponents and enemies in the party, one of whom was Wang Ming who returned to China having been the CCP's representative in Comintern. The factional struggle that went on in the party leadership, albeit in covert form, did not have the effect of weakening Mao's position; on the contrary, it made it all the more solid. The biggest ideological campaign conducted in the CCP in the early 1940s was that organized by Mao 'for an orderly style of work'. Under the slogans of struggling against dogmatism, subjectivism, sectarianism, and 'foreign stereotyped schemes', Mao managed to break the last serious vestiges of opposition to his leadership.

It should be noted, however, that the group led by Mao was the only one capable at that time of conducting an effective struggle in China against the KMT and the Japanese. For that reason he was supported by other leaders who differed from him in many ways, for example Zhou Enlai, Peng Dehuai, Liu Shaoqi, and later on Gao Gang, each one of whom had his own political base. The elements of nationalism in Mao's politics worked only in his favour during the time of the war for national liberation. Had not Stalin also exploited nationalist slogans during the prolonged and bitter war with Germany and the short war with Japan? China had been so utterly oppressed for over a hundred years that nationalism had become a great transforming force which it would have been absurd to ignore. Mao Zedong was being entirely sincere when he told American journalist Emmy Siao:

The Chinese people are not a flock of obedient sheep. They are a great people with a rich history, a noble national awareness and a lofty understanding of human justice. In the name of national self-respect, human justice and the desire to live on their own land, the Chinese people will never allow the Japanese fascists to turn them into slaves.[10]

It was precisely Communism or Marxism in national colours that led to the formation in China in the mid-1940s of a group of political and military leaders of great stature and experience, the like of which no other Communist party of the time could boast. Naturally, during the anti-Japanese war the Chinese generals deferred to the Soviet generals in their knowledge of modern military technology and the tactics of modern warfare, but they were simultaneously the political leaders of vast regions, whereas Stalin made sure his generals were kept away as far as possible from the political decision-making process. Mao's activities during that time in general helped the CCP to spread its influence in China, and nobody in 1945 could seriously have challenged his ruling position in the party Central Committee.

The Soviet press in the 1970s reproached Mao Zedong and his entourage for having attempted to make contact with the United States at the beginning of the 1940s. But what was criminal in that? America was engaged in a difficult war with Japan, and the main stream of American aid was going to the KMT government. It was perfectly understandable in these circumstances, therefore, to draw America's attention to the possibilities facing the armed forces of the CCP and their need for arms and ammunition. And, in any case, it was precisely at that time that the Soviet Union regarded the United States as an ally in the war against fascism and was not only enjoying substantial economic, military and technical aid from America, but was even insisting that it be increased. The Soviet Union was unable at that time to give the armies of the CCP even the modest degree of help it had given to the liberated regions of China before 22 June 1941, and hence P. P. Vladimirov's complaint that the leaders of the CCP did not give due attention to the small group of Soviet representatives in Yenan rings false and unconvincing.

The situation changed decisively in 1945, when the Soviet Union entered the war against Japan and gave enormous support and aid to the CCP and its armed forces, whereas the United States adopted the course of one-sided and unequivocal help for the KMT. Before the end of the war with Japan, the Seventh Congress of the CCP was convened in the Special Zone in order to set out the contours of the party's political line for the near future, to adopt a new party Statute and complete the formation of the new party leadership. The political report was given by Mao Zedong. Even its title – 'On the coalition government' – was an indication that, having just got rid of the Japanese occupiers, the party was proposing to avoid a civil war and to create a newly democratic society on the basis of a coalition with the KMT. This did not mean, however, that the CCP was prepared to relinquish control over the regions it had liberated, nor to abandon its military formations. The KMT was offered a compromise based on the enhanced role of the CCP and a proposal to introduce anti-feudal and national reforms in the country. In other words, the KMT was offered the chance to participate in the completion of the bourgeois-democratic and national revolution. The KMT of Jiang Gai-shi, however, had long ceased to be a revolutionary party.

The Congress report on the strategic advance against the Japanese was given by Zhu De, while Liu Shaoqi reported on the new party Statute. It was Liu Shaoqi who proclaimed Mao Zedong as 'the leader whom the party had found'. Mao's ideas, which 'united Marxism-Leninism with the experience of the Chinese revolution', were declared to be the ideological basis of the Chinese Communist Party. The cult of Mao, who was now to be called nothing less than the 'great leader of the Chinese revolution', became the political guideline and daily practice for the CCP in the belief that it would consolidate its strength and unity. Today nobody would dispute the harm that the cult of Mao did to both the Chinese Communist Party and the Chinese people. Nor is it disputable that in this the Chinese leaders used as a model the example of the Soviet Union. It was the time when all the large Communist parties emulated the CPSU and found their 'great leader', and the bigger the party or country, the greater or more of a 'genius' its leader.

The period comprising late 1945 and the greater part of 1946 was a time of complex political manoeuvring, with talks between the leaders of the CCP and the KMT, isolated armed confrontations, and preparations for a major civil war. The KMT reinforced its army, which now included troops which the Japanese had organized into puppet formations. The United States supplied Jiang Gai-shi with weapons, ammunition and aircraft, and also sent a number of strong military units, not to speak of countless military advisers and specialists. By the middle of 1946 the KMT had a threefold superiority over the CCP in the terms of regular army numbers.

On the other hand, the CCP was strengthening its own army, as well as its hold over the liberated areas. The Soviet Union withdrew its armies from Manchuria and handed over to the CCP not only a large part of the weaponry it had captured from the Japanese, but also a substantial amount of arms and ammunition taken from Soviet regiments and divisions. A group of Soviet representatives was set up in Manchuria with the task of implementing operational directives in collaboration with the North-Eastern Bureau of the Central Committee of the CCP. The Soviet Union helped with the reconstruction of many factories, highways and bridges; a steady stream of such essential goods as fuel, motor vehicles, cotton fabric, footwear, sugar, salt, medicines and so on flowed from the Soviet Union into Manchuria; Chinese military cadres were given training. To reinforce the rear, the Central Committee decided to resume agrarian reform in the liberated areas. Even though the regular army numbered about 1.5 million men, people's militia units were formed in the liberated areas amounting to more than 3 million men, and self-defence units accounted for a further 10 million.

In the autumn of 1946, the armies of Jiang Gai-shi began a general offensive against the Communist areas of China. In fierce battles the KMT army achieved a number of tactical successes, but it suffered heavy losses, became weary and was weakened by the fighting, and by the spring of 1947 the offensive had been halted. During the previous months the CCP had strengthened its rear and increased the number of its regular troops to 2 million men. Soon the Communists went over to a partial offensive and restored their control over the areas they had previously lost, including many of the large cities of the north-east. Whereas the CCP's control was very firm, the KMT government was incapable of creating a sound power structure in the rest of China, despite the considerable financial, political and military aid it was receiving from the United States.

The Chinese Communists' successes aroused unease in both Washington and Moscow. The Cold War was at its height and it was precisely through that lens that both Truman and Stalin viewed events in China. A 'two Chinas' situation suited Stalin perfectly, as did the analogous 'two Germanys' and 'two Koreas'. Stalin made it very clear that he wanted the CCP to try to obtain from the Kuomintang an arrangement that would somehow preserve a *modus vivendi*, that is to say a compromise by which Jiang Gai-shi's government would retain control of the southern, south-western and central provinces, while the Communists would be able to create their own 'People's Democratic' state in the northern and north-eastern territories where they were in control. This had essentially been Stalin's purpose even as early as the end of 1945, and pressure on the Chinese Communist leaders with that end in view was exerted throughout 1946 and 1947.

Stalin hinted at the desirability of a 'common Far East policy' with the United States during a meeting with the son of the late President Roosevelt. It was glaringly obvious in 1946–7 that neither the Soviet press nor that of the Western Communist parties was giving any information on what was happening in China. The Soviet newspaper reader learned virtually nothing of the large-scale battles between the KMT and Communist armies, nor of the revolutionary transformations going on in north-eastern China. Stalin was convinced that if the Communist offensive developed with further successes, the United States would openly intervene on a massive scale. American intervention would lead to the defeat of the Communists and the occupation of the whole of China by the United States: what Japan had failed to achieve, the United States would achieve with the help of Jiang Gai-shi. China would thus become a vassal of the United States which would hence be able to create its military bases not only in Europe and Japan, but even on the Sino-Soviet border. Stalin voiced these fears in his correspondence with the Chinese leadership.

But he had other still weightier feelings of disquiet, no doubt, about which he said nothing to anybody. He feared the emergence of a Communist state that was more powerful than the USSR and that would be independent of both the USSR and Stalin in its conduct of policy. He knew perfectly well that the Central Committee of the CCP had long been running its own policies and that it had not paid particular attention to Moscow's counsels. Stalin was already having some difficulties with the Communist leaders of Europe, a fact that had led to the creation of Cominform. The choice of Belgrade as the first location of this Communist 'Information Bureau', and of its editorial offices, was no accident. Chinese Communists had not been invited, even as observers, to the meeting in Poland where the decision to create Cominform had been taken.

In this way Stalin facilitated neither a victory for Jiang Gai-shi nor a complete victory for the CCP, since the strengthening of the Chinese Communist Party that would result could undermine the dominating position of the USSR and of Stalin personally in the world Communist movement. The spectre of eastern Titoism seemed to Stalin a greater threat than the Titoism of a relatively small Balkan country. Indeed, while the presence of Russians in Manchuria suited the Chinese Communists, Stalin would admit in 1948 that, after the war, he had advised the 'Chinese comrades' to desist from an actual attempt to come to power.[11]

The leaders of the CCP did not accept Stalin's advice on that occasion. In the latter half of 1947, the People's Liberation Army launched an offensive on a national scale. Led by Deng Xiaoping, Lin Biao, Liu Bocheng and other generals, the CCP armies began their successful drive south, putting pressure on Huai Hai and capturing several of the country's largest cities.

Events unfolded faster than even Mao Zedong had expected. He had reckoned that the war against the KMT would be a long-drawn-out affair, lasting at least five years; yet as early as the second half of 1948 the fundamental breakthrough in the civil war in China had been accomplished, and the main forces of the KMT had been wiped out in a series of systematically executed major military operations. One after another, the country's largest cities came under CCP control: Jinan, Jinru, Zhangzhu, Shenyang, the whole of the north-east and the central valley were liberated from the KMT. In January 1949 Tianjin and Peking were taken. The KMT was still hoping to consolidate its hold in the vast provinces of south-western China, but its hopes there were also dashed. After a short breathing-space, the armies of the CCP renewed their offensive which was now unstoppable. On 24 April 1949, Communist forces captured Nanjing, seat of the KMT government for some time. In May they took Wuhan, Nanchang, and Shanghai. In June all sources of KMT resistance north of the Yangtzijiang (Yangtze) were destroyed. In July and August the main cities and provinces of central-southern, south-eastern and south-western China came under CCP control. By the end of September practically the entire territory of continental China had been freed of KMT troops and only individual, isolated groups continued to show resistance, lasting up to the middle of 1950.

On 1 October 1949 at a solemn ceremony in Peking, the Chinese People's Republic was proclaimed. Mao Zedong was appointed Chairman of the Central People's Government. The revolution had won, even though the liberation of a number of isolated provinces in the south would take a few months more.

The first state officially to recognize the Chinese People's Republic was the Soviet Union, in a declaration published on 2 October, announcing the establishment of diplomatic relations with the new China. No personal letter to Mao Zedong to this effect came from Stalin, however, whose silence was all the more unusual in that only ten days later, on the occasion of the proclamation of the German Democratic Republic, he would send a long personal letter to the first President of the GDR, Wilhelm Pieck, and to the Prime Minister, Otto Grotewohl.

In October and November of 1949, the formation of the Chinese central state institutions took place relatively quickly, in particular the State administrative council, and by the beginning of December, the central government apparatus had virtually been brought up to full strength.

In mid-December 1949, Mao Zedong left China for the first time, heading a large and imposing Chinese delegation to the Soviet Union where, in the company of leaders of other Communist parties, he took part in the celebration of Stalin's 70th birthday. Talks followed, talks which turned out to be long and difficult.

Stalin had few meetings with Mao, and he declined to satisfy many of the requests made by the Chinese government, which was now made to appear in the humiliating role of petitioner. Moreover, difficulties also arose from the fact that Stalin had only recently suffered from a long and serious illness and was making a painful recovery. Finally, the Soviet Union's capacity to help was not yet very great.

Mao and his delegation greeted the New Year in Moscow, but it was not until the middle of February 1950 that a treaty of friendship, union and mutual assistance, to last for 30 years, was signed between the USSR and the Chinese People's Republic. At the same time, an agreement was concluded on the Chinese

Changchun railway, Port Arthur and Dalnii, under which the Soviet Union would retain its naval bases in Port Arthur (Lushun) and Luda (Dalian or Dairen) on the pretext of deterring possible new aggression from Japan.

Before departing, Mao Zedong gave a farewell address at the Yaroslav station in Moscow, in which he said: 'People can see that the unity of two great nations, China and the Soviet Union, reinforced by the treaty, will be eternal, indestructible, and that nobody will ever be able to tear us apart.'[12]

The formation of the Chinese People's Republic was undoubtedly one of the greatest events of the twentieth century. The fact alone of China's unification and the creation of a strong centralized state were of extreme importance. As with Germany and Italy in the nineteenth century, so now the days of a disunited China were past. All three cases came about as the result of historical forces and necessity, but just as Germany's unification without Bismarck, and Italy's without Garibaldi are unthinkable, it is equally hard to imagine China's unification without Mao, although there is no need for us to close our eyes either to his achievements or to his blunders and crimes.

The creation of the Chinese People's Republic changed the geo-political map of the world. Since China declared herself to be the faithful and eternal ally of the Soviet Union, there was no question yet of the formation of a 'strategic triangle'. The West now had to contend not only with the Soviet Union's acquisition of the atomic bomb – it was precisely in 1949–50 that the USSR built and tested its first atomic bombs – but also with the formation of a territorially vast block of allied states stretching from the frontier of West Germany to the South China Sea. Although everybody knew that China was the most populous state in the world, the exact size of the population was not known and was reckoned to be in the region of 450–500 million, but when the first census took place it turned out to be 100 million greater than expected.

The Soviet Union and China: ten years of eternal friendship

China's need for economic and indeed every other kind of aid was somewhat large, while the Soviet Union's capacity was strictly limited. Already, in the period 1946–9, the Soviet Union had done quite a lot to restore the economy of north-eastern China, and now it was said that China was requesting aid to the tune of 3 billion US dollars, but that Stalin would agree to only 300 million, still no mean sum in 1950. Between 1953 and 1960 the Soviet Union undertook responsibility for helping China to build 50 large industrial enterprises, as well as to refurbish and reconstruct the more important branches of its national economy. From the Soviet Union, and soon also from other countries, such as Czechoslovakia and the German Democratic Republic, China began taking delivery of equipment for power stations, metallurgical and mechanical-engineering factories, for coal mines, railway and road transport, and so on. Thousands of young Chinese arrived in the Soviet Union for training in all specialities. It was just at the time I was completing my studies in the Philosophy Faculty at Leningrad University, and in all departments we had Bulgarians, Romanians, Albanians, Czechs and, until 1948 when they had to leave the Soviet Union, Yugoslavs. Young Chinese men and women probably began to appear in our university hostels in the academic year 1949–50, but unlike the Czechs and Albanians, few of them ever made close friends with Soviet students. Nobody, it seemed, worked as hard as the Chinese students.

The basic job of restoring the national economy, which had been destroyed in the civil war, and of creating the various organs of national government and state administration, was completed in the years 1950 to 1952. Agrarian reform was carried out throughout the whole of China. The country's financial system was stabilized and unemployment was to all intents and purposes eliminated. The widespread banditry which was the usual legacy to be expected from civil war, was wiped out by harsh, swift means. All large-scale enterprises were nationalized, while small private industries were preserved.

At the end of 1952, the chairman of the State Council, Zhou Enlai, declared that the period of restoration had been completed and that the level of the national economy was higher than it had ever been before. Hence, from 1953, they would begin to implement the first Five Year Plan for the construction of China's national economy. This plan had been worked out on the assumption of growing technical, economic and scientific aid

from the Soviet Union: 'Learn from the USSR' had been virtually
the main slogan in the early 1950s. For example, in one of his
speeches at the beginning of 1953 Mao said:

> We intend to bring about a great national reconstruction. The work
> before us is hard and our experience is inadequate. Therefore we
> must toil stubbornly, and copy the advanced experience of the
> Soviet Union. Regardless of whether we are members of the Com-
> munist Party, old or young cadre workers, engineers or technolo-
> gists, intellectuals, workers or peasants, we must all learn from the
> Soviet Union. . . . In order to build our country, we must bring the
> job of learning from the Soviet Union up to nation-wide scale.[13]

The Soviet Union and China enjoyed their best relations in
the period 1953/4 to 1957/8. For China, it was a time both of
rapid economic development and major social and political
change. Chief among the social changes was the virtual completion of the collectivization of the peasant and artisan economies
and the transformation of the semi-capitalist economy. At the
end of 1957 the state sector of the entire Chinese economy
amounted to 33 per cent, that of the co-operatives 56 per cent,
the state-capitalist part accounted for 8 per cent, and the private
individual sector only 3 per cent. Private capitalism had practically disappeared from the economy.[14] Many of these social
changes were carried out too hurriedly and gave rise to the illusion that even faster progress was possible. Nevertheless, the
overall economic growth was remarkable and corresponded
more or less to both the needs and the demands of the country.

In the mid-1950s, China built more than 10,000 industrial
enterprises, of which 921 were major enterprises of national
significance, 428 of them being fully commissioned and 109
partially so during the Five Year Plan. Each year the growth of
industrial production averaged 19.2 per cent, instead of the pro-
jected 14.7 per cent, although in absolute terms China's industrial output was still insignificant. Steel output was 5.35 million
tonnes, cast iron 5.94 million tonnes, electricity 19.3 billion kilowatts, coal 130 million tonnes, metal-cutting lathes 28,000.[15] In
real terms, output of the most important kinds of production in
China in 1957 was comparable with Soviet indicators at the end
of the first Five Year Plan in 1932. However, the Soviet popula-

tion at the beginning of the 1930s was only one quarter that of China in 1957. Nevertheless, the results of the first Chinese Five Year Plan must be regarded as a considerable success and an important prerequisite of the country's future development.

Growth in production was not confined to heavy industry. Output of consumer goods went up 89 per cent, railways were extended by 22 per cent to 30,000 kilometres, highways to 250,000 kilometres, air routes to 25,000 kilometres. In five years the number of workers and employees rose from 8 to 24 million.

A tangible increase was also noticeable in the rural economy. The gross yield in food crops increased over the five year period by 22 per cent, and that of cotton by 26 per cent. Livestock numbers rose for pigs, cattle, horses and goats, and technical equipment for farms improved somewhat.[16]

During the first Five Year Plan, China established for herself important economic relations with several capitalist countries, with countries of the Third World and those of East Europe, but by far the greatest help she received in fulfilling the aims of the Five Year Plan in the years 1953–7 came from the Soviet Union.

We mentioned above that Stalin was reserved rather than helpful in promoting the spread of economic aid to China. Yet only two and a half weeks after the death of Stalin, an agreement was signed in Moscow by which the Soviet Union was to help the Chinese People's Republic in the expansion of existing and the construction of new power stations, and two months later another agreement was signed for assistance in the construction and reconstruction of 141 industrial sites, comprising 50 which had come under an agreement of 14 February 1950 and a supplement of 91 large enterprises.[17] The Soviet Union significantly broadened its technical help to China, and a substantial amount of technical documentation was handed over to Chinese enterprises and ministries without charge. By 1953 China's share of the USSR's total external trade turnover amounted to 20 per cent, while the Soviet Union's share of China's total volume of exports was 55.6 per cent.[18]

A Soviet government delegation, consisting of N. S. Khrushchev, N. A. Bulganin and A. I. Mikoyan, attended the fifth anniversary of the founding of the Chinese People's Republic at the end of September 1954. This was the first official visit abroad by the new Soviet leaders. Khrushchev and his colleagues met Mao Zedong several times and they also toured the country widely. Talks between the Soviet and Chinese leaders touched on practically every aspect of relations between the two countries. A large number of agreements were signed in the course of the talks, not all of which were published. The Soviet Union signed an agreement to withdraw its garrison from Port Arthur and to place without cost all military-strategic equipment from the base at the disposal of the Chinese. The Soviet Union gave China its share of the numerous joint stock companies and enterprises, involved in the manufacture of non-ferrous metals, in oil drilling, ship repair and air transport. The decision was taken to commence building railways to China from Ulan-Bator and Alma-Ata. The Soviet Union extended a large new long-term loan, and agreed to increase substantially the number of Soviet specialists working in China, while the number of Chinese undergoing various kinds of training in the Soviet Union was similarly increased. The Soviet Union undertook to increase its deliveries of equipment and to help in the construction of another 15 large-scale projects, and to give considerable aid to the Chinese army in the form of new types of weapons and the training of officers.

These agreements were supplemented over the next four years by a whole host of other agreements: to hand over to China a large quantity of drawings and scientific and technical documentation, to assist in the building of a Chinese experimental nuclear reactor and cyclotron, to exchange exhibitions of each country's achievements in cultural and economic activity, to co-operate in the fields of medicine and sport, education and literature.

In the course of the 1950s, nearly 800 Soviet films were screened in China. A Society for Chinese–Soviet Friendship was formed in China, and one for Soviet–Chinese Friendship came into being in the Soviet Union. When China launched its new Three Red Banners policy in 1958, and its notorious campaign of the Great Leap Forward, the Chinese government requested the acceleration of many deliveries and additions to the list of industrial enterprises being equipped by the Soviet Union. Numerous articles appeared in the Soviet press in the first half of 1958 praising the Great Leap Forward and the People's Communes, but by the latter half of the year it was virtually impossible to find such material any more. Alarming news from China began arriving in

Moscow by various routes, and the whole Three Red Banners policy was arousing considerable concern. Nevertheless, the Soviet Union set out to fulfil the majority of China's requests and greatly increased its aid in 1958 and 1959.

Considering the state and possibilities of the Soviet economy in the 1950s, the scope of Soviet aid to China was very considerable. More than 250 major industrial enterprises, workshops and sites were constructed with Soviet co-operation and equipped with the best Soviet machinery: for example, the Anshan and Wuhan metallurgical complexes, the Changchun automobile factory, the Luoyang factories making tractors, ball-bearings and mining equipment, the Harbin factories making electric motors, turbines and boilers, the Lanzhou oil refinery and synthetic rubber works, the nitrate fertilizer plants at Jilin and Taierzhuang, the slate works at Fujian, the heavy-machinery plant at Fulaerzi, several large power stations and a number of munitions factories, which even today constitute an important part of Chinese industry.

With Soviet help China acquired whole branches of industry that had never existed there before: aviation, automobile and tractor-building, radio and many branches of chemical production. Greatly enhanced capacity was introduced into those industries which had existed on a different technological basis. In overall terms, Chinese production in 1960 from enterprises built with Soviet technical assistance accounted for 35 per cent of cast iron, 40 per cent of steel, more than 50 per cent of rolled iron, 80 per cent of trucks, more than 90 per cent of tractors, 30 per cent of synthetic ammonia, 25 per cent of generated electricity, 55 per cent of steam and hydraulic turbines, about 20 per cent of generators, 25 per cent of aluminium, more than 10 per cent of heavy machinery, and so on.[19]

In the period 1950–60 more than 8,500 technical specialists and 1,500 specialists in science, higher education, health care and culture were sent for varying periods from the Soviet Union to China. The study of Chinese and the training of thousands of translators and interpreters were greatly expanded in the Soviet Union, while in China the study of Russian was even more widely taught. A large number of Soviet military experts worked in China, and at different times more than 1,000 Soviet teachers went there to lecture in the newly created institutes of higher learning. On the other hand, in the 1950s the Soviet Union received about 2,000 Chinese specialists and 1,000 scientists to acquaint them with the experience and achievements of Soviet science and technology.

With the aid of Soviet documentation, 160 sites were planned in China and more than 300 kinds of goods were produced. Joint scientific research projects on 124 subjects were carried out. More than 8,000 Chinese workers, employees and engineers went through production and technical training in Soviet factories in the 1950s, and 11,000 Chinese students and graduates went through Soviet institutes of higher learning and polytechnics. Nearly 900 Chinese scientists worked in the Soviet Academy of Sciences system. China published Soviet literature of all kinds in vast quantities. Chinese economists acknowledged that merely from the free use of the Soviet technical documentation that they had acquired, their country had saved itself several billion dollars. In practice, the Soviet Union and some of the East European countries were China's only source of modern production methods in the 1950s.

Against such a background of active and varied co-operation, isolated disagreements between the two countries went unnoticed. Already in the early 1950s the Soviet press began discussing the question of the so-called 'unequal treaties' in a different way from hitherto. All references to the Address of the Government of the RSFSR to China of 25 May 1919 vanished.[20] The Soviet leaders were clearly dissatisfied with some of the independent actions and decisions which China was taking in its relations with Asian countries and which had not been agreed with Moscow. On the other hand, the Soviet Union did not see any need to consult the Chinese over major acts of its own foreign policy: for example, the sudden *rapprochement* with Yugoslavia, which few expected, or the first attempts at closer relations with the West. The vast campaigns which the Chinese conducted in 1956–7 – building irrigation canals everywhere, the extermination of flies and mosquitoes – and which developed into the policy of the Three Red Banners, were purely Chinese inventions, and Soviet specialists were always critical of such initiatives. On the other hand, the Soviet Union at that time also indulged in adventuristic campaigns, attempting for example to catch up and overtake the United

States in the per capita production of meat, milk and butter. As early as 1954–5 the build-up began of the extremely complex process of Sino-Soviet ideological differences which would become more pronounced after the Twentieth Congress of the CPSU.

As is well known, the world Communist movement in the period from the 1920s to the 1940s was based on hierarchical principles, and although Comintern had been disbanded in 1943, it was still considered that strict unity of views on all basic issues should be adhered to, and that the movement should have a leader. This leader should be not merely one particular party, but one particular man, the most authoritative leader, or, still better, a Marxist–Leninist 'classic'. Up to 1953 there was no doubting that the CPSU was the leader of the world Communist movement, and that the universally recognized Marxist-Leninist 'classic' was obviously Stalin. After his death, however, the situation changed. The CPSU still presented itself as the most authoritative Communist party in the world, if only because it stood at the head of the most powerful socialist state; as for personal leadership, many Chinese believed that the Marx–Engels–Lenin–Stalin line could be continued by only one man, and that was Mao Zedong. In the opinion of many Chinese government people – and pre-eminent among them was Mao himself – not one of the new Soviet leaders could compare with Mao, either in terms of their services to the world Communist movement, or their theoretical contributions to the development of contemporary Marxism. These claims were not made openly, but the fact that the new Soviet leadership dealt with Mao much as they did with the leaders of other large Communist parties and governments of other socialist states, deeply offended Mao's self-esteem.

The Twentieth Congress of the CPSU did more than debunk the cult of Stalin – it also dealt a blow at the cults of other Communist leaders, including Mao Zedong, and this had to be taken into account in China as the materials of the Twentieth Congress became known among the most active members of the CCP. The Chinese press sharply curtailed its eulogies of Mao. The Eighth Congress of the CCP in Peking changed the formulation of the party's ideological foundations, passed at the Seventh Congress, and deleted the phrase: 'The Chinese Communist

Party is guided in all its actions by the thoughts of Mao Zedong, uniting as they do the theory of Marxism–Leninism with the experience of the Chinese revolution.'[21]

Deng Xiaoping devoted his Congress report to the principles of collective leadership and the broadening of internal party democracy, and said:

> Of course, the cult of personality is a social phenomenon with a long history and it could not but find its reflection to some degree in our party and social life. Our task is decisively to continue to carry out the policy of the Central Committee which is directed against over-emphasis on the personality and its glorification; our task is genuinely to strengthen the ties between the leaders and the masses, in order that in all spheres the line of the masses and the democratic principles of the party are carried out.[22]

The Twentieth Congress of the CPSU put forward a number of propositions which ran counter to the views of Mao Zedong, for example on the need to avert a new world war. Although the Chinese press formally upheld the line taken at the Twentieth Congress, on the unofficial level Mao Zedong criticized several of the Congress's propositions. The *People's Daily*, an organ over which Mao himself exercised ultimate editorial control, published barely masked criticism of Khrushchev's secret speech in the form of articles entitled 'On the historical experience of the dictatorship of the proletariat' and 'Once more on the historical experience of the dictatorship of the proletariat'; these were reprinted in *Pravda*.

A more moderate and ambiguous point of view expressed in Peking found its adherents in Moscow, where rumours were circulating about Chinese dissatisfaction with Khrushchev's 'high-risk' policies, and also about unofficial or even secret contacts between the Chinese leadership and Khrushchev's opponents in the Communist Party Central Committee. At any rate, it is clear that it was certainty of firm support from Peking that prompted Molotov, Malenkov, Kaganovich and their supporters to come out against Khrushchev in June 1957. The result of the June 1957 Plenum of the Party Central Committee, however, was a victory for Khrushchev and the consolidation of his position in the Party leadership. Mao Zedong would of course have been delighted had the Molotov group won the day, but he had nevertheless to accept the facts of the situation.

The Chinese leaders followed events in Eastern Europe and the Middle East closely, and all the main measures adopted by the Soviet Union in these areas were taken in consultation with China. However, both the Soviet Union and China dealt with many problems, domestic and foreign, totally independently of each other and without prior consultation. Almost nobody in the Soviet Union could understand the political campaigns of 1956–7, such as the struggle against the 'rightist' elements and the movement that went under the slogan 'let a hundred flowers blossom, let all scientists compete'.

Mao Zedong visited the Soviet Union for the second time in 1957 with a group of other Chinese leaders in order to take part in the 40th anniversary celebrations of the October Revolution. It is known that, following the celebrations, a conference of leaders from socialist countries took place, as well as an international conference of Communist parties. The reports of these conferences have never been published, but in short communiqués it was stated, in particular, that the participants had approved the decisions of the Twentieth Party Congress, as well as the foreign and domestic policies of the USSR. Criticism was aimed chiefly at Yugoslavia, which had not attended the Moscow meetings.

While Mao did not enter into open polemics with the Soviet speakers, his speeches were, however, different from those of many other Communist leaders. This even concerned the question of the possibility of another world war. The line taken by the Twentieth Congress had been that, if a new world war were nevertheless to be unleashed, it would be neither the whole world nor mankind, but imperialism that would perish. The Soviet press did not elaborate further on this formulation, but Mao was in general agreement with the Congress's new line and in his conversations and speeches he frequently elucidated his understanding of this particular thesis. His pronouncements on the subject were not just utterly frank, they seemed to his interlocutors at times even cynical, though it would be several years before the polemics began over many of his formulations. Some of Mao's utterances were not reproduced in the Soviet press until

1963. According to one source, Mao said at the Moscow conference of Communist parties:

> Can one guess at the number of human casualties a future war would cause? It might be one third of the entire 2,700 million of the world's population, that is, 900 million. I think that figure is too small, if atomic bombs really are going to be used. That is terrible, of course, but it would not be so bad if even half were killed. Why? Because it was not we who wanted the war, but they, they, who thrust it on us. If we fight, then atomic and hydrogen bombs will be used. I personally think that there would be such suffering in the whole world that half the world's population would perish, maybe more than half. I argued about this with Nehru. He was more pessimistic about this than I am. I told him that if half the world's population was destroyed, then the other half would be left, but then imperialism would have been utterly destroyed and throughout the world there would only be socialism, and in 50 or 100 years the population would increase, perhaps by more than half again.[23]

While both the CPSU and the CCP kept polemics out of their public speeches, the mutual criticism voiced at closed sessions mounted steadily. As early as January 1957 at a party meeting Mao Zedong – borrowing a quotation from Stalin – said that Khrushchev was obviously 'dizzy with success'. Mao was criticizing Soviet agricultural policy and defending Chinese domestic policy under the slogan 'let a hundred flowers blossom'. Some aspects of Soviet foreign policy were also subjected to criticism, but at the same time many facets of both Chinese domestic and foreign policy were being criticized at closed sessions in the Soviet Union. With some cause, the Soviet leadership doubted whether the Three Red Banners, the Great Leap Forward, the Liquidation of the Four Evils, and a number of other campaigns were correct courses for the Chinese to take. Both parties, let it be said, gave grounds for criticism at that time: both Khrushchev and Mao Zedong committed a number of errors of various kinds at the end of the 1950s.

Just when the Soviet Union was making efforts to improve relations with the United States, China was firing shells at Jiang Gai-shi's troops on the islands in the Straits of Formosa, thus putting great strain on US–Chinese relations. Differences arose between China and the Soviet Union in 1957–8 over military co-operation. The Soviet Union was evidently not keen to supply the Chinese with the technology and technical aid which they needed in order to create their own atomic and hydrogen bombs and rockets. On the other hand, China declined the Soviet proposal to build a special radio station on Chinese territory and also refused the Soviet request that Soviet naval vessels be allowed to enter Chinese ports. The Soviet Union for its part refused the Chinese request for a Soviet-built fleet of nuclear-powered submarines, which annoyed and offended Mao Zedong. To try to iron out these differences, Khrushchev decided to make a secret and unofficial visit to China, where he spent four days, 31 July to 3 August, 1958, meeting Mao every day. Their fundamental disagreements, however, remained unresolved.

A new spate of disagreements between the CPSU and the CCP erupted in the summer and autumn of 1959. The Chinese leaders did not hide their displeasure at Khrushchev's hurried trip to the USA and the prospect of improved Soviet–US relations, and when Khrushchev, soon after his return from Washington, flew to Peking for the tenth anniversary of the Chinese People's Republic, he found a very cold reception waiting for him. Mao Zedong and Liu Shaoqi were at the airport for a polite meeting, but their motorcade drove through empty streets. Mao Zedong, moreover, pleading a heavy workload, avoided long and serious discussion. It was hardly surprising, therefore, that as soon as the official ceremonies were done with, Khrushchev quit China. That was the last time a Soviet leader visited Peking. In the 25 years that have elapsed since that trip, not one summit meeting has been organized between the two countries.

The Soviet Union and China diverged further and further over questions of foreign policy. During the armed border conflict between China and India, the Soviet Union took a neutral position, sympathizing if anything with India rather than China. The differences between the two countries soon began to touch on a whole range of questions involving the national liberation movements in Asia, Africa and Latin America.

Economic relations between the Soviet Union and China also worsened. During China's first Five Year Plan, the USSR had been China's chief trading partner, but in 1959 the volume of

Sino-Soviet trade began to decline sharply. This was due in part to the collapse of the Great Leap Forward, but also to the deterioration of their political relations. Mutual criticism became more and more open; in the Soviet Union one could hear it in the tone of the propaganda, whereas in China it was carried out far more openly. At the same time an exchange of private letters took place. In the spring of 1960 the Soviet government invited Mao Zedong to come to the USSR for a rest and talks, but Mao declined the invitation. Gradually, the disagreements between the USSR and China became the object of discussion in other Communist parties when, in June 1960, the Central Committee of the CPSU sent a special 'Information Notice' to all Communist parties, containing criticism of the doctrinal views of the Chinese Communist leaders and their claims against the USSR. The Chinese leadership similarly sent a special letter to the leading organs of other Communist parties.

Then the Chinese began distributing some of the documents containing their criticisms of the USSR among the Soviet specialists working in China. After several protests, which the Chinese ignored, Khrushchev took a sudden and plainly mistaken decision. On 16 July 1960, the Chinese Ministry of Foreign Affairs was handed a note stating that the Soviet Union was recalling all its specialists. As later events would show, this was a decision that would have had to be taken sooner or later, but in the summer of 1960 it was hasty and politically ill thought out, an example of Khrushchev's impulsive actions that were to become more and more frequent, dictated not so much by sober reasoning as by irritation and impatience.

Just at that moment, China was going through particularly serious economic difficulties, brought about by the collapse of the Three Red Banners campaign; the recall of the Soviet specialists could only deepen and complicate her problems. Khrushchev's step cast doubt on the Soviet assertion that Soviet economic aid to the less developed countries was not bound up with political conditions. The Chinese, moreover, could now claim that many of their problems were precisely connected with the sudden cessation of Soviet economic and technical aid, although that was, of course, an obvious exaggeration. There were in all only 1,600 Soviet specialists working in China in 1960, not a large number for such a large country. However, one should not underestimate the scale of the damage to China, which for a while had to abandon several important projects; and the withdrawal of the specialists was accompanied by a considerable reduction of all other kinds of economic and technical aid.

The recall of the Soviet specialists did not yet signal the complete breakdown of relations between the two countries. Preparations began in the middle of the year for the new International Conference of Communist parties, in which all the Communist parties of the world, except Yugoslavia, would take part. The minutes have never been published, but it is known that the differences between the USSR and China were one of the most important items on the conference agenda. Practically every one of the 81 parties attending the conference in Moscow took the side of the CPSU. The Chinese delegation, headed by Liu Shaoqi, defended its position for many days, but they were isolated and, following the instructions of the Central Committee of the CCP, they signed the closing declaration of the conference.

At the Soviet government's invitation, Liu Shaoqi did not leave Moscow at once, but toured the country and had meetings with Khrushchev, who several times expressed the wish to open a new phase in the development of inter-state and inter-party relations. At first it looked as if this approach might be successful. The *People's Daily* wrote at the time: 'The current visit of President Liu Shaoqi has undoubtedly strengthened and developed still further the great friendship and bond of the peoples of China and the Soviet Union and it has written a golden page into the history of Soviet–Chinese friendship.'[24]

The same words were repeated in Mao's New Year greetings telegrams to Khrushchev and Brezhnev in 1961. But they were only words. The era of the 'great friendship and the bond between the Chinese and Soviet peoples' had come to an end.

The Soviet Union and China: 20 years of hostility

The compromise reached at the end of 1960 between the Soviet Union and China proved to be both unstable and short-lived. China's economic position deteriorated rapidly and this generated a sharp political struggle within the Chinese leadership. Mao Zedong managed to gain the upper hand over a group led by the Defence Minister, Peng Dehuai, which had severely criticized the Three Red Banners policy. Peng Dehuai was removed from office and placed under house arrest, his post now being occupied by Lin Biao who promptly launched a campaign 'to turn the army into a school for the thoughts of Mao Zedong'. In a matter of three months, from July 1960 to February 1961, he dismissed more than 3,000 defence staff. On the other hand, Mao was forced to step down from his post as Chairman of the Chinese People's Republic and to hand it over to Liu Shaoqi, whose supporters had been endeavouring to change, even if only partially, the reckless Three Red Banners policy. Mao remained chairman of the CCP, however, and continued to hold the main levers of power in his hands. The country began to experience hunger, the full scale of which was carefully concealed, and only after many years did it become known that in 1960–1 no less than 6 or 7 million people had died of starvation. Under the circumstances, it was prudent of Mao to move out of the limelight for the time being.

A painful policy of 'adjustment' was now proclaimed. Both industrial and agricultural output were reduced by approximately 30 per cent. Annual turnover of trade with the Soviet Union was cut to a third. The Chinese government declined Soviet help in the construction of 124 sites, but requested that co-operation continue on the construction of 66 existing sites. The volume of Soviet deliveries of complete equipment in 1961 shrank to one fifth.[25] At numerous closed meetings and conferences, the Chinese identified Soviet policy as the most important cause of the failures in the Chinese economy.

For its part, Soviet propaganda was also beginning noticeably to change its judgement and tone when the subject was 'our great and powerful eastern ally'; even as early as 1959–60, a stricter censorship was introduced in all publications about China, and all mention of the Great Leap Forward and the People's Communes was forbidden. I was working at that time in a large Soviet publishing house, and it was obvious to me that Chinese subjects were beginning to disappear from the forward plans of all the biggest publishing houses. As an odd example, a group of Soviet women workers from Ivanovo visited China in 1958 and were shown the latest textile factories and the best People's Communes. A book was written on the basis of their impressions and the materials they had collected, but the publishing authorities in their oblast held up its publication. The book did not come out until 1961, and then it drew sharp condemnation in Moscow. The gross error of the Ivanovo publishing authorities, oblast censorship offices and oblast party committee was discussed at a special session of the Central Committee Bureau for the RSFSR. In the 1950s such Chinese journals had appeared in Russian as *People's China* and *Friendship*, as well as occasional pamphlets, embassy leaflets and so on, but now they were all stopped.

Even so, when the Twenty-second Congress of the CPSU opened in Moscow in October 1962, there among the countless guests were the delegation from China, led by Zhou Enlai, whose speech at the Congress nevertheless contained some oblique criticism of CPSU policy. Pleading other commitments, the Chinese premier left Moscow before the end of the Congress. N. S. Khrushchev personally accompanied him to the airport, which indicated that the Soviet Union did not wish to sharpen the polemics. However, at the very next closed meeting of senior Chinese Communists, Zhou Enlai labelled the Twenty-second Congress 'revisionist', took up the defence of the Albanian delegation, which had left the Congress, and once again laid the chief blame for China's present economic difficulties squarely on the shoulders of the Soviet Union.

Suddenly, in 1962, China utterly refused to take delivery of complete equipment that had been ordered from the Soviet Union and Eastern Europe. Over the next two years, the Soviet Union repeatedly offered to send groups of specialists whose help was essential if the difficult economic problems the Chinese were experiencing were to be solved, but the Chinese government requested such help rarely, and even then they only wanted small groups of ten to fifteen. Cultural exchange between the two countries practically came to a standstill. China ceased publishing Soviet scientific and technical literature, or receiving Soviet documentation, or showing Soviet films. The exchange of all kinds of notes and letters containing every sort of accusation and criticism, however, expanded to greater and greater volume. Memoranda composed in Moscow were despatched to Peking, notes written in Peking went back to Moscow – all this correspondence, it should be noted, still of a confidential nature.

The political quarrel between the CCP and the CPSU – viewed

by President Kennedy as 'America's great hope' – became more open and much sharper in 1963. From the beginning of the year, the *People's Daily* and other Chinese organs began printing a series of articles attacking the policies of the Soviet Union and the CPSU; material that was even cruder and more hostile, both in style and content, was reprinted from the Albanian press; articles attacking the Italian, French, American and other Communist parties started appearing.

In the spring of 1963 the Soviet Union made a new effort to end the polemics which were becoming more and more intense. Khrushchev proposed a meeting of Soviet and Chinese leaders, either at the highest or at a 'high' level. The Chinese side responded by agreeing to a meeting at a 'high' level. Evidently not expecting a meeting to take place, however, they published a lengthy paper, outlining their view of the questions at issue and consisting of 25 points, entitled *Proposals on the general line of the international Communist movement*. There is no sense now in analysing that pretentious, scholastic, extremely dogmatic document. It was not published by the Soviet government, which did not wish to complicate the forthcoming meeting with the Chinese delegation, planned for July, but the Chinese embassy and several other Chinese organizations attempted wherever they could to distribute the *Proposals*, which had been translated into Russian for mass circulation as a sort of Chinese 'samizdat'. Chinese radio broadcasts to the Soviet Union throughout this time carried material and information all critical of CPSU policies. They were not jammed, but nobody listened to them anyway.

The meeting between CPSU and CCP representatives, which began on 5 July 1963, took place in an unpromising political atmosphere. The Chinese side was led by Party General Secretary Deng Xiaoping, and the Soviet side by M. A. Suslov. Just as the talks got under way, the Soviet press published all 25 points of the Chinese *Proposals*, as well as an *Open letter from the Central Committee of the CPSU to all party organizations and all Soviet Communists*, containing an all-out criticism of the 'general line' being proposed by the Chinese Communist Party.

In many respects, this extensive document gave a valid response to many of the issues then facing the international Communist movement, but it also contained not a few mistaken ideas, slipshod reasoning and demagogic assertions, and it was silent on many of the mistakes committed by and the problems facing the international Communist movement. The question of the general line of the international Communist movement was frequently identified with that of the Soviet Union's foreign policy. Indeed, the 'general line' itself was not always deeply thought out and often emerged as the product of extremely haphazard decisions and actions, and of major, frequently unjustified, zigzags in policy. This inconsistency and contradictoriness was the style and character of Soviet domestic as well as foreign policy. It was not, therefore, surprising that the talks between the CPSU and CCP did not lead to mutual agreement, and that they were broken off on 20 July 1963 at the insistence of the CCP. On their return to Peking, the Chinese delegation was given a triumphal reception and Mao Zedong himself turned up at the airport to greet them.

Economic relations between the Soviet Union and China were virtually broken off altogether in 1963, and both countries even removed their trade representatives and closed their consular offices. Various incidents began taking place on the Sino-Soviet border. On a number of occasions Chinese shepherds purposely crossed over into Soviet territory and refused to go back when asked to do so by Soviet border guards. Another issue that now became acute was that of Soviet citizens who had long been permanently settled in the Chinese western border province of Xinjiang, many of whom now wanted to get out of Chinese territory and were crossing the border illegally.

An escalation of the hostile polemics came after the treaty banning the testing of nuclear weapons in the atmosphere, in the air and under water was signed in Moscow on 5 August 1963 by the USSR, the USA and Great Britain, although the draft of it had been published long before. Most countries ratified the treaty, though France, which continued to generate its own nuclear potential, was unwilling to go over to underground testing, and did not join the ban. France did not, however, conduct a campaign of hostile propaganda against the USA, the USSR and Great Britain. China also did not ratify the Moscow Treaty, but the Chinese government and press chose to use the conclusion of this important agreement between the Soviet Union and the Western powers as an excuse to make crude and harsh comments. Describing the Moscow agreement as 'a gigantic fraud', the Chinese government went on to say:

> It will stupefy the peoples of the whole world, as it is utterly contradictory to the expectations of the peace-loving people of all nations. . . . It is unimaginable that the Chinese government would associate itself with this dirty fraud. . . . The indisputable facts show that the policy being followed by the Soviet government is a policy of uniting with the forces of war against the forces of peace, uniting with imperialism for the struggle against socialism, uniting with the USA for the struggle against China, uniting with the reactionary forces of different countries for the struggle against the peoples of the whole world.[26]

Even allowing for the general tendency for Chinese political rhetoric to be expressed rather powerfully, to all intents and purposes this statement, and the other articles, signalled the break in relations between the CPSU and the CCP, and soon that between the Soviet Union and the Chinese People's Republic as well.

Sino-Soviet relations were the object of special examination at the CPSU Central Committee Plenum held in Moscow in February 1964, with M. A. Suslov giving the report. At that moment, several Communist parties appealed to both the CPSU and the CCP to end the open polemics that had split the international Communist movement. The Soviet Union responded positively to this appeal, but the Chinese leadership turned it down, and hence the materials of the February Plenum were not published in the Soviet press until early April. The split and the break in relations between the two countries and the two parties were now accomplished facts.

We should note that the increasingly crude and sharp criticism levelled against the USSR and the CPSU by the Chinese press was often of a precisely personal kind and was aimed most frequently at N. S. Khrushchev and 'Khrushchevism'. The Chinese press customarily called Khrushchev 'the chief revisionist' who was leading the Soviet Union into a deal with the imperialists and was trying to change the USSR from a socialist country into a capitalist one. I used to listen sometimes to the Russian-language broadcasts from China in 1963–5, and I can confirm that the

Chinese propaganda had a much more demagogic and primitive character than the Stalinist propaganda of the 1930s and 1940s. Maybe it had some influence on the Chinese, but it certainly did not on Soviet listeners – even on those who were critical of the Soviet regime – for it was too much like a repetition of Stalinism, and a pretty crude and unpalatable repetition at that.

Soon after the CPSU Central Committee Plenum of October 1964, a number of articles were published in the West, including in Russian *émigré* periodicals, reporting alleged contacts between Khrushchev's opponents in the Soviet leadership and Chinese leaders.[27] The Central Committee conspirators supposedly wanted to know the Chinese terms for 'reconciliation' and received the terse response: 'Get rid of the revisionist Khrushchev, and then we'll see.' This is an unlikely story: although the October Plenum reproved Khrushchev for making tactless and rude remarks about Mao Zedong, he was not accused of damaging Sino-Soviet relations. Nevertheless, when Khrushchev was removed from office and was replaced as First Secretary of the Party Central Committee by L. I. Brezhnev and by A. N. Kosygin as Chairman of the Council of Ministers, certain circles in the East began to hope – and some in the West to fear – that the new Soviet leadership would manage to sort out new and more friendly relations with China.

China's economic situation in 1963–4, it should be noted, was extremely bad. The authorities had stopped publishing the basic statistics, but both Western and Soviet experts calculated that China's industrial production in 1963–4 had fallen to no more than 70 per cent of its 1959–60 level. Standards of food supply to the large cities were extremely poor and per capita the Chinese were getting about half the 1957 amounts of meat, fats, sugar and cereal products. Some of the Chinese leaders believed under these circumstances that the maintenance of external tension provided a valuable guarantee for internal stability.

In addition to 'revisionism', a new note came into Chinese propaganda in 1964, namely that the Soviet Union had held on to Chinese territory, allegedly seized by tsarist Russia. As early as March 1963 an editorial in the *People's Daily* raised the question of reassessing the treaties of Aigun (1858), Peking (1860), and St. Petersburg (1881) which had defined practically the entire line of the Sino-Soviet border.[28] In an interview given to a group of Japanese socialists on 10 July 1964, and published on 11 August in the Japanese press, Mao Zedong openly accused the Soviet Union of practising an annexationist policy. In evidence he not only cited the Soviet–Finnish war of 1939–40, and the absorption of the Baltic states, the Western Ukraine and Western Belorussia, Bessarabia, the Bukovina and part of East Prussia, as well as a number of Japanese islands, but also declared that Khabarovsk and Vladivostok were on territory that had belonged to China a hundred years before, as had Mongolia.[29] The total area of Soviet territory now put in dispute by China was around 1.5 million square kilometres.

The first successful test of China's atomic bomb was carried out at the end of October 1964, and it was followed by a noisy propaganda campaign with posters pasted up everywhere in millions of copies depicting the explosion of the 'Chinese' atomic bomb.

The sharp factional struggle among China's leaders was being carried on against Mao Zedong by an impressive coalition led by Liu Shaoqi. Mao left Peking temporarily in the belief that he had a more secure political base in the southern provinces. He appeared to those around him as sick and weak. He took to writing poetry and would talk with those close to him about death and his imminent meeting with God – or with Marx. He was often attended by nurses at meetings with foreign leaders. Throughout the period 1961–6, only one Plenum of the Chinese Communist Party Central Committee took place. While the practical business of governing the country was in the hands of Zhou Enlai, Liu Shaoqi, Deng Xiaoping, and Lin Biao, the personal cult of Mao Zedong continued and indeed intensified. All the recommendations on this issue made by the party's Eighth Congress were ignored. The Western journalist Edgar Snow, who had become friendly with Mao, once asked him about the Mao cult that had developed in China. Mao replied that Khrushchev had been overthrown and removed from power largely because he had not created his own cult, and he added that after a thousand years of imperial administration, it would be too difficult for the Chinese to free themselves of traditions of power that had been created over so many generations.[30]

Given the situations in Moscow and Peking, it was difficult to expect a change in relations between the two countries, yet at the same time it was not a simple matter for the Chinese leaders to decline a Soviet invitation to hold talks, hence at the beginning of November 1964, an imposing delegation, headed by Zhou Enlai, arrived in Moscow on the occasion of the 47th anniversary of the October revolution. There Zhou Enlai, following the practice of all official visitors, laid a wreath at Lenin's mausoleum, but then went on and paid a demonstrative visit to Stalin's grave and laid a wreath there, too – not that this gesture would necessarily have upset L. I. Brezhnev and his colleagues. Soon after the festivities, however, the talks began, and it quickly became evident that the new Soviet leadership found the Chinese demands unacceptable. The Chinese wanted the CPSU to express total repudiation of its own previous policy on the international labour movement, to make fundamental changes in Soviet foreign policy and concede unconditional recognition that the CCP had been correct in its ideological dispute with the CPSU in the period 1960–4. Understandably, the talks, which were conducted by Brezhnev, Kosygin and Suslov, did not last long and led to nothing. Although Zhou Enlai was regarded as a 'centrist' in the factional struggle among the Chinese leadership, and a man who had shown himself to be an experienced diplomat and a master of the art of compromise, the delegation also included Gang Shang, a man who was close to Mao and one of the most important of the 'leftists'. A delegation composed in this way was not likely to produce a successful outcome.

By 14 November 1964 the delegation was already back in Peking, where once again they were given a triumphal welcome. Soon the Chinese press, which had briefly soft-pedalled its criticism of the CPSU, renewed its concentrated anti-Soviet campaign. The new Soviet leaders were variously labelled 'Khrushchevists without Khrushchev', 'politicians of the Khrushchev type' and, naturally, 'revisionists' and 'opportunists'. In articles of various kinds, authors again tried to show that a shift from socialism to capitalism was taking place in the USSR, or that it had already taken place, that a 'collapse of the economy' had occurred, that there was 'degradation of culture', that 'capitalist forces were rampant' and so on. At an All-China meeting of people's representatives, which took place in December 1964, Zhou Enlai's speech was of a frankly anti-Soviet character.

In an effort to change the position with the help of others, the

Soviet leadership arranged a consultative meeting of delegations from the most influential and powerful Communist parties in the world. Of the 26 parties invited to send a delegation to Moscow, 19 accepted. Nobody came from China, Albania, North Korea, North Vietnam, Romania, Indonesia or Japan.

Relations between the Soviet Union and China were not even affected by the need to send help to Vietnam in its fight against the direct and open intervention of American armed forces, and Soviet and Chinese advisers were working there independently of each other. China was sending Vietnam small arms and part of its essential food supplies, and Chinese sappers were repairing roads and important installations in North Vietnam. The Soviet Union supplied more complex weapons, such as ground-to-air missiles, fighter planes and anti-tank guns, as well as industrial equipment, transport vehicles, and medical supplies. The greater part of this aid went by sea to the ports of North Vietnam. A Soviet request to allow this military aid to go by a faster route through Chinese territory was refused.

At the beginning of 1965, A. N. Kosygin led a Soviet party and government delegation to Vietnam and North Korea and, with the agreement of the Chinese authorities, twice during these visits he stopped over in Peking. There he had talks with both Zhou Enlai and Mao Zedong, but nothing came of them, neither an improvement in Sino-Soviet relations, nor the co-ordination of Soviet and Chinese aid to Vietnam. China even refused to issue a joint declaration condemning the mass bombardment of North Vietnam by the US Air Force, or to mark in any way the 15th anniversary in 1965 of the signing of the Sino-Soviet Treaty of Friendship.

There were still quite a few Chinese students in Moscow and Leningrad in 1964–5, and when at the beginning of March 1965 a mass demonstration of Soviet citizens – most of them students – was organized outside the US embassy to protest against the bombing of North Vietnam, a large group of Chinese students – probably in company with North Vietnamese students – separated from the main demonstration and made an attempt to break into the embassy grounds. Soviet demonstrations of this sort generally pass off peacefully, but on this occasion the US embassy was protected by reinforced units of the militia and KGB, in case there were going to be any incidents, and fighting indeed occurred between the Chinese students and the militia, at times quite fierce. Many Chinese students were forcibly thrown into closed trucks, but they were all released from custody after a few hours. Some had been injured during the skirmish and needed hospital treatment. This blatantly organized confrontation sparked off a new anti-Soviet campaign in China. Mass meetings were held everywhere. A vast demonstration was organized, this time in front not of the US embassy, but the Soviet embassy in Peking. The incident in Moscow was described as 'a massacre of Chinese students'. After these events it became impossible for Chinese students to remain in the Soviet Union and they were all recalled home.

Violations of the Sino-Soviet border occurred more frequently, with the Chinese military becoming increasingly involved. Clashes took place in isolated incidents, but as yet there had been no resort to arms. In the correspondence which still went on unabated between the CPSU and the CCP, the tone and content of the Chinese contributions became closer and closer to that of their published articles. Up to the end of 1965, despite the crudeness and sharply polemical character of their articles, they were still accompanying them with qualified remarks, such as 'the CCP and the CPSU have a small quarrel but a great unity', or 'we are separated by only one finger out of ten' and so on. On 11 November, however, the *People's Daily* carried an editorial which ran: 'That which exists separates us, and there is nothing that unites us; what exists is in opposition, and there is nothing in common. The chief task for the CCP now is totally to demarcate itself from the CPSU both politically and organizationally.'

Even from the formal point of view this meant a cessation of the polemics, a break in all relations between the CPSU and the CCP on party matters. When in early 1966 the Chinese leadership received an invitation to send a delegation to the Twenty-third Congress of the CPSU, due to open in March, their reply was to decline in a public and rude way.

China had not yet recovered fully from the consequences of the Great Leap Forward and the Three Red Banners policy when, from the middle of 1966, another destructive political campaign began to spread rapidly throughout the country, namely the policy known as the Cultural Revolution. In this outline we cannot give even a general picture of the causes and essential stages of this 'revolution' which temporarily destroyed the fundamental structure of the Chinese Communist Party, the Komsomol, the trade unions and many of the country's state institutions, and disrupted the Chinese economy and system of education, neither of which at the best of times were fully functional. It must be said, nevertheless, that the Cultural Revolution also turned out to be a severe test of Sino-Soviet relations. Any relations that had survived up to the middle of 1966 were broken off. The few Soviet students still studying in Chinese institutions of higher learning were recalled home. Chinese working under contract in enterprises in Siberia and the Far East were similarly called home. It was now dangerous for Soviet citizens still living in China to appear on the streets of Peking and other cities. The street in Peking where the Soviet embassy was located was renamed 'The Struggle against Revisionism Street', and anti-Soviet slogans and portraits of Mao Zedong were hung all around the embassy. Almost incessant mass demonstrations outside the embassy proclaimed the slogan 'The Soviet Union is our fatal enemy.' Diplomats leaving the embassy were subjected to insults.

At the beginning of 1967 the Chinese diplomats and those Chinese citizens still remaining in Moscow provoked a series of incidents, among other places in front of the Lenin Mausoleum in Red Square, at Yaroslavskii Station and right at their own embassy, where they fixed loudspeakers to the outside walls and broadcast slogans attacking the CPSU and the Soviet leaders. Incidents of various kinds were calculatedly provoked a number of times by the crew of the Peking–Moscow express, as well as on airlines and shipping routes, and each occasion was made the subject of a detailed and biased report in the Chinese press. It was the Soviet embassy in Peking, however, that became the chief object of provocation. From 26 January 1967, day and night, it was surrounded and blockaded by a vast crowd of Red Guards. Day and night, loudspeakers which had been installed around the embassy proclaimed the slogans of the Cultural Revolution and abused the 'Soviet revisionists'. The Soviet government decided to evacuate the families of its diplomats, mainly women and children, but although the Chinese government gave permission for a specially fitted plane to land, the Chinese Ministry of Internal Affairs announced that it could not guarantee the safety either of the plane crew or of the departing Soviet citizens. And indeed the Soviet citizens who were leaving the country were subjected to abuse and insults from the raving mobs which spat at them and forced them to walk bent double. A number of women and even children were beaten up at the airport. Diplomats of other socialist countries who had come to escort them were subjected to the same treatment. The entire incident was no doubt engineered in order to secure the breaking-off of diplomatic relations and was indeed sufficient cause for such a course of action. The Soviet government, however, restricted itself to sending some notes of protest and staging a number of demonstrations at the Chinese embassy in Moscow.

The mass demonstrations of Red Guards around the embassy in Peking ceased in the middle of February, but it was still dangerous for Soviet diplomats to go outside the embassy grounds. Even their food supplies had to be brought in by transport from the embassies of other socialist countries. Outbursts of frenzy and hatred, however, were to occur again on more than one occasion outside the embassy. For example, on 17 August 1967 a crowd of Red Guards broke into the embassy grounds, ran riot in a number of buildings, burnt down the sentry-box and set fire to some motor vehicles. The Chinese guards at the embassy did nothing to prevent this outrage. On many occasions in 1967 diplomats of other socialist countries, including Bulgaria, Hungary, East Germany and Mongolia, were subjected to various offences.

Planned infringements of the Sino-Soviet border greatly increased in frequency during 1967, with the Soviet border guards registering around 2,000 violations of different kinds, of which nine were sufficiently serious to be made the object of special representations by the Soviet Ministry of Foreign Affairs. However, during 1968, the number of provocative incidents involving either Soviet diplomats, journalists or merchant navy men, greatly diminished, even though conflicts and incidents in general could still be counted by the hundred. Relations between the Soviet Union and China were stretched to the limit by the beginning of 1969, but now the political confrontation began to escalate rapidly into military confrontation, beginning with the events which took place on Damansky Island (Zhenbao) in the River Ussuri.

The Chinese–Russian border along the River Ussuri had been established at the end of the nineteenth century on the basis of one of the so-called 'unequal treaties', and it is indeed not a fair border, ceding as it did the whole of the river to Russia. According to international law, where a navigable river divides two states, the border is deemed to be within the navigation channel, or fairway, whereas in the case of non-navigable rivers it follows the centre-line of the river. For many Chinese settlements and a few large Russian villages on the banks of the Ussuri, the river provided a supply of water, a means of communication and a source of fishing, benefits which the Chinese, however, could exercise only with the permission of the Soviet border authorities. Moreover, the Ussuri frequently changes course, and in doing so detaches pieces of the bank, usually from the Chinese side, thus forming islands which thereby become part of Soviet territory. When friendly relations existed between the two countries, these matters were dealt with amicably, but in conditions of hostility they easily became a constant cause of contention and conflict. It would have been sensible for the Soviet Union to announce unilaterally that it had changed its attitude over the Ussuri issue, and for China it would have been sensible to seek a solution at the negotiating table, but with the circumstances so utterly embittered by the Cultural Revolution, a peaceful settlement of the border problems seemed impossible to achieve.

There are various versions of what happened on the River Ussuri. According to the Soviet version, a specially trained sub-unit of 300 Chinese troops occupied Damansky Island on the night of 2 March 1969, and there they secretly concentrated mortars, grenade-launchers, machine-guns and anti-tank weapons.[31] When a unit of Soviet border guards approached the Chinese positions and demanded the removal of the sub-unit from Soviet territory, the Chinese opened fire on them without warning, virtually at point-blank range. The Soviet guards called up reinforcements and, after a battle in which lives were lost, occupied Damansky Island and forced the Chinese to withdraw. The Chinese in turn brought in their reinforcements and on 14–15 March again tried to capture the island; they were again beaten and compelled to retreat, this time under heavy Soviet rocket fire on Chinese territory.

The armed skirmishes on Damansky Island provoked a fierce

anti-Soviet campaign in China. The Soviet embassy in Peking was again subjected to an organized siege, the Chinese press carried increasingly open Chinese territorial claims, a Soviet proposal for immediate talks to settle the contentious border issue was ignored, and soon armed incidents started to occur at other outposts along the border. In April 1969 a large group of Chinese under the protection of army units tried to occupy the island of Kultuk in the River Amur. In May border incidents took place near the town of Blagoveshchensk and in various areas in Kazakhstan. From the beginning of June to the middle of August 1969 the Soviet border authorities registered no less than 488 infringements of the border and armed incidents.[32] A comparatively serious armed skirmish took place between Chinese army units and Soviet border guards on 13 May 1969 in Semipalatinsk Oblast near the settlement of Zhalashakol.

These border conflicts attracted world attention, and as the possibility of a major war in the Far East between the Soviet Union and China was raised, political and military leaders examined possible scenarios. The Soviet leaders had to make a hasty assessment of the country's strategic position, given that the occupation of Czechoslovakia had caused a sharp deterioration in the Soviet Union's relations with the West, and now there was this added problem of military confrontation with China.

Some hope of reducing this confrontation came in the autumn of 1969 when A. N. Kosygin, on his way home from the funeral of Ho Chi-minh, stopped briefly in Peking and had a meeting with Zhou Enlai. They agreed to reopen discussions on the border issue and talks began in Peking in October 1969. At that moment, however, a huge campaign was launched throughout China to 'prepare for war', and the press made no secret of the fact that what it had in mind was the 'inevitable war with the Soviet Union', for there were, according to the *People's Daily* 'irreconcilable differences of principle between China and the USSR', and therefore 'the struggle between them will continue for a long time'.[33]

The 'prepare for war' campaign was more than mere propaganda. Whole populations from the border regions, where they had long-established links with the Soviet population, were transported into the central and southern areas of the country, and hundreds of thousands of recently enrolled Red Guards were shipped to the border territory. A considerable number of factories were transferred from the northern areas of China to other provinces. In towns and villages food supplies were stored up 'in case of war'. In large cities the entire population was conscripted to begin building gigantic bomb-shelters, and regular training in case of air raids was given. The press was full of anti-Soviet material and warnings of the threat from the north. Large army units were moved to areas bordering the Soviet Union, and the Chinese defence minister, Lin Biao, who had been named at the Ninth Congress of the CCP as Mao Zedong's official 'heir', transferred his staff headquarters to a place near the border.

Naturally, the Soviet Union began making its own extensive war preparations on its border with China. Earlier, in the mid-1950s on Khrushchev's orders, various fortifications that had been built in the 1930s and 1940s had been blown up. Now the border was fortified once again. Dozens of military settlements were established to house large army formations. When yet another border clash took place in 1970, Soviet troops were given orders to open massive missile and artillery fire on Chinese territory up to a depth of 10 kilometres. This 'preventive' strike was meant to serve as a warning to the Chinese leaders. Large concentrations of Chinese troops had been fired on and their losses must have been considerable. Lin Biao's headquarters were not far from the area of fire, but this was not known to Soviet military intelligence, otherwise it is safe to assume that it too would have been detroyed by missile attack. The Chinese army was large, but in terms of weaponry it lagged far behind the Soviet army. The Chinese response to the Soviet missiles was to intensify their propaganda campaign. Hundreds of burnt corpses of Chinese soldiers were carried through the streets of Chinese cities in order to arouse hatred for the Soviet Union and to underline the 'threat from the north'. At the same time the Chinese government resolved to accelerate the production of atomic bombs and missile weapons. The Soviet Union was declared China's 'Enemy No. 1'.

In the early 1970s, L. I. Brezhnev and many of those around him believed that war with China was a real possibility. Fear of war with a poorly armed but extremely populous and fanatical China was undoubtedly one of the reasons prompting the policy of *détente*, which the Soviet Union pursued energetically in the early 1970s and which entailed making a number of concessions to the West, such as permitting the mass emigration of Soviet Jews and Germans, allowing many dissidents to leave the country, ending the jamming of Western radio stations, and broadening contacts with the West on many levels. Brezhnev even discussed with Henry Kissinger and President Nixon the possibility of Western support in the event of war with China.

The danger of total war with China at the end of the 1960s and beginning of the 1970s even alarmed Soviet dissidents and occupied an important place in their thinking, as well as in their letters and articles. Andrei Amalrik devoted almost half of his well-known essay *Can the Soviet Union Survive Until 1984?* to discussing various aspects of a war with China, which he regarded as both inevitable and fatal for the Soviet Union. China's expansionism, seen for example in her conflict with India, was, in Amalrik's view, a possible solution to her economic problems, as well as gaining redress for the centuries of humiliation and dependence on foreign powers suffered by the Chinese. Only the United States and the Soviet Union stood between China and her ambitions, and they would not unite because of their own differences. Therefore, China would make every effort to achieve an adequate supply of nuclear weapons – it did not have to be equal to the Soviet Union's – and that alone would determine when the war would start, in his view sometime between 1980 and 1984.[34] Amalrik's essay was written in 1969 and was translated and published in ten Western countries, where it created considerable interest.

Even greater resonance, both in the Soviet Union and abroad, was generated by *A Letter to the Soviet Leaders*, written by Alexander Solzhenitsyn in the autumn of 1973 and published in the spring of 1974, in which he expressed his alarm at the thought of a war with China in which the best of Soviet youth would perish, 'in which 60 million of our compatriots would allow themselves to be killed'. Unlike Amalrik, Solzhenitsyn believed that the chief cause of a war with China lay in their growing ideological differences, and he therefore urged the Soviet leadership to abandon altogether the 'dead letter' of Marxist ideology and acknowledge the value of 'live' Christian Orthodox ideology. The Soviet leaders should let the Chinese keep their pride, the dissension would fade, and with it the prospect of war. 'And if war should nevertheless come in the distant future, it should be a defensive one, a truly patriotic one.'[35]

Solzhenitsyn's letter provoked an extremely wide discussion not only in the Western press but also in the Soviet Union. A collection of articles by dissident writers was even compiled, with the title *What Awaits the Soviet Union?*, in which a minority agreed with Solzhenitsyn, while a majority took issue with him. For example, Academician A. D. Sakharov wrote that, whereas he had also, like Solzhenitsyn, once had the same fear of total war with China, with utter destruction as the result, without victors or vanquished, he now felt this was an over-dramatization of the position, complicated though it was. In his view, the Chinese did not have, nor for a long time would have, enough strength to unleash war against the Soviet Union – not that the Soviet Union would succeed should it take the aggressive path itself – and he went on: 'One might even suggest that the inflation of the Chinese threat is one element in a game being played by the Soviet leadership. The over-estimate of the Chinese threat ill serves the cause of democratization and demilitarization that our country so badly needs, that the whole world so badly needs.' For Sakharov, the contest between the Soviet Union and China was not, as Solzhenitsyn claimed, one of ideology, but was an essentially non-political struggle for leadership of the Communist world, and in this respect he regarded the Chinese leaders as no less pragmatic than their Soviet counterparts.[36]

The Russian nationalist, L. Borodin, assessed Solzhenitsyn's letter quite differently. Citing earlier Russian thinkers, he recalled that fear of China was nothing new, and he accepted Solzhenitsyn's idea that the rational opening up of Siberia by the Russians was the way to protect Russia from this threat. Solzhenitsyn was wrong, however, in Borodin's view, to let the Chinese have the monopoly on ideology, for Marxism had an eternal horizon that is aimed at world government, and when harnessed to a national idea – and China's was to expand beyond her present borders – then the outcome was as inevitable as Germany's suicidal world adventure had been. The only way to withstand the attack was to defend oneself, and in that sense Solzhenitsyn's proposals for the rebirth of true national consciousness in Russia were timely.[37]

In my own reply to Solzhenitsyn's *Letter*, published in the German magazine *Der Spiegel* in 1974, I wrote that I also felt that, dangerous though the threat of war with China was, it should not be exaggerated. The Chinese, who still had enormous areas of undeveloped territory, would not go to war over Siberia, still less over some ideological disagreements, and that despite the disparity of arms, neither the Soviet nor the Chinese army could long sustain a war in the wastes of either Siberia or the border regions of China. I agreed that strategic imperatives dictated that we develop the borderlands more energetically, and in ways that were also beneficial to the Soviet economy, but to attempt to 'unfreeze' the north-east as a response to the threat from China would be a senseless waste of resources.[38]

The danger of war with China was one of the reasons that prompted the Soviet Union in 1970 to increase its military spending significantly and to force the expansion of Soviet industry. The Soviet Union now had two strategic enemies: if President Nixon could instruct his military strategists to bear in mind that America must be prepared to fight one large war and one or two small wars at the same time, then the Soviet government had to give its General Staff a far more daunting task: the Soviet Union must be ready to fight two large wars at the same time, one in the West and one in the East.

The armed confrontation with China was an unexpected factor for the Soviet Union, compromising socialism as a whole to some extent, as it did, for such a situation had been thought impossible between two socialist states. The armed invasion of Czechoslovakia had dealt this particular dogma a shattering blow, but the incidents on the Sino-Soviet border put the final nail in the coffin. The issue had not been one only of theory, but a question of purely military necessity and the Soviet Union's economic capacity.

Naturally, China could not compare with the Soviet Union in terms of the technical level of its armed forces, but China was a country with a vast and well-organized population which could be mobilized by the tens of millions in the event of a war with the Soviet Union. The occupation of Czechoslovakia had been a possibility, but the occupation of China with its 700–800 million-strong hostile population was an impossibility. The Sino-Soviet border runs through areas of the Far East, Siberia,

Kazakhstan, that is to say areas of relatively low density of population, and the only line of communication between the European part of the country and the Far East and eastern Siberia ran through the southern part of Siberia in immediate proximity to the Chinese border. With only one railway and one highway of strategic importance in that area, Soviet defence did not have the necessary depth, while its 'width', that is its extent along the Chinese border, was all of 7,000 kilometres. To create a secure defence along such a border required enormous numbers of troops and military engineering operations of colossal dimensions.

The work of construction was begun. Along the border in the first half of the 1970s dozens of divisions were gradually deployed; fortifications and roads, military cantonments and everything that constitutes a military infrastructure were built. Siberia-based nuclear missiles were now targeted on China, and it is reckoned that during the 1970s roughly one third of the total military potential of the Soviet Union was swung round to face Mao Zedong's China. Together with various kinds of auxiliary units, the eastern military commands had placed at their disposal more than 100 infantry, motorized, tank and air force divisions combined. If the memoirs of such American politicians as Nixon and Kissinger are to be believed, Brezhnev and his advisers were weighing up the possibility of launching a preventive strike against a number of areas where the Chinese maintained their nuclear arsenals; and apparently Brezhnev was not merely 'feeling out' the possible reaction of the United States and other Western countries to such an act, he was also trying to gain Western support and using the 'yellow peril' as a means to scare the Americans into giving it.

It is quite possible that such an action was being discussed, and fortunately it must have been decided that the outcome was too unpredictable and that it would anyway most likely be negative both for the Soviet Union and the rest of the world, to say nothing of China. Be that as it may, once the main part of the Soviet Union's defence potential had been deployed along the border, the idea of a preventive strike was no longer discussed, even as a theoretical possibility.

The Sino-Soviet armed confrontation of the 1970s prompted the building of a second line of communications between the

European parts of the USSR, the Urals and the eastern regions, namely the Baikal–Amur mainline (BAM) and the industrial and housing zone running along it, with the prospect of gradually transferring the armed forces from their more southerly deployment in close proximity to the border and establishing a second line of defence for the eastern regions.

One may assert with complete assurance that the chief part in creating the danger of war on the Sino-Soviet border was played by the Chinese leadership, although it is probably also true that the Soviet leadership did not always come up with the right response.

Although the Chinese leaders' massive propaganda campaign was against the 'threat from the north', it was of great importance for Mao Zedong in internal political terms. Already in the 1950s, Chinese foreign policy had been linked to a significant extent to the country's internal situation. The bombardment of the offshore islands, occupied by Jiang Gai-shi's forces, and the worsening of relations with the United States and Japan, had been linked to the policy of the Great Leap Forward, one important component of which had been the militarization of the entire population, in particular the Peoples' Communes then being established throughout the country. Tension in foreign policy helped in 1959–60 to mask the failure of the Great Leap Forward and to divert the nation's attention from the worsening economic situation. The 'regulation' of the economy, undertaken in 1962–5, was, however, interrupted by the Cultural Revolution, and when that episode came to an end, or rather when the end of its first phase was announced, when millions of Red Guards had to be sent out to work into the countryside, sometimes with troops to keep them under control, when work was begun to reconstruct the administrative and economic institutions that had been destroyed by the Cultural Revolution, and when it became clear that the country's economy at the end of the 1960s was in an even more lamentable condition than it had been at the beginning of the decade, then Mao Zedong and his group tried to divert the attention of the nation, the party and the army from their domestic problems by provoking and then blowing up an external threat. A big war with the Soviet Union had certainly never been part of Mao's plans. He knew that China could not win such a war, that the Chinese army would be utterly destroyed once it had penetrated Siberia and the Far East. But maintaining tension, blowing up the myth of the 'threat from the north', and engaging in limited skirmishes on the border, were useful to him for internal political reasons.

The Cultural Revolution brought about a considerable change in the composition of the Chinese leadership. Most of those who had come into prominence between the 1930s and 1950s were removed from power. Some of them died, for instance Liu Shaoqi and Peng Dehuai, but the majority of the Party Central Committee, the Politburo, as well as military and economic leaders, were defamed, exposed to public humiliation and insult, and exiled to remote provinces for 're-education', though they were permitted to remain alive, and were not physically exterminated, as Stalin's victims had been in the bloody purges of 1936–8 and the post-war years. Mao's enemies had to remain as live witnesses to his triumph and some of them, including Deng Xiaoping, even managed to get back into the ranks of the ruling elite after a few years.

New arrangements in the party and army leadership came again with the end of the Cultural Revolution. Mao Zedong's closest supporters and the organizers of the Cultural Revolution, including Lin Biao and Zhen Boda, were removed from power and denounced not only as traitors, adventurers, careerists and conspirators, but also as agents of social imperialism. It was no accident that the plane in which Lin Biao was allegedly trying to escape abroad crashed in Mongolian territory. A special commission, which examined the remains that had been found in the plane's wreckage, came to the conclusion that all the 'passengers' had been shot on the ground even before take-off. The plane had been on a course for the Soviet Union but had crashed before reaching its destination, most likely due either to sabotage or a bomb.

A younger group of 'leftists' headed by Mao Zedong's wife, Jiang Qing, came to power, and continued to repeat many of the slogans of the Cultural Revolution and to support Mao's personal cult. China, however, could not go on any longer in a state of chaos and isolation that threatened the very existence of the country and the nation. The Maoists therefore had to introduce measures that would lead to greater stability in the political and economic leadership, and to get production going again in the country. As a result there was some lessening of tension between the Soviet Union and China between 1971 and 1975, despite which the Tenth Congress of the Chinese Communist Party retained for approval among its basic slogans 'prepare for war', 'dig deep tunnels', 'save grain' and so on, though it also put forward demands for the development of agriculture and industry.

China continued with its forced programme of nuclear missile production, building medium-range missiles and the first Chinese satellites. It was plain, however, that the development of its defence industry was not possible without the development and modernization of the entire economy, without the scientific and technical development of the country and the restoration of the higher education system.

China began to emerge from the state of diplomatic and cultural isolation that had characterized the period of the Cultural Revolution. While this shift in foreign policy was generally 'Western' in orientation, some changes also occurred in relations with the socialist countries, with whom China once again exchanged ambassadors. The Soviet Union actively supported the return of China to the United Nations General Assembly and Security Council, where China's place had long been occupied illegally by the representative from Taiwan. Trade between the Soviet Union and China had almost ceased by 1970 and no trade agreements had been made, yet in 1971 the two countries signed an agreement on trade. Volume, it is true, was re-established only very slowly. Thus, in 1970 trade between the two countries had amounted to 42 million roubles, and in 1975 it reached 200 million roubles,[39] but these were negligible sums for countries the size of China and the Soviet Union. The chief items of export from the Soviet Union were machinery, equipment, transport facilities and essential spare parts. The chief items of China's exports remained the products of the food and textile industries.

Talks over the border dispute went on, but the anti-Soviet propaganda in China continued on the previous scale, while for their part Soviet publications of all kinds were coming out with more and more critical material on the Chinese leadership and its policies. In 1975 a new constitution was adopted by the All-China Assembly of People's Deputies which included a clause to the effect that the threat to China from 'social imperialism' would persist throughout the entire existence of the socialist society. In defining the tasks of the Chinese armed forces, the constitution stated directly that they must prepare for the struggle against 'social imperialism'. The term 'social imperialism' in the Chinese lexicon of the 1970s meant the Soviet Union and the struggle against it was now elevated to the rank of state policy.

In 1974 a Soviet helicopter with three officers on board went off course due to bad weather and was forced to land on Chinese territory in Xinjiang. The crew were kept in custody for more than one and a half years on spying charges, but then in December 1975, together with their helicopter, they were returned to the Soviet side, accompanied by an admission from the Chinese Ministry of Foreign Affairs that the charge of spying had not been substantiated.[40] On 29 April 1976 a bomb was exploded next to the Soviet embassy in Peking, killing three Chinese, of whom two were the militiamen on duty. By pure chance, no Soviet personnel were injured.

The year from the autumn of 1975 to the autumn of 1976 was a watershed in Chinese history. At the end of 1975 one of Mao Zedong's closest comrades-in-arms, Gang Shang, died. A man who had preferred to remain in the background, he had undoubtedly been one of the creators and mainstays of Mao's regime. Then on 8 January 1976 Zhou Enlai died, for 70 years having firmly held second place in the Chinese hierarchy, despite his reputation as a 'centrist' and master of compromise. He was one of the best- known figures of the Chinese revolution and had become a member of the Politburo of the Central Committee of the CCP five years before Mao. His death sharpened the struggle for power in the leadership, but it was also made to serve as the trigger for mass demonstrations in Peking, reflecting the people's dissatisfaction with the difficult material conditions they were facing. On 6 July 1976 Zhu De died in his 90th year, again a veteran of the revolution, a former commander of the Red Army and the Eighth People's Revolutionary Army, long regarded as second in command of the revolution. Zhu De hardly involved himself in politics during the 1970s, though he was chairman of the Permanent Committee of the Chinese Supreme Soviet and a member of the Politburo.

Then, on 9 September 1976 at the age of 83, Mao Zedong himself died. An 'Address' from the chief party and state institutions to the Chinese people contained a catalogue of all the main Maoist slogans of the 1960s and 1970s, including 'the struggle against social imperialism' and 'prepare for war'. Foreign delegations were not admitted to the funeral ceremonies, but telegrams were sent from most countries in the world. Telegrams of condolence were also sent by the Central Committee of the CPSU and leaders of other Communist parties, but they were not published and were even demonstratively refused.

The death of Mao triggered a sharp political struggle between various groups in the leadership of the Chinese Communist Party. Only a month after Mao's death, the group led by his widow, Jiang Qing, and three other members of the Politburo, who had emerged during the Cultural Revolution as the most radical Maoists, were deposed and arrested. They were from then on dubbed the Gang of Four in the press. A group of more moderate Maoists came to power led by the prime minister, Hua Guofeng, who had succeeded to the post on the death of Zhou Enlai. A group of 'pragmatists', led by Deng Xiaoping – who only recently had been dubbed a 'defeatist', 'bourgeois oppositionist', 'organizer of counter-revolution' – also quickly began to consolidate its position and increase its influence.

The changes of leadership led to substantial changes in many aspects of the CCP's domestic policies. Little changed in 1977–8, however, in respect of Sino-Soviet relations. The anti-Soviet thrust of previous policy was so deep and strong that neither Hua Guofeng's followers, nor those of Deng Xiaoping, could expect to succeed, except by resorting to anti-Soviet rhetoric. Speaking at the CCP Eleventh Party Congress in August 1977, Hua Guofeng castigated both the United States and the Soviet Union as sources of a new world war, but he pointed to the Soviet Union as the more dangerous, stating: 'The Soviet revisionists are not giving up the idea of enslaving our country, so we must be ready to fight.'[41]

Similarly, when in September 1977 Deng Xiaoping met the West German politician and future defence minister, Manfred Werner of the Christian Democratic Union, he called the prospect of *rapprochement* between China and the Soviet Union senseless, and he expressed his certainty that he, at any rate, would not live to see it, adding that he doubted such an outcome 'even for the next generation'.[42] Significantly, the new 'revised' version of the Constitution, passed at the beginning of 1978, excluded the clause enjoining citizens 'to prepare for war'; on the contrary, it included a paragraph on the need 'to struggle against a new world war'; but it also preserved and even reinforced the clauses on the struggle against 'social imperialism'.

Mao Zedong's legacy, however, was so painful that it could hardly have been revised without also changing some of the emphases connected with Sino-Soviet relations. In 1977–9 the rehabilitation took place of the victims of the Cultural Revolution. We have already noted that during this 'revolution' the majority of officials removed from their positions in government, army and cultural institutions, were not physically annihilated, but were sent to remote districts for 're-education'. Now they were brought back to Peking and other large cities and given responsible posts in the party and state apparatus. Many people who had been the victims of earlier political campaigns were similarly rehabilitated and returned to their families, and so also were not a few social, cultural and artistic figures who had the reputation of being friends of the Soviet Union. (An example is the writer Ding Ling, who in 1952 had won the Stalin Prize and who had been called a 'rightist' element and sent for 20 years to a remote village to do heavy farm labour.) Without loud publicity, the Chinese began publishing the works of Russian and Soviet authors in translation, and books by Chinese writers were correspondingly published in the Soviet Union. On the other hand, the Chinese chose to publish either Russian classics or works with a critical content, such as the 'village prose' of the 1960s, while for their part Soviet publishers brought out either Chinese classics or stories critical of the times and values of the Cultural Revolution.

In July 1977, the Soviet Union announced its agreement to an understanding between Soviet and Chinese authorities allowing Chinese civilian vessels to pass Khabarovsk by means of internal Soviet waterways at times when the Kazakevich Channel, which lies on the border, was too shallow.[43] This arrangement began to operate from 1 September, and talks on the border issues continued into 1978.

On 24 February the Presidium of the Supreme Soviet of the USSR approached the Permanent Committee of the All-China Assembly with an appeal to end the abnormal state of relations between the two countries and to arrest the dangerous trend of those relations worsening still further. To this end, the Presidium of the Supreme Soviet proposed a meeting, to take place either in Moscow or Peking, of sufficiently senior representatives of both countries, charged with the job of producing an appropriate document.[44] The Chinese government replied in a note from the Ministry of Foreign Affairs dated 9 March 1978 which in practical terms rejected the Soviet proposal. Furthermore, at the beginning of April 1979, the Chinese government officially announced that it did not intend to prolong the Sino-Soviet treaty of friendship, union and mutual assistance which was due to expire in April 1980 after 30 years. In a moderately worded special statement expressing its regret at this, the Soviet government declared, among other things, that there were no objective reasons for the alienation, and still less for the confrontation, and it concluded that the enemies of Sino-Soviet friendship, however hard they tried to erase the memory of past co-operation and mutual effort and to build a wall of hatred between the two peoples, would not succeed.[45] The Chinese government, however, ignored all such statements and the tone of the Chinese press remained exclusively hostile.

The inner party struggle in China resulted in 1979 in victory for the 'pragmatists' and 'reformers', led by Deng Xiaoping, Hu Yaobang and Zhao Ziyang, while the moderate Maoists, led by Hua Guofeng, were defeated. Twelve men who had occupied important party and state posts even before the Cultural Revolution were now included in the Party Central Committee. The scale of rehabilitations was widened and the reputations of people who had suffered in earlier campaigns were restored. Thus, for example, on 8 December 1978 the Third Plenum of the Central Committee rehabilitated Peng Dehuai and many other leading officials and military commanders. Most of these rehabilitations were, unfortunately, posthumous. The urn containing the ashes of Peng Dehuai, who had died 'as the result of treachery by Lin Biao and the Gang of Four', was buried at the cemetery for heroes of the revolution.[46]

Criticism of Mao's policies during the last 20 years of his life became more and more openly expressed in 1979. The basic principles of economic policy in town and country were subjected to a broader and deeper reappraisal than ever before. The partial liberalization of the political and economic regime in China was not, however, accompanied by an improvement in Sino-Soviet relations. On the contrary, relations deteriorated still further, while in contrast a rapid *rapprochement*, initiated by a visit to the United States by Deng Xiaoping at the beginning of the year, was taking place between China and the United States and was acquiring the contours of a military-political alliance aimed against the Soviet Union.

Relations again became strained to an extremely dangerous degree in the spring of 1979 as a result of events which were taking place in South-East Asia. Kampuchea, regarded as a loyal ally of China, had for several years already endured bloody atrocities in the course of which the military junta of Pol Pot had exterminated almost 3 million of the 7 million population of that small country. The Khmer Rouge had physically annihilated all representatives of the bourgeoisie, feudal landlords, clergy, as well as the entire Kampuchean intelligentsia, and all students, in a word all educated people. Towns were demolished along with industrial and financial enterprises, and a large number of workers and peasants were exterminated, while those who survived were driven into forced labour camps.

It is impossible to know how the bloody carnage would all have ended had not a group of Kampuchean patriots organized armed resistance and turned to Vietnam for help. Vietnamese troops entered Kampuchea and quickly destroyed the main forces of the Khmer Rouge. A government friendly to Vietnam was set up in Kampuchea and economic and cultural life began to return. Interference by one state in the internal affairs of another had undoubtedly taken place, but among the many examples of such interference, amply provided by the history of the twentieth century, that of Vietnam in Kampuchea must surely rank as one of the most justified. The West, however, which only recently had watched the Kampuchean tragedy with horror, and also recently had approved Tanzania's intervention in the internal affairs of Amin's Uganda, and France's in the Central African 'Empire' of Bokassa, now condemned Vietnam's invasion of Kampuchea in unison.

The most vehement opposition to Vietnam's action, however, came from the Chinese leadership who decided 'to teach Vietnam a lesson' and ordered the 600,000-strong regular

Chinese army, stationed in the southern provinces, to invade and 'punish' Vietnam, a country whose government and people had already suffered so much. The action was completely illegal, stupid and ill prepared, and the 'lesson' which the Chinese army was supposed to give the Vietnamese was first and foremost a lesson for the Chinese political and military leaders themselves. During the three weeks of the war, the Vietnamese did not yield a single important base in Kampuchea, nor did they send so much as one of their regular divisions into battle. It was a test of strength between the Chinese regular army, armed and equipped with thousands of tanks and weapons, suddenly invading the six northern provinces of Vietnam, against Vietnamese territorial regional defence formations and the border militia.

The Chinese army, however, was equipped with weapons that were 20 years out of date, and its troops had had no experience of fighting, whereas the far less numerous Vietnamese local troops and militia were using modern defence weapons and consisted mostly of seasoned fighters. As a result, after a month of fighting the Chinese had lost one tenth of their troop strength, more than 500 armoured vehicles and a huge quantity of equipment. The Chinese army was bogged down in bloody fighting and could have gone deeper into Vietnam only with reinforcements of 20–30 new divisions. On the other hand, the nature of the local terrain allowed Vietnam to choose at will whether to commit its regular divisions of battle-hardened troops, armed with the most up-to-date weapons, and to encircle and completely destroy the Chinese army. The Vietnamese leadership wisely decided to restrain itself and instead to allow the Chinese army to make its way out of their country and back to China. Although the Chinese leaders proclaimed that their army had fulfilled its mission, they knew perfectly well that it had suffered a heavy defeat in Vietnam.

The Chinese invasion of Vietnam caused Sino-Soviet relations to deteriorate sharply. Soviet troops on the Chinese border were put on full alert. The Soviet government made it sufficiently clear that if China widened its aggression in Vietnam, the Soviet Union would feel compelled to take action of a similar kind in North Korea. Fortunately, things did not go that far, and the Soviet government limited itself to sending a large amount of new military equipment to Vietnam and to helping Vietnam build large-scale fortifications on its border with China. The defence of Vietnam's northern borders was also strengthened by the deployment of regular army units. In all, China's 'armed expedition' into Vietnam had led to the decline of China's influence in South-East Asia and to the strengthening of the ties between Vietnam, Laos and Kampuchea and the Soviet Union.

Despite the continuation of border conflicts between China and Vietnam, by June 1979 there were signs of a certain *détente*. The Soviet Union proposed talks 'with the aim of reducing tension and establishing friendly relations'. The proposal was accepted, something that could hardly have happened had Mao Zedong still been alive. An exchange of memoranda took place between the two countries' foreign ministries and it was agreed to start talks in July–August 1979. The number of anti-Chinese articles in the Soviet press diminished noticeably. Moreover, on 8 June *Pravda* carried a notice about the fight against the pollution of the atmosphere in the Chinese capital, the first article for many years in the Soviet press showing measures taken by the Chinese authorities in a positive light. The long-forgotten Sino-Soviet Friendship Society was back in business: in February its Third All-Union Conference took place in Moscow and was attended by 240 delegates from various parts of the Soviet Union and a group of Chinese embassy staff, and in the summer it gave wide notice to the 60th anniversary of the Soviet Union's 'Address to the Chinese people and governments of North and South China'. Thereafter its meetings and conferences – which were mostly devoted to the memory of the better-known figures of the Chinese revolution and Chinese culture – took place on a regular basis.

The talks began only in September and were utterly fruitless. They were broken off on 30 November 1979. The amount of anti-Soviet material published during the summer and autumn of 1979 in the Chinese press, far from diminishing, had increased still further. This was no doubt one of the weightier considerations in the chain of other reasons and motives that prompted the Soviet government to take the decision – an extremely risky one in many respects – to put Soviet troops into Afghanistan in order to prop up the regime which had come into being after the so-called April revolution. It was a decision that had resulted from the considerable worsening of the Soviet Union's relations with the West and China and which in turn only made those relations still worse. In the West, for all practical purposes it brought about the end of the *détente* of the 1970s. While in the East things had never got as far as *détente*, in 1980 Soviet–Chinese relations reached their lowest ebb since the time of the armed clashes on the border in 1969–70. The Soviet Union was once again China's 'Enemy No. 1'. Some foreign observers believed there was a strong possibility of renewed armed conflicts on the border, and there were not a few Western politicians who were pleased rather than saddened by such a prospect.

2

The United States and China: some pages of history

Before the Second World War

The Americans 'discovered' China much later than had the countries of Western Europe, Russia or Japan. When England began her first war against China and imposed the first enslaving Nanjing Treaty of 1842, California had not yet been finally joined to the United States. American traders and missionaries appeared in China in the middle of the nineteenth century, but America's own internal problems and the Civil War held up American expansion in the Pacific Basin for a long time. It was only at the end of the century that the Unites States established its first naval base in the Hawaiian Islands which it eventually took over. A large part of American society viewed China and the Chinese with open hostility and even contempt. In 1882 the US Congress passed a law, signed by President Arthur, banning the entry of Chinese to the United States.

When, after her victory in the Spanish–American War, the United States began to see, and comport, herself as a great world power, most of developed China had already been carved up into 'spheres of influence' between England, France, Germany, Russia and Japan. The United States was not willing to be satisfied with the left-overs of this division and declared an 'open door' policy, demanding freedom for its commercial and industrial expansion throughout the whole of China.[1]

From the beginning of the twentieth century, China and the countries of the Pacific Basin became the second most important region of active foreign policy for the United States. As a result of the American–Philippines War of 1899–1901, the United States turned the Philippines into its largest colony and began vigorously to increase its commercial and economic penetration of

China. After the Russo-Japanese War, and especially after the First World War, the United States and Japan became chief rivals in the struggle for influence in China, thrusting the other large capitalist powers into second place. By the 1930s hundreds of small, medium and large American companies were operating on Chinese soil and deploying quite large investments by contemporary standards. While it is true that the Chinese portion of trade within the overall external trade balance of the US did not exceed 3–4 per cent, interest nevertheless grew continually, for American businessmen were intrigued by China, by its size and enormous, untapped potential as a foreign trade market.[2]

United States foreign policy in the 1920s and 1930s, however, was in the grip of isolationism. The Senate defeated President Wilson by refusing to ratify the Treaty of Versailles and join the League of Nations. With their vast domestic market and overwhelming influence in Latin America, and securely defended by two oceans, the majority of conservative-minded Americans did not want their country to become involved in new conflicts in Asia or Europe or beyond the limits of the western hemisphere, indeed they shunned the problems of the Old World in general, and this despite the fact that they themselves were mainly emigrants or the descendants of emigrants from that selfsame Old World.

Only a small number of Americans in ruling circles were troubled when Japan occupied Manchuria and set up a pro-Japanese puppet government. The majority of influential American politicians agreed with the view expressed by President Hoover who in 1931 commented on the Japanese aggression: 'Neither our obligations to China, nor our interests or dignity demand that we should go to war over this.'[3]

America's policy of 'non-intervention' was not motivated solely by isolationism, nor only by the behaviour of Japan. Of still greater concern was the existence and development of the Soviet Union with whom the United States had still not established diplomatic relations. The successes of the revolutionary movement in China where the Kuomintang was suffering defeat after defeat in its campaigns against the country's sovietized areas were a further cause for concern. President Hoover explained his policy to his cabinet colleagues in an *aide-mémoire* which said, among other things, that, as far as the Sino-Japanese conflict was concerned, it was not America's business to maintain the peace between states by force. He went on, if the Japanese were to say to America outright that they could no longer observe the Washington Agreement because order had not been re-established in China, since half of China had been Bolshevized and was collaborating with Russia; and if they were to say that Japan's existence could come under threat if, as well as having Bolshevist Russia to the North, they had on their flank a possibly Bolshevized China; and if, therefore, they asked the US for the opportunity to re-establish order in China, the United States, according to Hoover, would have no objections.[4]

In other words, the United States was hoping that Japan would succeed where the Kuomintang was failing and that Japanese expansion would be limited to the northern regions of China or still better to areas of the Soviet Far East. The same motives guided extreme conservative circles in England and France in their policies towards Nazi Germany in the mid-1930s.

The higher the tension rose in Western Europe and the Far East, the greater the desire of the US Congress to avoid being dragged into a new world war, at least in its early stages. In 1935 Congress passed a bill on neutrality, amended in 1936–7, which in particular banned the export of weapons to warring countries unless it was for the direct defence of a republic on the American continent. Undoubtedly, this policy could only help to strengthen the position of the extreme militarist groups in Japan and facilitate Japan's decision in 1937 to launch an all-out war to conquer the whole of China.

But even the start of the Sino-Japanese war did not change US policy. In July 1937 the US government declined a British proposal to undertake joint action against Japan. Even when Japan announced its blockade of the coast of Korea in August 1937 and closed the mouth of the Yangtzijiang (Yangtze) to the ships of all nations, and in the process shelled the American liner the *President Hoover*, US policy did not change. American business continued to export millions of dollars' worth of goods to Japan in 1937–8 – the value of military exports alone was in excess of $150 million – and in 1936–9 Japan was buying the greater part of its aviation fuel from the US.[5]

President Roosevelt gained support neither in Congress, nor from the country's ruling circles, nor even in the State department itself, for his famous 'quarantine' speech of 5 December 1937, in which he called for a halt to 'the epidemic of international lawlessness', and proposed co-ordinated action with the aim of operating a 'quarantine' against aggressive nations.

American public opinion was shocked by the Japanese sinking of the US gunboat *Panay* and three other US vessels. Some US admirals proposed mounting a naval blockade of Japan as an appropriate response, but the government turned down the idea. It was even suggested that Japanese control of East Asia, guaranteeing order and stability as it did, would lead to the increase of American trade with China and thus it served the American interest.[6]

Between 1936 and 1939 the United States gave a certain amount of help to the KMT government and also subscribed to the League of Nations' decision giving 'moral support' to China. The Council of the League of Nations, however, three times turned down China's demand, supported by the Soviet Union, that the Western countries, above all the United States, stop sending strategic raw materials to Japan.

In 1938 the Japanese forces made a significant advance towards the southern provinces of China, occupying Shanghai, Nanjing, Wuhan and Guangzhou. There were no serious obstacles in the way of further advance south and the capture of the whole of southern China, as well as the British, French and Dutch colonies of South-East Asia. The Japanese made their aggressive intentions clear by blocking the international settlements and the English concessions in China. The US government sent several protests to the Japanese in 1938; at the end of the year it advanced a loan of $25 million to the government of Jiang Gai-shi, and finally in the middle of 1939 it renounced the Japanese–US trade agreement. Goods needed by the Japanese, however, continued to be delivered on a private basis. In 1938 the US redeployed a large part of its fleet from the Atlantic to the Pacific.

During the Second World War

The beginning of the Second World War and Hitler's success in Europe – the defeat of Poland and France, the occupation of

Denmark, Norway, Belgium and Holland – also changed the strategic situation in the Far East.

In August 1940, Japan announced the inclusion of South-East Asia in its sphere of influence, known as the 'Greater East Asia Co-Prosperity Sphere'.[7] With the agreement of the puppet Pétain government in Vichy, the Japanese landed troops in northern Indo-China, and a month later Germany, Italy and Japan signed their triple pact aimed unambiguously against the United States and Britain. The latter in turn responded by signing an agreement on 7 November 1940 for the combined defence of the Pacific.[8] A united war council of the United States, Britain and China was set up in the beginning of 1941 at Chunjing, the US substantially increased its financial aid to China and soon also extended its lease-lend facilities. Events were rapidly moving towards a military conflict. In the summer of 1941 President Roosevelt froze all Japanese assets in the US and set up government controls on all trade and finance deals with Japan; and a few days later the export of American fuel to Japan ceased. Secret talks between America and Japan were nevertheless going on in Washington throughout this time. Highly influential political circles in the US still wanted to conclude an acceptable agreement with Japan and prevent the entry of their country into the world war.

On 7 December 1941, Japanese carrier-based planes approached the Hawaiian Islands unnoticed and carried out a devastating bombing raid on Pearl Harbor, the main US naval base in the Pacific, sinking a substantial part of the American fleet. Next day, 8 December, the US Congress declared war on Japan, Germany declared war on the United States and hence China became a direct ally of the United States. Jiang Gai-shi was formally appointed Commander Allied Forces in China, Indo-China and Burma, with US General Stilwell as his chief of staff. The US 14th Army Air Corps was formed on Chinese territory, and the US stepped up its deliveries of weapons and war supplies to China.

The United States and Britain were hoping that the Chinese would be able to withstand Japanese pressure on South-East Asia, but in 1941–3 the Japanese still held the military advantage on every front and occupied nearly all of the European colonies in Asia, the Philippines and a much expanded zone of occupation in China itself.

The military situation in the Pacific began to change in 1943–4 in favour of the Americans, who were gradually building up vast naval and air strength. The role of Jiang Gai-shi's armies was not very significant and for a while the Americans' main concern was to prevent a separate peace between Jiang and the Japanese.

While Jiang Gai-shi's armies were being defeated and in 1943–4 lost some 2 million square kilometres of territory, the Communist Eighth and new Fourth Armies were developing their operations in the Japanese rear with more and more success. The strategy of the Chinese Communist Party, however, based as it was on a real relationship of forces, was the strategy of the prolonged, or long-drawn-out, war. Without major victories on external fronts, this strategy could bring success only after many years, and that, naturally, suited neither the USA nor Britain. Their efforts to stimulate Jiang Gai-shi's fighting activities against Japan were not very successful, however. A substantial part of his forces were blocking the Communist areas with an eye on the civil war to come.

The United States did not relish the thought of China becoming a Communist power after the war, which was entering its final phase. They therefore not only continued to support Jiang Gai-shi but also made considerable efforts to enhance the international prestige of Nationalist (Kuomintang) China by seeing that it took part in a number of the most important conferences and meetings of the Allied powers. With America's active support, but also with Soviet agreement, China was made one of the four great powers which, together with the United States, Great Britain and the Soviet Union, took upon themselves the responsibility not only for the joint effort in the war, but also for the establishment of a more secure system of international co-operation after it. The Statute of the United Nations Organization, which was soon drawn up, gave China a place as a permanent member of the UN Security Council. Many American politicians and army personnel were well acquainted with the situation in the areas under Jiang's control, and were therefore extremely sceptical about both the Kuomintang regime and its prospects for the future. General Stilwell later described the Kuomintang as a band of thieves, that was guided only by the single thought of securing their own supremacy and that of their system. Its leaders were eaten up with the greed for money, influence and jobs.[9]

In 1944 the United States significantly stepped up its military operations against Japan and scored a number of major victories over the Japanese navy. The American generals decided that the main strike should be carried out in the Pacific, a policy requiring the gradual conquest of strategically important islands. Individual landings on Chinese territory would serve only as auxiliary diversionary operations. Although the Americans supported Jiang Gai-shi, they were not keen to increase their military aid to his regime. Roosevelt commented sarcastically that it would take the teaching and training of three generations before China became a serious factor.[10]

Meanwhile, by February 1945, it was clear that the war in Europe was coming to a close and that the defeat of Nazi Germany was only a matter of two or three months away. In the Pacific, by contrast, Japan was preparing to put up desperate resistance, even using suicide-fighters, and hoping to be able to achieve a relatively honourable peace. Despite the Allies' obvious superiority, military operations involving the use of large forces could still drag on for a long time. The Americans were getting close to the completion of the atomic bomb, but tests had not yet been carried out and its possibilities were still unclear. Not wanting to miss important opportunities in Europe because of their commitments in the Pacific, the US and Britain asked the USSR for help. At a meeting in the Kremlin in February 1945, Roosevelt, Churchill and Stalin took the then secret decision that, two or three months after the capitulation of Germany and the end of the war in Europe, the Soviet Union would enter the war against Japan on the side of the Allies.[11]

Two months after the Yalta Conference of 1945 President Roosevelt died and was succeeded by Harry Truman, whose attitude to co-operation with the Soviet Union was very different. He was delighted by the successful results of the atom bomb tests in the New Mexico desert, not only because the United States now had a powerful new weapon, but, as one of the American researchers later observed, Truman and his closest advisers thought they could use the bomb as a means of diplomatic deterrence to the Russians. They were hoping that it would produce the necessary shock to make the Japanese surrender before the Russians entered the war in the Far East.[12]

Events were moving fast. The first atom bomb was dropped on

Hiroshima on 6 August 1945 and was indeed a great shock to Japan. The Japanese government had not yet properly understood the significance of this tragedy when on 8 August the Soviet Union declared war on Japan. The second atom bomb was dropped on Nagasaki on 9 August and the Soviet Union began to advance into Manchuria. On 14 August the Japanese military and political leaders announced that they were ready to capitulate and the final act of Japan's unconditional surrender was signed on board the US battleship *Missouri* on 2 September 1945. American troops began landing on Japanese soil and setting up the administration for their military occupation.

From 1945 to the beginning of the Korean War

The situation in China, meanwhile, was exceptionally complicated. A vast part of the country was still under the control of the Japanese army and the puppet forces created and armed by Japan. The US command and Jiang Gai-shi were demanding the surrender of Japanese troops only in situations where their weapons and their control over the territory could be transferred either to the Americans or to Jiang's forces. Meanwhile, by the end of the war, Jiang Gai-shi's main forces had been driven into remote areas of south-east China and, fearing that the Communists would be able to broaden their zone of control and even occupy the country's large cities, Jiang Gai-shi ordered the Japanese commanders to put up an 'effective' defence against the People's Army and even 'to liberate' the strongpoints they had already surrendered to it.[13] Simultaneously, he appealed to the Chinese puppet forces, who had hitherto been subordinate to the collaborationist pro-Japanese government in Nanjing, to stand firm at their posts and to carry out his orders, promising their officers that their military ranks and privileges would be protected. It should be noted that the command of the puppet forces had earlier had secret relations with Jiang Gai-shi and that many of them were KMT generals who had gone over to the Japanese on Jiang's secret instructions, their main task being to conduct the struggle against liberated areas that were under the control of the CCP.[14]

Immediately after the Japanese surrender, the Americans

began landing US Marines in the main Chinese ports, where dozens of US warships now appeared and cast anchor. In the middle of September 1945, for example, an 18,000-strong unit of marines landed not far from Tianjin, while other units landed in Nanjing and Shanghai and soon US ships were sailing into all the ports of Northern China. US paratroops were dropped on Peking and rail junctions, and soon the total number of US troops in China amounted to more than 100,000.[15] This was not enough, however, for control over a country as vast as China, nor indeed even for the purpose of accepting the Japanese surrender. Therefore at the end of August 1945, on President Truman's orders, US air and naval forces commenced the huge operation of airlifting and shipping KMT troops out of south-west China and into the main cities of central, southern, south-east and, where possible, also northern China. Within weeks of the Japanese surrender they had transferred three KMT armies to the Shanghai, Peking and Nanjing regions. Hundreds of thousands of KMT troops were shipped by sea and air in this way to key regions. In his memoirs, President Truman frankly explained that Jiang Gai-shi needed US help to get his troops to the places where the Japanese were ready to lay down their arms, and that if they had not got there, the Japanese might have handed over their weapons to the Chinese Communists who would have hence been able to take over the territory then under Japanese occupation.[16] Truman recalled that, if the Japanese had been told to lay down their arms immediately and move to the coast, the whole of China would have been occupied by the Communists. The Japanese were therefore told to stay where they were and maintain order. This was a joint operation of the Departments of Defense and State and was approved by Truman.[17]

With the end of the war the Americans had increased their economic aid to Jiang Gai-shi and now, having helped to transfer his troops to key cities, they proceeded in the autumn of 1945 also to undertake their intensive re-arming, reorganization and training, their numbers having been greatly enhanced at the expense of the puppet armies and new mobilizations.

In the autumn of 1945, as we have already noted, the Communists were also strengthening their influence and their armed forces, using the help they were getting from the Soviet Union and its army. Jiang Gai-shi, however, was confident of his own supremacy, for by the autumnn of 1945 he was controlling more than twice as much territory as the CCP and he had a well-equipped army more than three times larger than the regular forces of the People's Liberation Army. The nation's desire for peace during those months was so great, however, that the leaders of the KMT could not bring themselves to turn down a proposal from the CCP to hold talks, with a view to averting a new civil war and to creating a coalition government. The talks opened in Chunjing at the end of August 1945, with both Jiang Gai-shi and Mao Zedong taking part, and they ended on 10 October with the issue of a joint communiqué in which both sides undertook 'determinedly to avoid civil war in order to guarantee the building of a new, independent, free and flourishing China'. They further agreed that political democratization, the transfer of all troops to the state and the recognition of equal legal status for all political parties and groups were absolutely necessary to guarantee the peaceful construction of the state.[18]

It was one thing to sign such an undertaking, but it was quite another to see that it was carried out, and neither new talks and agreements, nor the Moscow conference of the Soviet, American and British foreign ministers, nor the Political Consultative Conference in Chunjing, which included the KMT, the CCP, small intermediate parties, and authoritative non-party figures, could avert a new major civil war. Nearly 200 KMT divisions, massed on the border of areas under CCP control, launched a large-scale offensive in March 1946 in north-east China, and in June–July the civil war was being fought on a nation-wide scale.

In the first part of this study, we referred briefly to the course of the civil war in China, to the KMT's partial success and the early collapse of its 'general offensive' against the areas liberated by the Chinese Communist Party. We also mentioned the advance of the People's Liberation Army following this and we noted Stalin's qualified attitude to this advance. Stalin's fears regarding possible open intervention by the USA in the Chinese civil war were not, however, confirmed.

The threat of defeat for Jiang Gai-shi and the obvious weakening of KMT control over a wide expanse of the country aroused great alarm in American government circles. The Democrats were in power at the time, and President Truman and Secretary of State Marshall decided to increase military and economic aid to the KMT. They turned down at once, however, plans submitted by more reactionary American politicians for direct military intervention in the civil war. For the United States, a war with China would have been a very different proposition from the war with Japan. It would have required vast land forces and been protracted, costly and unpopular, and since the Communists were most likely to get support from the Soviet Union, the chances of success for the United States would be minimal.

The principal differences between the Democrats and Republicans were soon concentrated on the scale of American help that should be given to Jiang Gai-shi's China. The Republicans demanded that it be increased several-fold and that many more thousands of American military advisers and specialists should be sent out to help Jiang Gai-shi. General Wedemeyer, who for several years had been a chief of staff in Jiang Gai-shi's army and until the summer of 1946 commander of US forces in China, was sent out to study the situation on the ground. Wedemeyer, who had the reputation of a reactionary anti-Communist, was staggered by the scale both of Jiang Gai-shi's unpopularity and his defeats. He nevertheless recommended that aid to the Chinese leader should be both of large dimension and extended duration, but his proposals were not accepted. United States policy in late 1947 was based on the principle that the solution to the Chinese problem must be for the Chinese themselves to find, and the US did not intend by its aid programme to put itself in the position of bearing responsibility, either for the conduct of the fighting or the economy of China. It did not wish to assume the role of the Chinese government, realizing that such a stance would drag the US down the path of intervention from which it would be unable to extricate itself, regardless of the circumstances or actions of the Chinese government. This policy greatly dissatisfied Jiang Gai-shi who was demanding much more aid from the United States but refusing to introduce any domestic reforms as a means of consolidating the social and political base of his government, as even General Wedemeyer advised him to do.

Meanwhile, events in China were moving faster than either the Americans or Jiang Gai-shi had expected, or even Mao Zedong, who had thought the war with the KMT could be a very prolonged one, lasting at least five years. A radical turning-point came in the second half of 1948 when the main forces of the

KMT were destroyed in a series of major encounters. One after another, the large cities came under CCP control: Chingjiang, Zhengzhou, Changchun, Shenyang. The entire north-east and the central plain were liberated from the KMT, and in January 1949 the People's Liberation Armies took Tianjin and Peking. Still the KMT hoped to consolidate in the vast provinces of the south-west.

The United States had greatly increased its financial and military aid to Jiang Gai-shi in 1948, but in a statement to Congress Secretary of State Marshall warned of the possibility that the Nationalist government – as the Kuomintang came more commonly to be known after the civil war – might not hold out and that it might leave under pressure either from the Communists or from some outside forces which could enter China. It was not in America's interests, Marshall continued, to go on absorbing Jiang Gai-shi's failures and scattering US forces to the detriment of significantly more important areas where there was the possibility of resisting the Commmunist threat or upsetting the Communists' plans, that was to say in the main area of Western Europe with its traditions of free institutions.[19]

In November 1948, realizing that his army had fallen apart and that the end of the regime he had created was near, Jiang Gai-shi asked the United States to take over command of his army, to put American officers in charge of Chinese units and to appoint an American general to direct stategic planning. Secretary of State Marshall and President Truman turned down his request. They knew perfectly well that the transfer of Chinese troops to US command would not bring victory. The US moreover was beginning to recall its military advisers from China.

There was no unity in US governing circles on the issues of China policy, and many influential people, especially top figures in the Republican Party, were arguing for greater and more active American help for Jiang Gai-shi. 1948 was an election year in the US, and naturally Jiang Gai-shi and his friends were hoping that Truman would be defeated and that the Republicans and their presidential candidate, Thomas Dewey, would win.

The Democrats' pre-election platform, which was published in the summer of 1948, said no more about aid to China than it did about military aid to Greece or Turkey. In this respect the Republicans were more decisive, and in his first interview, on

25 June, Dewey declared that, if he were elected, one of the cardinal principles of his administration would be to give more effective aid in the struggle against Communist influence in China.[20] The Republican election platform, indeed, contained a promise to defend and develop the historic friendship with China and 'to show America's deep concern by supporting China's integrity and freedom'.[21] Jiang Gai-shi's emissaries were actively lobbying in Washington and in General MacArthur's headquarters in Tokyo, trying to scare American public opinion with the spectre of a Communist victory in China as 'the beginning of a new world catastrophe'. They contributed to Republican party funds, and they looked for opportunities to provoke an armed confrontation between the United States and the Soviet Union. In several Chinese cities under KMT control demonstrations took place under the slogan 'Long live President Dewey!'

Even without the efforts of the Jiang Gai-shi lobby, Dewey had the support of a majority of Americans, according to pre-election polls, but quite unexpectedly it was Truman who won on the day, an outcome, needless to say, that bitterly disappointed the Jiang Gai-shi camp in China. The Truman administration was, of course, extremely hostile to the Chinese Communists and to the revolution they were leading, but still the Democrats took a more sober view of America's ability to influence the course and outcome of events in so vast a country as China; it was unrealistic to imagine that what Truman had been able to achieve in Greece he would also be able to do in China. After taking the oath for his new term, President Truman set out the main points of his future foreign policy before the American people, and the problem of China was totally ignored, a fact which aroused great indignation among the Republican opposition, both in Congress and outside. The US ambassador in Peking, John Leighton Stuart, received telegrams calling for 'constructive help' for Jiang Gai-shi, and Republicans demanded that the government make a large loan. But the new Secretary of State, Dean Acheson, refused, arguing that it would be a catastrophe to give large credit to a government that was already in no condition to withstand a decisive push by the Communists even in the south of the country.[22]

To explain the government's position and its policy to the American public, the State Department hurriedly produced a 'white book', cited above, which was compiled by a specially formed group of State Department staff. Published in 1949, it remains the main source for the study and analysis of US policy on China between 1944 and 1949.

By the end of 1949 the whole of continental China, apart from Tibet, had been cleared of KMT forces. The United States, however, refused to recognize the new government and state, the Chinese People's Republic. American forces had already left the country, and with American help the remnants of Jiang Gai-shi's army and the leaders of the Kuomintang had managed to get across to Taiwan, an island of some 35,000 square kilometres with a population of 15 million, and where, under the protection of the US navy, a new and formally independent state of China was set up. The United States established diplomatic relations, concluded a mutual security treaty which bound the US to defend Taiwan, and for many years guaranteed Taiwan a seat on the Security Council and General Assembly of the United Nations. On Taiwan, however, the KMT at last managed to gain a 'lasting' victory by annihilating the greater part of the Taiwanese peasant rebellion which had erupted in 1947 and which was still in control of much of the island when the new Chinese state was set up.

A wave of criticism was levelled against the Truman administration over the collapse of all its calculations about China. In an accompanying note to the 'white book', Dean Acheson defended the record by pointing out that the huge amount of aid given to Jiang Gai-shi had been more than enough for them to win against the Communists, and that it was Nationalist, or KMT, incompetence that had been to blame. The only alternative open to the United States had been direct and massive intervention, but in defence of a government that had already squandered the trust both of its army and its people. Intervention, moreover, would have angered the Chinese people, would have run entirely counter to historic US policy, and would have been condemned by the American people. 'The sinister outcome of the civil war in China was outside the control of the United States,' he concluded.[23] Even before the proclamation of the Chinese People's Republic, the United States government was faced with the problem of establishing contact of some sort with the Chinese Communist Party. John Leighton Stuart, the US ambassador in

Nanjing, where the KMT had its government at the time, was instructed to conduct talks with the CCP in the strictest secrecy, but when he was invited to Peking to raise the level of the talks, President Truman, sensitive to the loud criticism his policy had already aroused, refused his permission and recalled Stuart to Washington for 'consultations'.

After the proclamation of the Chinese People's Republic, Zhou Enlai officially informed the United States, through the US Consul General in Peking, of his government's willingness to establish diplomatic relations.[24] A wave of anti-Communism, however, was sweeping the United States, with Senator Joseph McCarthy even declaring that the Truman administration had fallen under Communist influence and lost China.[25] Peking's approach was turned down and official circles in the United States began to push for a policy of 'encirclement', which meant building US bases in South Korea, on Okinawa, in Japan and Taiwan, in Indo-China and the Philippines. A long period of bitter hostility and military and political confrontation between the United States and the Chinese People's Republic was now inaugurated.

Twenty years of hostility

The formation of the Chinese People's Republic, followed by the treaty of friendship and mutual aid signed by China and the Soviet Union, was greeted by ruling circles in the United States with extreme hostility. While the Soviet press described the success of the Chinese revolution as the greatest defeat for capitalism since the October revolution, the American press said much the same thing, though in a different sense, and a sense moreover that was reinforced by US policy.

The central position in the anti-Communist front which the United States was creating soon came to be occupied by Taiwan, where the salvaged remnant of Jiang Gai-shi's army numbered more than half a million men, and whither China's relatively small navy, her archives and her gold reserve had also been evacuated. The United States provided substantial financial and military aid to Taiwan and a large military establishment was developed there under American direction. Sixteen warships and the supplies for five divisions were handed over to Jiang Gai-shi. Several large airforce bases were built and the main ports of the island became anchorages for the ships of the United States Pacific Fleet.

Having recalled all her diplomats from China by the end of 1949, the United States banned the sale of 'strategic goods' to China, including metals, chemicals, equipment for many branches of industry, motor vehicles and petroleum products. Although China officially appointed her representatives to the Security Council and other United Nations organizations, the USA virtually barred them from their functions. Not surprisingly, the Chinese press during this time was extremely hostile in its assessment of American policy.

Relations between the two countries became still more hostile with the outbreak in the summer of 1950 of the Korean War, the history of which can be outlined simply. In 1948 two states had been set up in Korea: in the southern part of the Korean peninsula, where the Japanese surrender was received by the Americans, the Korean Republic was formed under the protection of the United States; in the northern half of the peninsula the Korean People's Democratic Republic was created under the protection of the Soviet Union and China. Complicated talks and political manoeuvres were going on at the time with a view to uniting Korea and forming a single coalition government for the whole country. When the negotiating table proved inadequate, the matter was taken to the battlefield for resolution. At the end of June 1950, after some short border clashes, the army of North Korea launched a massive offensive on the south and within a short space of time had inflicted serious defeats on the forces of the South Korean dictator, Li Sing-man (or Syngman Rhee, as he was known to the West). Despite US air support, within 20 days Li Sing-man had lost practically the whole of South Korea, managing to hold on to only a small bridgehead at the city of Pusan.

In the first days of the conflict the United States moved its Seventh Fleet into the Straits of Taiwan, landed its 13th Air Corps in Taiwan and started a blockade of the Chinese coast. In the absence of the Soviet delegate, the UN Security Council passed a resolution declaring North Korea to be the aggressor and appealing to member states to come to the aid of South

Korea. On the basis of this decision, troops from the United States and 15 other nations entered the war under the command of US General Douglas MacArthur, who had distinguished himself in the war against Japan. With air and sea cover provided by hundreds of planes and ships, a large landing was effected at the port of Inchon, deep in the rear of the North Korean army, which was thus compelled to make a hasty retreat to the north after suffering heavy losses. US troops, together with the remnants of the South Korean army, began to move north above the 38th parallel and were soon occupying the whole of North Korea, reaching the Chinese border at the Yalu River. From the end of August US planes were carrying out attacks on areas bordering China. In the autumn of 1950 it looked as if North Korea had been thoroughly defeated.

Although the war in Korea originally developed as a conflict between North and South Korea, there can be little doubt that various scenarios had been discussed well before June 1950 in the political and military centres of Moscow and Peking and possibly also in the recent talks in Moscow between Stalin and Mao Zedong. It is difficult to say which of the two had been the prime initiator of the action. Some present-day Western historians take the view that Stalin wanted to weaken the Chinese People's Republic by dragging the young state into a war with the United States. It is equally possible, however, that neither in Moscow nor Peking, nor in Pyongyang, did they have a proper understanding of the present mood of the American leadership and its desire to take political and military revenge for the recent defeat in China. For President Truman, who was still being accused of having been too soft on the Communists – practically of having made a deal with them – it was crucially important that he demonstrate his firmness and his anti-Communism.

Washington had, however, underrated the determination and resolve of the new Chinese leadership. As early as the end of October 1950 individual units of Chinese volunteers, and in fact several Chinese regular army units, had crossed over into North Korea to give help to the beaten and demoralized North Korean People's Army which was retreating back to the north. On 25 November large units of the Chinese army under the command of Peng Dehuai crossed the Sino-Korean border and launched a major and successful offensive, thanks to a combination of the element of surprise and superior numbers. The Americans suffered defeat and it was now their turn to beat a rapid retreat. By early January Chinese forces were occupying not only Pyongyang, the capital of North Korea, but also Seoul, that of South Korea. The Americans were forced to bring in large contingents of fresh troops and after fierce fighting managed to halt the Chinese advance, reoccupy Seoul and again advance to within 20–25 kilometres of the 38th parallel, where the fighting continued for more than six months with neither side able to win a decisive victory. The United States had manifest technical as well as aerial and naval superiority, but the Chinese, despite their losses, had far greater numbers.

The war was a very bloody affair. According to American statistics, by the end of 1951 the United States had lost 135,000 men, dead, wounded or missing, the South Koreans 260,000, and United Nations contingents from other countries 12,000. China's human resources, of course, far outweighed those of the United States. According to Kim Ir-sen, up to 800,000 Chinese volunteers were buried on Korean territory, while the armies of North Korea and China together lost up to 1.5 million, dead or wounded.[26] Among them was the son of Mao Zedong.

Reporting to the White House on the situation, General MacArthur said there were three possible solutions to the Korean problem: either continue a bloody war against the Chinese within the framework of one Korea, or accept the 38th parallel as an armistice line – always assuming the Chinese would agree to peace talks – or, finally, broaden the scale of the war, that is launch a large-scale attack on China using every means available. Among the options under consideration were the total blockade of the Chinese coast, the despatch of Jiang Gai-shi's army to the mainland, and the bombing of large Chinese cities, with the possible use of the atomic bomb. General MacArthur was personally in favour of this last option, despite the obvious threat of war it would pose in view of the fact that the Chinese People's Republic had already signed its mutual aid treaty with the Soviet Union.

President Truman did not support MacArthur's views, which nevertheless many Americans shared, and, relying instead on the support of the chiefs of the combined staffs, he favoured a limited war with a view to achieving an armistice. General MacArthur, however, came out with a public statement demanding the spread of the war to China's internal bases and coastal provinces, as a result of which he was relieved of his command. He was received as a national hero by the city of San Francisco, given a triumphal welcome in Washington, where he made a speech to a joint session of Congress, and millions turned out to greet him in New York. The argument between the politicians and the military nevertheless ended in the triumph of the more moderate line, and by July 1951 armistice talks had begun in the ancient Korean capital city of Kesong. With interruptions they lasted two years and were concluded in July 1953 by the signing of an armistice agreement which is still in force today. By this time the United States had a new president, the Republican Dwight Eisenhower, while in the Soviet Union, Stalin having died in March 1953, there was a new leadership consisting of a small group, among whom the most influential were G. M. Malenkov, N. A. Bulganin and N. S. Khrushchev.

These changes in the US and Soviet leadership were to have far-reaching consequences for relations between the two countries. The new Soviet leadership gradually began practising a new foreign policy, of which one important element was to find ways of improving relations with Western countries in general and the United States in particular. It was the successful development of this policy that led to the July 1955 meeting in Geneva of the heads of government of the USSR, the USA, Britain and France. For a short time relations between the USSR and the Western countries were greatly improved. The situation in the Far East, however, was very different and even after the armistice in Korea, relations between the Chinese People's Republic and the United States hardly improved.

The early 1950s in the United States were the time of McCarthyism and the witch-hunt. Anti-Chinese feeling predominated both in the Senate, where the greatest influence was wielded by Senators McCarthy and McCarran, and in the State Department, where anti-Communism became fundamental policy for the new Secretary of State, John Foster Dulles. Under pressure from a Senate committee headed by McCarthy, many leading China specialists, who did not share the administration's views, were smeared by interrogations and fired from their jobs. Dulles carried out a similar 'purge' in the State Department and other government institutions. Between 1953 and 1957, in the words of the American scholar J. C. Thompson, an entire generation of extremely valuable, well-trained American specialists on China were thrown out of their jobs or simply disappeared. The elaboration of US China policy was now put in the hands of people who did not know China and had no idea about the problems of the Chinese revolution. American policy on the Far East, in Thompson's view, was distorted, deeply flawed, and a future result of this would be the war in Vietnam.[27]

Throughout the 1950s, the United States continually strengthened and increased its military and naval bases in the Far East and South-East Asia. In making American forces responsible for defending Taiwan at the beginning of the Korean War, the US government was in effect revising the island's status. Economic and military aid to Taiwan were significantly stepped up. Between 1945 and 1965 US investment amounted to $4.76 billion dollars, of which $2.53 billion was in the form of military aid.[28] On 2 December 1954 the United States and the 'Government of the Chinese Republic' signed a mutual defence treaty without time limit, under which the United States was granted the right to maintain its troops on the island, while for its part it undertook both to give military aid and also to assist in the economic progress and social welfare of Taiwan.[29]

Jiang Gai-shi's government had under its control not only Taiwan, but also the small islands located between Taiwan and the mainland. These offshore islands – Quemoy, Matsu and the Dazhens, all part of the Pescadores group – were gradually turned into military bases by the forces of Jiang Gai-shi. At the beginning of September 1954 China shelled these islands for the first time, greatly heightening tension in the Taiwan–China conflict, into which the United States was now to be dragged. In January 1955, on a proposal from President Eisenhower, the US Congress passed a special bill giving the President wide discretionary powers to use US forces in the defence of Taiwan, the Pescadores Islands and the positions and territories connected with them.[30] Using naval cover, the Americans effected the evacuation of the sparse population of the Dazhens, situated some 300 kilometres from Taiwan and close to the Chinese coastline, and where the Nationalists maintained a garrison of 15,000 troops. At the same time the US navy undertook the defence of the larger islands of Quemoy and Matsu which lay closer to Taiwan and which were under fire from the Chinese mainland artillery.

In demonstrating their determination to defend the Nationalist regime, American naval vessels and aircraft were in frequent violation of Chinese territorial waters and airspace, but the Chinese were wary of widening the conflict and merely sent 'serious warnings' to the US government.

Both the civil war in China and the Korean War had given rise to several problems which could only be resolved through direct discussion between representatives of the United States and China. Such discussions indeed opened in Geneva in 1954 and it was quickly agreed that they should continue on a regular basis at ambassadorial level, with China represented by its ambassador to Poland. Already during the first phase of the talks, agreement was reached over the repatriation of most of the US citizens still in China and of those Chinese in the United States who wished to return home. On more complicated issues, such as the use of force in the region of Taiwan, the Sino-American talks went no further than statements by the two sides of their respective positions.

Relations between the Soviet Union and the West, meanwhile, took a sharp turn for the worse in the autumn of 1956, as a result of the Soviet suppression of the Hungarian uprising, and also the assault by Britain, France and Israel on Egypt, which was at that time the Soviet Union's chief ally in the Middle East. By 1958, however, the Soviet Union was making strenuous efforts once more to improve relations with the countries of Western Europe and the United States. Some improvement took place in China's political and economic relations both with Japan and the countries of Western Europe, but her relations with the United States remained extremely strained, not that either side made especially noticeable efforts to improve them.

China's internal political situation at the time had become extremely complicated. In late 1957 and early 1958 Mao Zedong was promulgating his policy of the Great Leap Forward. This was to be a frenzied attempt to multiply industrial and agricultural output several times over a three- or four-year period and, in thus overcoming the country's inveterate backwardness, to proceed to the immediate introduction of Communist relations in Chinese society. In Mao's thinking, a tense situation in external relations would admirably serve the purpose of mobilizing hundreds of millions of Chinese to carry out the most varied grandiose schemes. Chinese peasants marched to work in military formation and carried a rifle on their backs as they worked.

The situation in the Straits of Taiwan became so strained in the autumn of 1958 that the possibility of war with China was being seriously contemplated in Washington. The Chinese were stepping up their shelling of the offshore islands and moving units of their army into the area, and it looked as though they were preparing to land on Matsu and Quemoy. Explaining these moves to Soviet Foreign Minister Gromyko, Mao Zedong suggested that international tension, especially in connection with what was happening in the Taiwan region, was of greater advantage at the moment to the Soviet Union and China than it was to the imperialists.[31] A special Chinese government announcement declared that Chinese territorial waters now extended to a width of 12 nautical miles and that this would apply to all Chinese territories, including the mainland, the offshore islands and other islands that were separated from the mainland by open sea. Foreign warships and warplanes were prohibited from entering Chinese territorial waters and airspace without the prior permission of the Chinese People's Republic.[32]

In the autumn of 1958, as a matter of urgency, the United States despatched 130 warships to the Straits of Taiwan, including seven of her thirteen aircraft carriers, three cruisers and forty destroyers. Large contingents of air-force and marine units were sent to Taiwan, where the building of rocket launch-pads was begun. Threats of all kinds issued from both sides, but China's shelling of the offshore islands grew less and less frequent and much less intense. The lessening of tension in the Taiwan region, however, was accompanied by a gradual deterioration of relations in South-East Asia, above all in Vietnam.

Much earlier, in the second half of the 1940s, France had been fighting a war in Vietnam in an effort to retain the entire peninsula of Indo-China as a French colony, but despite the constant increase of the French expeditionary forces, by 1951–2 the military initiative had passed to the government of the Democratic Republic of Vietnam and its People's Army.

The United States kept a close watch on the situation in Indo-China, which State Secretary Dean Acheson described as 'part of America's defence perimeter in the Far East',[33] and when the Republicans came to power the United States greatly increased its financial and military aid to France. In 1953–4 France was given credit of $1 billion, and in that same period she took delivery of 340 US aircraft, 1,400 tanks and armoured vehicles, 350 landing craft and great quantities of light arms and ammunition.[34] As it became clear that France was losing the war in Vietnam, the extreme anti-Communist movement in the United States gathered momentum and began demanding direct US intervention. However, even a special military mission which was sent to Indo-China to assess the situation reported back to President Eisenhower that large contingents of US troops would need to be sent if the People's Army of the Democratic Republic of Vietnam (DRV or North Vietnam) was to be defeated. This was more than Eisenhower was prepared to do, and after the defeat of the French at Dien Bien Phu, the United States had to agree to talks in Geneva where not only France, Britain and the United States took part, but also representatives of Vietnam, China, the Soviet Union, Laos and Kampuchea. The great powers pledged themselves at the Geneva Conference not to interfere in the internal affairs of the countries of Indo-China. Political normalization in those countries was to be brought about by means of free elections. A temporary demarcation line running more or less along the 17th parallel was established between North and South Vietnam.

The United States administration saw the Geneva accord as a defeat, and in order to 'compensate' for this loss it created the South-East Asian Treaty Organization (SEATO) in the region, a military-political bloc that included the USA, Britain, France, Australia, New Zealand, Pakistan, Thailand, the Philippines and soon South Vietnam. It was precisely in South Vietnam that the United States was intending to establish a reliable military and political bridgehead directed above all at North Vietnam. It had been possible to build such a bridgehead in South Korea without particular difficulty, but in South Vietnam the government of Ngo Din-Diem, despite the use of terror, was unable to extend its firm control over the territory and population, and during the period 1954–60 the United States broadened both its economic and military presence in the country. In addition to providing military aid to South Vietnam amounting in all to $2 billion, the United States was also mainly responsible for reorganizing and rearming the South Vietnamese army, and between 1955 and 1960 it raised the number of its military advisers from 500 to 3,000.

As the internal situation in China worsened during 1960–3, and the polemics with the Soviet Union grew more intense, the Chinese stepped up their anti-American propaganda. China's main accusation against the Communist Party of the Soviet Union was precisely that it did not conduct the struggle against the 'paper tiger' of US imperialism with enough energy. In practice, the Chinese themselves were somewhat changing their own approach to the United States. They stopped shelling the offshore islands, transferred elsewhere forces which had been brought to the coast of the Straits of Taiwan, and hence allowed the United States to remove most of its fleet from the area.

In his first State of the Nation message to Congress on 30 January 1961, newly elected President Kennedy declared that the constant pressure of the Chinese Communists in Asia, from the Indian frontier to South Vietnam to the jungles of Laos, constituted a threat to the security of the entire area, and that in order to respond to this audacious challenge and fulfil its role, the United States could not walk away from the world arena, but must reassess and review the whole arsenal of means that it had at its disposal.[35]

This same theme was attacked more decisively and in sharper terms by Vice President Lyndon Johnson, who was to become President on 22 November 1963 on the assassination of John Kennedy. After touring the countries of Asia in May 1961, Johnson concluded that the United States must throw its might into the struggle against Communism in South-East Asia, and be determined to win, otherwise it would inevitably have to concede the Pacific Ocean and look to the defence of its own shores. Asiatic Communism, Johnson claimed, was preventing the existence of free nations on the sub-continent, and unless America made the effort, the island outposts – that is, the Philippines, Japan, Taiwan – would not be safe and the great Pacific Ocean would be turned into a 'Red Sea'.[36]

Even during Kennedy's years in office the United States

increased the number of its military advisers in Vietnam by several thousand and was gradually becoming more and more involved in the civil war that was unfolding implacably in the Vietnamese jungles, villages and towns. The scale of American intervention in South Vietnam grew significantly in 1964, although it did not prevent the Communist Party and partisans from achieving considerable success and creating several zones over which they exercised control. Now President Johnson took the decision that Eisenhower had refused to take ten years earlier, and in February 1965 US Air Force planes bombed North Vietnam and units of the American army began to take a direct part in the fighting on South Vietnamese territory.

It goes without saying that American political and military leaders during those years kept a close watch on political events in China and the sharpening ideological and political conflict going on between the Soviet Union and China. American politicians were heartened by the widening of this rift, believing as they did that it made it easier for them to confront each of their adversaries separately, for the fact of the Sino-Soviet split in itself did nothing to alter the extremely hostile relations existing between the United States and China. To many American politicians, indeed, Chinese Communism seemed much more militant, radical and anti-American than Soviet-style Communism at that time. State Secretary Dean Rusk had warned as early as 1961 against counting too heavily on the differences between the Soviet Union and China, for the question was one of 'two systems of power which are as a whole united, and which have a definite common interest in opposing the rest of the world'.[37] In later years he would go on to assert that both China and the Soviet Union were equally hostile to the United States and 'freedom', and that they only differed in the methods they chose to struggle against the 'free world'.

Nevertheless, the split between the Soviet Union and China gradually began to cause changes in important aspects of Sino-American relations, changes which were initiated not so much by politicians as by various influential business circles. As we have already noted, Sino-Soviet economic relations shrank dramatically at the beginning of the 1960s, China's trade with Japan and the countries of Western Europe began to grow, while America, by its boycott, excluded itself from the potentially vast Chinese market. One of John Kennedy's most appealing slogans had been a call for new ideas, and among such new ideas emerging from some of the young politicians in his circle was the modification of US policy in relation to China, which would involve the admission of China to the United Nations and the Security Council, while safeguarding Taiwan's UN membership and its status as an independent state. The Chinese People's Republic, however, decisively rejected the 'two Chinas' policy, and Jiang Gai-shi's government would similarly not hear of it. The exacerbation of China's internal situation, following the collapse of the Great Leap Forward, had given the Nationalists hopes of returning to power in China. They believed that all they had to do was land on the mainland and the majority of Chinese who were fed up with Communism would join them. It was a dangerous illusion. Nevertheless general mobilization was declared in Taiwan, a supreme war council was formed to supervise 'counter-offensive activities', road and sea transport facilities were mobilized, and hurried preparations for an invasion of the mainland were made on the offshore islands, all of which aroused anxiety not only in Peking but also in Washington. Jiang Gai-shi could not so much as begin his active war policy without American help, but the use of the American naval and air forces to give him direct support was neither in the United States' interest nor its capability. John Kennedy therefore made it clear to Jiang that the US would not support the Nationalists in, for example, a landing on the mainland, although it would defend Taiwan if the mainland Chinese were to resort to force.

The search for new ideas on America's China policy continued after Kennedy was assassinated, virtually by momentum. For example, three weeks after that event, a public statement by Assistant Secretary of State R. Hillsman on the need to begin a process of 'normalizing' relations with the People's Republic of China evoked a loud response in the press. In 1964 quite a few influential American newspapers and journals called on the government to 'seize the initiative' and 'exploit the Sino-Soviet rivalry in America's interests'. The 1960s saw a great increase in the number of different government groups that were studying the Chinese problem, and hundreds of plans and schemes of all kinds for the future course of American policy were sent in to

Washington and the White House. Even the Senate sub-committee on the Far East and Pacific Ocean sent the President recommendations 'to take the initiative at a suitable time in the question of re-establishing direct contact with Red China'.[38] On several occasions in the mid-1960s both Houses of Congress organized hearings on China and on the possible ways open to the United States to alter its policy in the light of the Sino-Soviet split.

Such voices became rarer and quieter, drowned by the thunder of bombs and shells exploding in Vietnam. The advocates of a hard line on China gradually got the upper hand in the Johnson administration and one of its keenest proponents was Secretary of State Dean Rusk, not to mention President Johnson himself. The United States was drawn deeper and deeper into the war in Vietnam, while for its part the Chinese People's Republic increased its aid to North Vietnam. By 1967-8 the Americans had 570,000 troops in South Vietnam, while their losses could be counted in tens of thousands dead and many more wounded. There was, however, no breakthrough in the fighting, and success, if anything, was increasingly on the side of their enemies. The influence of the top brass on White House policy grew steadily, and fear of a humiliating defeat gave rise to the idea in the minds of the generals of some new show of strength, including direct invasion of North Vietnam by US troops and even preventive strikes against China's nuclear installations. The White House did not take up these ideas, however, and US and South Vietnamese forces never crossed the 17th parallel, limiting themselves to the heavy bombing of the North. The United States government was wary of another clash with 'Chinese volunteers', but the war nevertheless became more and more bitter and did nothing to encourage a review of America's official, negative policy towards China.[39]

The Cultural Revolution created anarchy within the country and greater isolation for China in the international arena. Her ambassadors were recalled from capitalist and socialist countries alike and were not replaced. In the eyes of many American politicians, however, the Cultural Revolution, for all its outer radicalism, had certain intrinsic qualities. First of all, it was accompanied by an extremely sharp and seemingly final break with the Soviet Union. Secondly, it administered severe shocks to the Chinese economy which was already shaky enough as it was, and since China was not going to be able to manage without foreign aid in the future, business circles in America counted on benefitting themselves from these circumstances. The Cultural Revolution was accompanied by a fierce internal struggle for power, the weakening and partial destruction of the Chinese Communist Party, the devastation of normal state structures and the general debilitation of China as a great power. The United States no longer feared an invasion of Taiwan or the arrival of Chinese forces in Vietnam. All these circumstances seemed far more important to ruling circles in America than any amount of anti-American rhetoric from the Red Guards or hostile *émigrés*. As the eminent American historian George Kennan commented at the time, one of the most encouraging facts for the last 20 years had appeared on the world scene, and it would be foolish for the Americans to sit idly by and ignore the conflict between China and the Soviet Union and not to profit from the favourable consequences that it might have.[40]

Official Washington, however, reacted very slowly to China's changing domestic and international situation. The State Department announced at the end of 1965 that doctors and medical scientists could now go on trips to China, and a short while later it announced that Chinese journalists could visit the United States, and then a number of American universities were permitted to establish scientific exchanges with China. The number of visas issued by the State Department during this period, however, could be counted in tens, and there were no hints as yet of any change in the position.

Far more activity in the field of US–Chinese relations was achieved by American business circles, individual Congressmen and academic specialists on China. As a result of the efforts of interested individuals and groups, in July 1966 a National Committee for American–Chinese Relations was founded, on an unofficial basis, in order to make propaganda in favour of normal relations with China. Influential politicians, prominent businessmen and well-known scholars took part in its activities. The Committee received donations from the Ford and Rockefeller Foundations and support from some of the biggest enterprises, including General Motors.

In 1966 special congressional hearings took place on the question of relations with China. The general conclusion reached by participants was that America's policy towards China should be one of 'containment without isolation'. Powerfully convincing voices were raised against America's current policy of embargo. The embargo, it was argued, did not hurt the Chinese who could in any case buy what they needed from other countries in the West, but, on the contrary, it isolated America from its allies in Europe and Asia and deprived American business circles of both real and potential opportunities to widen their commercial links with the biggest country in the world.[41] The same thoughts were expressed the following year during hearings before the Congressional Joint Economic Committee on the subject of 'Mainland China in the world economy'.[42]

The Johnson administration was still unable to carry out any substantive change in Sino-American relations, its chief foreign policy concerns being the confrontation with the Soviet Union and the escalation of the war in Vietnam. The Republicans were able to exploit the growing dissatisfaction with this policy during the 1968 election campaign. In 1967 Richard Nixon, not yet a presidential candidate, had published an article entitled 'Asia after Vietnam' in the journal *Foreign Affairs*, in which he wrote that in the long-term perspective the policy of isolating China was irrational. He therefore advocated that the 'reality of China' be recognized and that a policy be pursued that would help to bring China back into the international community as a 'great and progressive nation, rather than the epicenter of world revolution'.[43]

The Chinese were following these American debates very attentively. The 134th meeting of the ambassadors took place in Warsaw in January 1968, but China postponed the 135th, at first to February 1969 and then to an even later date. Peking was obviously waiting for the change of administration in the United States and also waiting to see its first steps in Far East policy.

During 1969, the first year of the Nixon–Kissinger administration, American foreign policy followed the beaten track of anti-Sovietism and anti-Communism, even though the character of some important statements by American politicians began to change. It should not be forgotten that it was precisely during 1969 that the Cultural Revolution in China officially came to a close and at the same time fierce skirmishing began on the Sino-Soviet border. In the middle of 1969, at a special session of the US National Security Council in Washington, a number of general questions of US–Chinese relations was discussed and the President was advised to take steps which would give the Chinese to understand that Washington wished to start the process of normalization. At the same time, the Council indicated to the media that they should refrain from publishing anything that could arouse Chinese public opinion against the United States.[44] Nixon and Kissinger decided to take a number of unilateral measures, of little practical importance in themselves but of considerable political significance, that were later dubbed the policy of 'small steps'.

For example, in June–July 1969 the administration lifted the ban on travel to China for seven categories of US citizens: Congressmen, journalists, teachers, students (both undergraduate and graduate), scientists, doctors and Red Cross workers. US citizens were permitted to bring back with them goods of Chinese manufacture to the value of $100. In December 1969 foreign branches of US companies were allowed to trade in 'non-strategic' goods with China. The Seventh Fleet ceased to patrol the Straits of Taiwan from December 1969 and the number of US vessels in the area was greatly reduced.

The policy of 'small steps' continued in 1970. The maximum of $100 on US purchases of Chinese goods was abolished, the trade embargo was eased and US private individuals and firms were permitted to import Chinese goods for 'non-commercial purposes'. In February 1970, President Nixon sent legislation to Congress making provision for the sale of US grain to China in exchange for Chinese hard currency. In the autumn of 1970, Nixon and Kissinger proposed setting up a commercial telephone link between San Fransciso and Shanghai and a 'hot line' between Washington and Peking. In October during an official visit to the USA by President Ceauşescu of Romania, Nixon used the official name of the Chinese People's Republic for the first time, and many observers took this as a hint at the possibility of official recognition of China.

China for her part in no way responded to these purely symbolic moves and anti-American propaganda went on as furiously as before. In his speech to the Ninth Congress of the Chinese

Communist Party, Lin Biao – Mao's 'heir' – attacked not only 'Soviet revisionism', but also 'American imperialism' which he called the 'main enemy of all the peoples' and which, he claimed, 'was sliding lower and lower'. According to Lin Biao, Nixon had only adopted a 'peace-loving posture for the sake of appearances, but in fact he is still leading the arms race on an even greater scale'.[45]

At the same time, Peking broke off the ambassadors' talks being held in Warsaw and refused to discuss their resumption with the US. Nor did the Chinese leadership respond to the unilateral measures taken by the US in the fields of trade and cultural exchange, although China did make use of the easing of trade restrictions in order to purchase large consignments of goods of American–European manufacture in Western Europe. In summing up the results of the policy of 'small steps', Assistant Secretary of State M. Green commented that China's lack of response was hardly surprising, since labelling the US as the devil was part of the means of maintaining unity inside the country in face of an alleged threat from outside, and he concluded that the US would have to wait until Peking realized that friendship with the US would be more valuable to the regime than the existing anti-American propaganda.[46]

Nixon, however, was not discouraged by the Chinese lack of a clear response to his 'goodwill' gestures. Through intermediaries he supplemented his 'small steps' policy with secret talks at which the Chinese were able to state more clearly what they expected from the USA as 'payment' for the normalization of relations. For their part, the American politicians made clearer to the Chinese how far they could go without losing face in the complex world of the American political establishment. Acting as intermediaries between the American and Chinese governments were first, in 1969, President de Gaulle and later President Ceauşescu. In 1970 the chief intermediary was General Yahya Khan, President of Pakistan, with whom, given the hostile relations with India, China was trying to have friendly relations. But it was the United States that was on extremely friendly terms with this harsh Muslim dictator. .

While openly ignoring America's soundings and her policy of 'small steps' in 1969–70, the Chinese government nevertheless had to give serious consideration to the pros and cons of the change that was being offered, and it did so at the Second Plenum of the CCP Central Committee, held from 25 August to 6 September 1970 at the resort of Lushan in Jiangxi province. Many questions of China's internal politics were discussed there. Since the Cultural Revolution and the Ninth Party Congress three main groups had formed among the CCP leaders: the 'administrators', headed by Zhou Enlai, the 'ideologues' led by Mao's wife, Jiang Qing, and a group headed by Lin Biao and Zhen Boda who had been the leaders of the Cultural Revolution and Mao's closest associates in the Politburo.

Reports appeared in the Soviet press, without any reference to their sources, to the effect that at the Lushan Plenum a group of army leaders had proposed that the post of President of the People's Republic be restored and that Lin Biao be elected to fill it. This proposal allegedly provoked objections from the 'administrators' and the 'ideologues', as well as from Mao Zedong himself who reproached his 'heir' with 'straining too hard for power'. Mao informed the conference about the talks with the United States on settling relations between the two countries. Reasserting his slogan on being prepared for war, Mao made it clear that in the short term this applied only to the possibility of war with the Soviet Union. Lin Biao and Zhen Boda are said to have spoken out against the policy of *rapprochement* with the United States and this is said to have angered Mao. Zhen Boda was excluded from the Politburo and disappeared completely from the political scene. Lin Biao remained in the leadership, but his influence was plainly reduced.[47]

Through the mediation of Pakistan, Washington received Zhou Enlai's message of reply in early December 1970. The Chinese Premier announced China's willingness to receive a special representative of the United States President in Peking 'to discuss the question of the liberation of the Chinese territory known as Taiwan'.[48] The Americans were not bothered by the wording of this reply, and set about preparing for the visits to China. On 10 December 1970 Mao Zedong received the American journalist Edgar Snow, whom he had known as far back as the civil war period in the 1930s. In his book on 'Red China', which had been published before the Second World War, Snow had drawn an extremely flattering portrait of Mao as the leader of the Chinese Communist Party. Now Snow asked Mao whether such right-wingers as Nixon, who represented the capitalist monopolies, were going to be allowed into China, to which Mao replied that Nixon had to be received because at the present moment only he could resolve the problems of relations between China and the USA, and he added that he would be happy to chat with Nixon either as a tourist or as the President.[49] A new era in United States–Chinese relations had begun.

Ten years of normalization and rapprochement, 1971–80

The normalization of relations between the United States and China was a long and complex affair, yet the turning-point in this process appears to have been as insignificant an event as the invitation to China of the American table-tennis team which had been competing in the world championships in Japan. The press reported that Mao himself had issued the invitation. The American sportsmen, who were given an unusual amount of attention, had a 'cordial conversation' with Zhou Enlai, who described the visit as a 'new chapter in relations between the Chinese and American peoples' and expressed assurance that other Americans would soon be able to come to China.[50] The trip was commented on widely and at great length by the world's press, and it even gave rise to the new concept of 'ping-pong diplomacy'. The White House was satisfied. The American table-tennis players had been in China only in March 1971 and already in April Nixon announced America's willingness to issue visas to individuals and groups from China who wished to visit the USA. American currency restrictions were relaxed, a long list was published of goods which could now be exported to China without special permits from the US Department of Trade, the ban on the commercial import of all goods of Chinese manufacture was lifted, and Nixon further announced the ending of some (though not all) discriminatory limitations in trade relations between the United States and China.

By agreement between both sides, in July 1971 Henry Kissinger paid a secret visit to Peking. Officially, Kissinger flew to Pakistan where, after talks with Yahya Khan, he accepted the latter's invitation to rest for a few days in the mountains. In fact, those few days were spent in Peking in conversation with Zhou

Enlai, Huang Hua and other high officials of the People's Republic of China. A wide range of questions was discussed, chief
among them being a visit to China by President Nixon, which was
decided affirmatively. After Kissinger's return to Washington, a
communiqué was published simultaneously in China and the
United States to this effect, adding that the object of the visit
would be to seek to establish normal relations and to exchange
opinions on matters of interest to both sides.[51]

Intensive preparations for this summit meeting began in both
the United States and China, in the course of which a split
occurred in the Chinese leadership, and Mao's official heir, Lin
Biao, who had for years been extolled by Chinese propaganda
almost as persistently as Mao himself, disappeared from the political scene. As recently as 12 September 1971, that is to say the
very day when, according to the later version, Lin Biao had
attempted to carry out a 'counter-revolutionary coup', the newspaper People's Daily wrote: 'Comrade Lin Biao has always held
aloft the banner of the thoughts of Mao Zedong, firmly implemented and defended the proletarian revolutionary line of
Chairman Mao Zedong, and has always been a shining example
for the whole party, the army and the people of the entire
country.'

On 13 September, all aircraft in China, military as well as civil,
were suddenly grounded. One military aircraft nevertheless did
take off from an unknown aerodrome and took a course in the
direction of Mongolia. Apparently it was not pursued and that
night it crossed the Mongolian frontier. Then suddenly it went off
course, crashed and blew up in the region of Aimak Khentei.
According to the Mongolian telegraph agency, the remains of
nine half-burnt corpses and some weapons were found among
the wreckage. No information was given as to the identities of the
victims. Only later did it emerge that the plane was carrying Lin
Biao, his wife, who was also a member of the Politburo, their son
and a number of other people. Lin Biao's name disappeared
from the pages of the Chinese press, and instead the formula
'scoundrels of the Liu Shaoqi type' would occasionally pop up,
this being a surrogate label above all for Lin Biao, as it soon
became clear.

The disappearance and reported death of Lin Biao was connected by the American press with Nixon's forthcoming visit to

China and the *New York Times* commented that the Chinese decision to receive the US President had no doubt fostered the hitherto secret political rift which had turned China's defence minister from a 'close comrade-in-arms of Mao' into a nothing, and maybe had even led to his death.[52]

This version was accepted by the Soviet press with evident sympathy. Lin Biao and his close associates may well have had objections to the *rapprochement* with the United States. However, the political crisis in China in the autumn of 1971 was undoubtedly more complicated than that. It was part of the general crisis of the regime in the years following the Cultural Revolution which, like all regimes based on a personal cult whether Stalin's in the Soviet Union or Mao's in China, have a need to find scapegoats among the people closest to the 'leader'. In 1971 Mao needed a 'scoundrel' like Liu Shaoqi and the man most suited to the role was Lin Biao. It is very rare for the official 'heir' or 'successor' to come to power in an authoritarian or totalitarian regime.

The change in relations between the United States and China was quickly reflected in the question of China's admission to the United Nations. According to the United Nations Statute, the question of whether one state or another is accepted into the United Nations is decided not by the Security Council but by the General Assembly. At every session of the General Assembly the Soviet Union had tabled a resolution in favour of the admission of the People's Republic and the consequent exclusion of Taiwan. For more than 20 years this resolution had been rejected, although the number of member states supporting the Soviet position grew steadily. Thus, in 1952, for example, 9 of the 60 member states voted to admit the People's Republic, while 42 voted against and 9 abstained. In 1960, with total membership now at 98, 34 voted in favour, 42 against and 22 abstained.[53] In 1970 there were 127 member states, of which 51 voted in favour, 49 against and 25 abstained.[54] A year later the situation changed and even the United States voted in favour of admitting China, while retaining the simultaneous presence of Taiwan, a proposition that was not acceptable to the majority of member states. When the delegates voted on the resolution to admit the People's Republic and exclude Taiwan, the voting was now 76 in favour, 17 abstentions, and 35 against, including the United States and Japan.[55]

The result surprised even President Nixon who had felt sure that the 'two Chinas' resolution proposed by the United States would be accepted. The People's Republic was equally surprised by the result, a fact Zhou Enlai mentioned in an interview for the Japanese newspaper *Asahi* on 8 November 1971, and it aroused the indignation of right-wing politicians in America, where there was talk of the United States quitting the United Nations. Particular indignation was expressed by the Governor of California, Ronald Reagan, who sent a special telegram to Jiang Gai-shi, conveying his resolute disagreement with the position taken in the United Nations. As for President Nixon, he only expressed his dissatisfaction outwardly. While noting that the conservatives were furious, the editor of the American right-wing magazine *Human Events* expressed the belief that the administration had thought it could save Taiwan, but that if it came to a choice between helping China to get into the United Nations or sacrificing Taiwan, the government would prefer to have Red China in the UN.[56]

The admission of the People's Republic to the United Nations opened up a whole range of possible contacts and consultations with the United States through their permanent delegations.

President Nixon's visit to China in February 1972 was an important new step in the process of normalizing relations between China and the US. A week before the visit, the United States announced the abolition of the so-called 'Chinese differential' and put China on an equal footing with the Soviet Union and the other socialist countries in terms of trade. Many restrictions on trade between the US and China were thus removed, and at the same time more favourable circumstances were created for the success of the visit, which took place from 21 to 28 February 1972. Nixon, who was accompanied by a large retinue of advisers and assistants, met and talked with Mao Zedong, but by far the greater part of his talks were with Zhou Enlai, some 40 hours in all. After Peking, the American delegation visited Hangzhou and Shanghai, where the joint Shanghai Communiqué, as it has become known, was signed. We shall not describe the visit in detail, nor analyse the contents of the extensive communiqué which registered both the problems on which the two sides had found agreement, and those for which solutions had still to be found.

The visit was the subject of very noisy propaganda in China and was proclaimed as a huge success for Chinese foreign policy and an important step towards the restoration of 'the traditional friendship between the Chinese and American peoples'. It was even more extravagantly proclaimed in the United States where newpapers and magazines wrote about 'the week that changed the world' and 'the historic events of fundamental importance for future generations'. Nixon himself compared the visit with the trip to the Moon. Public opinion surveys showed that the overwhelming majority of Americans viewed both the idea of the visit and its results favourably, and it was indeed a very important historic event, even if it far from justified all the expectations the leadership in both Peking and Washington had invested in it. As the future President Carter's national security adviser Zbygniew Brzezinski commented shortly before Nixon's arrival in Peking, the visit would only make sense if it served two purposes, neither of which the President could acknowledge publicly. The first was to influence the voters in the United States, an aim that was adequately met. The second was to influence Moscow, despite the administration's denial that the trip had any secondary foreign policy purpose. Nevertheless, the spectacle of President Nixon chatting with Chairman Mao, Brzezinski mused, must have given Moscow food for thought.[57]

The aims indicated by Brzezinski were undoubtedly of great importance for the Nixon administration, but Brzezinski was mistaken in thinking these were the main purposes of the visit: they lay in the realm of American–Chinese relations, not American–Soviet relations. The point at issue was America's policies in Asia in general, not putting on a pre-election show for Nixon. The visit was above all an act of recognition of China that went beyond mere *de facto* recognition. In essence it was the diplomatic recognition of China without the formal establishment of diplomatic relations. The year following the visit, special contact missions were set up in Peking and Washington which substantially did the work normally carried out by both a trade mission and an embassy.

The normalization of relations between the United States and China greatly increased the possibilities for United States foreign policy in Asia and throughout the world. With all its internal disorder and convulsions, China still remained the biggest country in Asia and the world, and its influence on events, already considerable in 1972, would continue to grow in the future. To ignore that fact, as American politicians had done for 20 years, had been as big a mistake as their prolonged refusal to give diplomatic recognition to the Soviet Union. To be sure, Nixon was counting on China's help in resolving the Vietnam problem, the most painful problem of American foreign policy at the end of the 1960s and beginning of the 1970s.

America's new relations with China met the aims and aspirations of an influential part of American business circles who had observed the gradual penetration of the Chinese market by their competitors in Japan and Western Europe. Only a year after Nixon's visit, and as a result of the accords registered in the Shanghai Communiqué, a National Council for the Promotion of American–Chinese Trade was set up in Washington, in which nearly all the leading corporations were represented. In 1972–3 trips to China by all kinds of business groups from America became a common occurrence, and a little later the exchange of official trade delegations took place.

The *rapprochement* between the United States and China put an end to the state of permanent confrontation that had existed in the 1950s and 1960s, and that had become increasingly onerous and pointless. In 1947–9 America had managed to avoid becoming directly involved in the civil war in China and now she could count on being able to avoid the sort of situations arising in the Far East that had led to the Korean War in 1950 which many Americans still remembered very well.

No doubt, in giving the go-ahead for the American President's visit, the Chinese leaders were also thinking of the problems that had arisen out of the Sino-Soviet conflict, but equally that was not the only, nor most likely the main motive of Chinese foreign policy in signing the Shanghai Communiqué. On the one hand, recognition by the United States increased the authority and influence of China and its leaders, and on the other hand, it diminished the sense of a lack of national self-esteem which many Chinese were feeling after a 15-year stretch of economic and political failure and disorder. Dozens of delegations and groups of all kinds from all over the world were now visiting China, and one after the other, heads of government and state were following suit. The figures for the number of states with whom China had diplomatic relations speak for themselves: in 1957 – 29; 1969 – 42; 1970 – 55; 1971 – 77; 1972 – 88, including the Federal Republic of Germany and Japan; 1974 – 99; 1975 – 107. China's economic relations with the outside world also broadened, though at a much slower pace.

Thus, even allowing for the various personal motives of both the American and the Chinese leaders, and despite the fact that it aroused some concern in the Soviet Union and India, and in Japan and some of the other Asian countries, as a whole the process of *rapprochement* between these two great powers was a generally positive one. The Nixon visit did not of course resolve the fundamental differences between the USA and China, but it did create an important channel of communication between them and it replaced confrontation with dialogue.

The suddenness and somewhat sensational nature of the visit generated a host of assumptions in terms of a rapid friendship developing between the two countries, assumptions which were not realized in the succeeding years, nor were realizable. The United States had set important but limited goals for its China policy, and most of those were achieved by the President's visit itself. Nixon's policy of *détente* still had as its major priority the improvement of relations with the Soviet Union, and that excluded rapid progress in Sino-American relations at that time. It was not therefore surprising that the development of relations between the USA and China in the period 1973 to 1976 was slow and difficult. Moreover, the United States was entering its own internal crisis with the 'Watergate affair' and it lacked stable leadership. China was on the threshold of big changes. The era of Mao Zedong was past and that fact had led to a power struggle for his 'legacy' among different factions in the Chinese leadership. Exploiting their closeness to Mao, the group of 'ideologues', led by Jiang Qing, managed to constrict the 'pragmatists' and the 'administrators', headed by Zhou Enlai and Deng Xiaoping. The 'ideologues' or 'radicals', who controlled the mass media, organized a series of noisy ideological campaigns in the mid-1970s targeted against people who had underestimated the danger of 'social imperialism' and American imperialism alike, and none of this facilitated progress in Sino-American relations.

Trade between the United States and China increased soon after Nixon's visit. The volume of trade between the two countries in 1971 had been about $5 million, in 1972 it rose to nearly $100 million and in 1974 it grew to practically $1 billion. Most of it was in the form of US exports of grain and a few other American goods to China, however, rather than Chinese exports to the USA. The Chinese then became concerned about their excessive indebtedness and, not wishing to accept credit from the USA, they sharply curtailed their purchases in 1975 and 1976, and in that year the volume of Sino-American trade was only $357 million, with US exports to China falling to $135 million and US imports from China amounting to $222 million. These were extremely insignificant sums for countries as large as the USA and China: in 1976 the overall volume of trade between the United States and Taiwan stood at nearly $5 billion.[58] Scientific and cultural exchange between China and the United States also developed only slowly between 1973 and 1976.

China was disconcerted by the continued close links between the United States and Taiwan and by America's refusal to establish full diplomatic relations. America's efforts in developing US–Soviet co-operation, and the whole policy of *détente* between the Soviet Union and the countries of Western Europe, aroused even greater dissatisfaction in the ageing Mao Zedong and his 'radical' associates. Every new agreement between the Soviet Union and Western countries was greeted by China with disapproval, if not outright hostility, starting with the SALT 1 treaty and ending with the Final Act on Security and Co-operation signed at the Helsinki Conference of European nations, the United States, Canada and the Soviet Union. Fearing their northern neighbour, the Chinese leaders were seeking allies in the West, and they were extremely disappointed by the development of the international situation in 1973–6. In the United States also there were influential circles, however, which considered that the USA should not go too far in the *rapprochement* with China.

Henry Kissinger, by now Secretary of State, visited China in 1973 and 1974, but his visits did nothing to advance Sino-American relations. Nor did a visit from 1 to 5 December 1975 by the new President, Gerald Ford, produce any noticeable change in relations, although this visit was not calculated to resolve any important questions. The Americans knew that Zhou Enlai was seriously ill and that his days were numbered.

During his long talk with Mao Zedong, President Ford could see that Mao was also in a poor state of health. The big question exercising American officials, therefore, was what kind of new leaders were going to emerge in China? Nobody had the precise answer to this question. Ford's lack of success in China was underlined by the fact that no communiqué was issued after this summit meeting. Of course, both the American and Chinese leaders tried to create the impression for world public opinion, as well as that of their own countries, that this was an important and significant visit. Deng Xiaoping made a number of statements along these lines, and Assistant Secretary of State Philip Habib, in summing up the results of the trip, said that while relations between the two countries were not yet normalized, the visit nevertheless showed that they were what could be called good. The talks had demonstrated that some important points of view were held in common, though of course a number of incongruities had also been exposed.[59]

To show their irritation at the slow progress of Sino-American relations, the Chinese leadership extended an invitation in 1976 on a private and personal basis to ex-President Richard Nixon, who had had to leave office as a result of the 'Watergate affair', and after narrowly escaping impeachment. Nixon of course accepted the invitation and undertook the trip with pleasure.

Both the United States and China were preoccupied in 1976–7 with their own internal domestic problems. President Ford was defeated in the election and a new administration came to power under Jimmy Carter, a completely new face, both on the international stage and the American political scene. The new administration needed time to formulate its foreign policy ideas and priorities. Changes going on in China at the same time were hardly less significant in scale. Zhou Enlai died and his closest associate, Deng Xiaoping, disappeared from the scene for a while. Soon, however, Mao Zedong also died. The triumph of the 'radicals' and 'ideologues', however, was short lived. Only one month after Mao's death, his widow, Jiang Qing, was arrested together with her close comrades, and the 'moderate Maoists', led by Hua Guofeng, came to power.

Unfortunately, the Carter administration, with Zbygniew Brzezinski as its chief foreign policy adviser, was not noted either for its competence or consistent behaviour in the international arena. During Carter's term of office no new impetus was initiated in the process of *détente* in US–Soviet relations, on the contrary in many respects relations began to deteriorate from the very first months of Carter's stay in the White House.

On the other hand, not much progress was discernible in 1977–8 in Sino-American relations either. Even during the election campaign, while Carter's rival, the incumbent President Gerald Ford, took every opportunity to emphasize the Republican administration's great achievement in 'opening up China', Carter himself avoided discussing the subject, and although he underlined the fact that the previous administration had hit an impasse in its relations with China, he advanced no proposals of his own for getting out of it.

The United States had no influence on either the course or character of the changes taking place in China after the death of Mao Zedong, and was therefore compelled to wait for a stable and strong new leadership to be established, and for the main principles of its foreign policy to emerge, before it could formulate the broad direction of its own policy in relation to China.

As we have noted above, soon after the death of Mao and the removal of the Gang of Four from the political scene, the movement to rehabilitate the victims of the Cultural Revolution gathered pace. For the second time, after suffering recent humiliation and loud abuse, Deng Xiaoping, the acknowleged leader of the 'pragmatists', returned to political life, and many other prominent Communist party officials, who had suffered persecution during the Cultural Revolution, were appointed to important jobs in the state and party apparatus. These moves were viewed with concern by some of President Carter's advisers, notably Zbygniew Brzezinski, who saw in them the possibility of *rapprochement* between China and the Soviet Union. Moreover, by this time President Carter had proclaimed the basis of his administration's foreign policy to be America's concern for human rights throughout the world, a sphere in which China could hardly figure as a model state.

President Carter recognized the importance of continuing the dialogue with China and its new leaders, however, and a visit to China by Secretary of State Cyrus Vance in August 1977 was intended to serve that end. Vance promised China very little and he avoided the most difficult problems of Sino-American relations, concentrating instead on studying, analysing and asking questions, and if the American side soon expressed its satisfaction with the visit, the Chinese leaders openly and directly expressed their disappointment with its results. They insisted on the full recognition of China by the United States which they claimed had been promised by President Ford. At the beginning of September 1977 Deng Xiaoping gave an interview to Associated Press in which he accused the United States of 'being attached to the old policy', and 'causing harm' to the relations which had taken shape under Presidents Nixon and Ford.[60] Replying to Deng Xiaoping, Assistant Secretary of State John Cisco stated that there were no weighty reasons compelling the Carter administration to take immediate steps towards normalizing relations.[61]

American public opinion in 1977 was very much divided over the future development of relations with China. One could find extremely different views among politicians who could reasonably be included in the conservative wing of American society, and also among those with a liberal reputation. A number of Republican Congressmen came out in favour of immediate normalization of relations. Among them was Senator Henry Jackson who had been favoured with a personal invitation to visit China, where he met nearly all the Chinese leaders, and who now made statements demanding not merely normalization of relations with China, but the organization of the supply and sale to China of consignments of American arms in order to safeguard Chinese security against the Soviet threat. During his visit, Jackson demonstratively visited areas along the Sino-Soviet border.

On the other hand, there were those in right-wing circles who, both from pro-Taiwan sympathies and a determined rejection of any sort of Communism – whether 'Chinese' or 'Soviet' – were as decisively against diplomatic recognition of China as they were against breaking off diplomatic relations with Taiwan. The influential Congressman, Senator Barry Goldwater, for example, regarded the latter as so utterly unacceptable that he announced that he would demand impeachment, that is the court examination by the Senate of the President's action, should Washington break off the treaty of mutual security with Taiwan. Many people in business circles also spoke up in favour of preserving the previous relations with Taiwan. Direct American investment in Taiwan in 1977 amounted to more than $2 billion and the volume of trade stood at some $5 billion, which was 12 times greater than that with the People's Republic. Five hundred American companies were supported by the business carried on with the island state. Many Asian countries which looked towards the United States measured America's loyalty to her allies in terms of the conduct of her relations with Taiwan. After the American withdrawal from South Vietnam, her departure from Taiwan could easily undermine her influence in many non-Communist countries in Asia.

The Taiwan lobby, or network of lobby organizations which had been created in the late 1940s by supporters of Jiang Gai-shi, exercised a definite influence on American public opinion. With names like the Committee for Free China, the Economic Council of the United States and the Republic of China, the Student Committee for Free China, the American Friends of Free China in Taiwan, the American Council for Free Asia, and so on, these groups had substantial sources of funding within the United States, but they also received considerable support from the Nationalist government and business circles in Taiwan itself. In 1977–8 the Taiwan lobby launched an active campaign against the *rapprochement* between the US and the People's Republic, sending tens of thousands of letters to American politicians and placing countless paid advertisements in the press.

An even more active campaign, however, was launched by groups forming the 'New China lobby', that is American organizations, committees and groups which were in favour of improving and normalizing relations with the People's Republic. The National Council for the Promotion of American–Chinese Trade, which was set up in 1973, was one such organization to which we have referred earlier. By the mid-1970s it already included 140 large and medium-sized companies and on its board of directors sat such eminent figures in American business as T. Wilson, the head of the Boeing Aircraft Corporation, David Rockefeller, the president of the Chase Manhattan Bank, O. Klausen, the president of the Bank of America, M. Blumenthal, the future United States Secretary to the Treasury, and many others. The Council promoted the idea that the Chinese market offered practically unlimited possibilities, that there were vast reserves of oil and many other raw materials in China, as well as the notion that none of these possibilities could be realized unless the United States established normal diplomatic relations with China and made the most favourable concessions to the Chinese regime.[62]

The National Committee for American–Chinese Relations (NCACR) had been formed as early as 1966 and included representatives from business, scientific, and journalistic circles and Congress. It organized hundreds of seminars and conferences, assisted in the publication of books and articles on the need for *rapprochement* and normalization of relations with the People's Republic, and it played no small part in the change of American Far East policy carried out by President Nixon's administration in 1970–3. In 1977–8 the NCACR lobbied in favour of Sino-American *rapprochement* with the help of such powerful corporations as Ford Motors, Exxon and others, and it was instrumental in arranging numerous exchanges of business, educational and cultural delegations.

Also in 1966 the Committee for Scientific Relations with China had been formed with the support of the National Academy of Sciences, the American Council of Learned Societies, and the Research Council for the Social Sciences, among others. In time the Council for Scientific Relations began to function as a lobby, agitating in favour of normalization of relations with China. Numerous scientific exchanges and study tours were arranged through the Committee after 1972. Finally, another influential lobby organization that was formed in 1974 was the Association for American–Chinese Friendship, a powerful national body that was not, however, connected with ruling circles. Its membership included many left-wing intellectuals, radical students, American Maoists, activists from among the Chinese-American community, a number of Black American activists and some Hispanics. This was not an organization that could exert much influence on the American government's position directly, but its activities, which were supported by social organizations in China itself, did have a certain influence on the attitudes and statements of many important liberals, some of whom were members of the Association, for the same absence of unison on this issue among conservatives was to be found also among liberals.

For example, Senator Edward Kennedy was decisively in favour of the urgent normalization of relations with China and the acceptance in full of all of China's conditions for such normalization. As for Taiwan, Kennedy's position was that the United States should retain only unofficial relations in order to guarantee Taiwan's security and economic viability. George Kennan, on the other hand, was more cautious. In 1977 he published his book, *The Cloud of Danger*, which was devoted to American foreign policy. On American–Chinese relations, Kennan advised not going too far too quickly. In particular, he attacked the view that closer relations with China would serve America's interest *vis-à-vis* the Soviet Union, for this view, he claimed, presupposed that America had more long-term interests in common with China than she had with the Soviet Union, an assumption which was far from proven. Furthermore, such an arrangement would place a heavy burden on the United States in its relations with the Soviet Union and also would weaken its position if the two Communist powers chose to settle their differences without regard to America, should it be in their interests to do so.[63]

Thus, the first year of the Carter administration was a time of reflection, disagreement, discussion and declining interest in China as a partner for the United States, whether in foreign policy or trade. The political commentator S. Carnow observed in an article of September 1977 that Americans were sick to death of endless descriptions of acupuncture and the Great Wall, scientific organizations were put off by Peking's obsessive need to introduce political meaning into every scientific and cultural exchange, businessmen who had imagined that China would be a goldmine were disappointed to find that their sales had not yet reached the level of trade with Honduras, and the internal unrest and sense of continuing tension inside China, along with these other factors, explained why polls showed that as many as 52 per cent of Americans were negative on China, while only 26 per cent were favourable.[64]

From the spring of 1978, however, American–Chinese relations began to warm up again, thanks to a number of factors, of which we will consider only the most important. Although the internal struggle in the Chinese leadership did not cease, things had become noticeably more stable following the Eleventh Party

Congress of August 1977 and the First Session of the Fifth People's Assembly of February–March 1978. The Chinese Communist Party was clearly dominated by two men, Hua Guofeng, who gave the keynote speech at the Congress, and Deng Xiaoping, who gave the closing address.

The Americans were especially disturbed by the development of Sino-Soviet relations. In the preface to *China's Future*, published in 1977, the American political scientist B. Manning asked where China and the Soviet Union would be in the 1980s · on the spectrum from war to alliance, and he commented that the global balance of power would be substantially destabilized if Moscow and Peking were to find their common interests.[65] These fears were, however, largely dispelled in the first half of 1978 when China, far from smoothing out its anti-Soviet line, rather intensified it. Hua Guofeng announced at the Eleventh Congress that 'the quarrel with the USSR on matters of principle will go on for a long time to come', and he called upon the Chinese people and the People's Army 'to maintain a high state of vigilance and to be totally ready for war to be unleashed by imperialism or social-imperialism'.[66] On this occasion he spoke first of imperialism and secondly of social-imperialism, but the People's Assembly had already reinforced those clauses in the Constitution which dealt with the struggle against 'social imperialism', and 'social imperialism' occupied first place throughout as the object of struggle, with imperialism in second place. In private conversation, the Chinese leaders called on the United States not only to normalize relations with China, but to make an alliance with China aimed against the Soviet Union. Deng Xiaoping, whom Western journalists likened to Khrushchev because of his impetuous reforming zeal, outward spontaneity and coarseness of expression, said in an interview that only an alliance between China and the United States aimed against the 'white bear' could assure peace and stability for the whole world.[67]

Despite the fact that in 1976–7 industrial and agricultural output in China rose, the general economic condition of the country remained extremely poor and indeed in many provinces the situation could fairly be described as desperate. A course for the 'modernization' of the economy, the army and science had been set in 1975–6, but progress was still totally inadequate. The new government called on the people to speed up the country's development, and the National Assembly set as guidelines for 1985 the following tasks: steel production was to be raised to 60 million tonnes, and grain to 400 million tonnes; the rate of growth in agricultural output must rise by 4–5 per cent per year and that of industry by not less than 10 per cent; the volume of investment must exceed all investment made during the period 1950–75; the construction of 120 large projects was proposed, including 10 iron works, 8 coal fields, 10 natural-gas fields and 30 hydroelectric stations; huge targets were similarly set for all other branches of industry and for scientific and technological research; foreign trade was to be actively pursued and the scientific and cultural level of the entire nation was to be raised.

The People's Republic had neither the capital, nor the human resources and skills to accomplish so vast a programme of industrial construction in so short a time. For example, China's under-mechanized and backward agricultural sector had achieved an average annual growth rate in output of no more than 1.2–1.3 per cent. Such an ambitious programme could not possibly be achieved by sticking to the slogan of 'relying on our own forces'. The Chinese leaders were clearly counting on combining the country's vast labour resources with major foreign credits and loans which they intended to use to buy entire enterprises and industrial plants, equipment and technology from abroad. Large numbers of Chinese students would study abroad and many foreign experts would be brought to China. These calculations were not without foundation.

By the end of the 1970s the West was gradually recovering from the consequences of the 1974–5 crisis which had arisen only in part from the sudden rise in the price of oil. In countries such as the United States, West Germany and Japan, huge amounts of capital had been accumulated which were looking for some practical use. Large-scale investment was not in the offing at home, and as a result the banks went in search of reliable borrowers abroad. It was precisely in those years that countries with an average level of economic development but above-average ambitions were making efforts to escape from the bounds of their backwardness by relying on the financial assistance of the more developed countries. Countries like Mexico, Argentina, Brazil, Poland, Yugoslavia and others piled up the

huge debts which today have become the source of many political and economic disasters for them. The biggest demands for
credits and industrial schemes, however, came from China in the
years 1977–8, and American industrialists and financiers did not
want to be left out.

It is well known that in the United States and the West in general
there are, apart from official government institutions, many influential unofficial bodies of all kinds whose opinions have to be
taken into account. We have already mentioned the lobby organizations with their relatively narrow interests. There are, however,
other very important organizations and groups in the United
States which discuss and formulate general principles of domestic
and foreign policy and which exert considerable influence over
the advancement of particular political leaders and ideas. I have
little faith in the oft-repeated assertions of the Soviet press about
the enormous, if not virtually decisive, influence exerted on
United States policy by the Freemasons and other similar secret
organizations. On the other hand, an organization like the Committee on the Present Danger, formed ten years ago and including
many senior politicians and leading businessmen, must surely
exercise great influence. One of the oldest of such bodies is the
Council on Foreign Relations, formed in the 1920s by top people
in the New York business world. A younger organization of the
ruling élite is the Trilateral Commission which includes not only
representatives from California and Texas, but also from a
number of other leading Western countries. Such research establishments as the Rand Corporation also enjoy substantial prestige
in the United States. With Henry Kissinger among its members,
the Council on Foreign Relations put its considerable influence
behind the Republican administration, while the Trilateral Commission, with Zbygniew Brzezinski as its long-term executive
director, played an important part in Jimmy Carter's emergence
as President.

In 1977–8 many of these bodies were seeking to establish a
model of foreign policy relations for the 1980s. Their general
conclusion was that a certain 'cooling' of relations between the
United States and the Soviet Union was needed, which in effect
meant a renewal of confrontation. They came to a different
conclusion about China. There it was felt that if the new Chinese
leaders showed willingness to concede certain American con-

ditions, the policy should be to develop and further US–Chinese relations and co-operation. The motivation for such a new direction of policy lay not only in hopes for an economic boom in China.

In reviewing the development of international events during the period from 1970 to 1977, influential American politicians and political observers could not fail to come to the conclusion that the United States' influence throughout the world had diminished, especially following the defeat in Vietnam. Ruling circles experienced a sense of growing alarm at the trends in events, not only in South-East Asia, but also in Africa, in the Middle East, and in Central America. The revolutions in Iran and Nicaragua, which despite all their differences had a sharply expressed anti-American character, were a clear indication that such fears were not groundless.

On the other hand, all political observers noted that the Soviet Union's influence in the world in general, which had been weakened by the events of the 1960s, had begun to grow noticeably on all continents during the 1970s. Reunited Vietnam, which had become the militarily most powerful country in the region, was now a firm and reliable ally of the Soviet Union. The former Portuguese colonies in Africa, on achieving independence, adopted a pro-Soviet orientation, particularly Angola, where well-armed Cuban troops were sent at the request of the Angolan government. After the overthrow of the monarchy and feudal regime in Ethiopia, a powerful and influential country, the Soviet Union acquired an important ally.

It was also during the 1970s that, for the first time since the Second World War, the Soviet Union achieved parity with the United States in the field of strategic weapons. The Soviet Union openly declared that it would never again be reconciled to the superiority in strategic arms which until then had given the United States tangible foreign policy advantages.

After so many failures, it was hardly surprising that ruling circles in the United States should have a strong desire to compensate by gaining such an important ally as China. Friendship with China, the White House calculated, would quickly restore America's former dominating position among the countries of the Third World and allow it to regain the advantage in its relations with the Soviet Union.

A host of extremely varied official American groups and delegations visited China in 1978, among them Secretary of State Cyrus Vance who twice met the Chinese Foreign Minister Huang Hua; Secretary for Energy James Schlesinger who signed a number of important agreements; Secretary for Agriculture R. S. Berglund and Presidential Adviser on Science F. Press. However, the most significant of the flood of visits and contacts was that of the President's National Security Adviser, Zbygniew Brzezinski, which took place in May 1978.

It would both wrong and crude to see American political leaders solely as the simple executors of the will of powerful corporations and the unofficial organizations, clubs and groups that we have discussed above. Politicians such as Nixon, Kissinger, Carter, Brzezinski, Kennedy or Reagan can also 'make policy' and exert influence on America's destiny and position in the world. In this respect the role of Brzezinski is especially instructive, for although he was a very welcome guest in Peking, he was never sent as President Carter's representative to Moscow. If Nixon and Kissinger tried somehow to pursue a policy of balancing relations with China against the policy of *détente* in relations with the Soviet Union, then clearly Brzezinski's prevailing thought was to establish some sort of union or bloc with China which would be aimed against the Soviet Union. And China in 1978–9 not only did not rebuff, but rather encouraged such thoughts among American politicians.

During his visit, Brzezinski and the Chinese leaders discussed many problems, not all the details of which were made public. As it emerged later, the most important issue was that of the diplomatic recognition of China, which was agreed in principle, with both sides receiving the assurances they had sought. The Carter administration conducted this part of the talks in almost complete secrecy, however, only making it known to leading figures in Congress at the last moment. The question was discussed of selling China military equipment and technology with 'dual application', and China succeeded here in gaining a number of advantages and promises. As it later emerged, already during his 1977 visit and again during the 1978 visit, Brzezinski informed Chinese officials of the course of the US–Soviet disarmament talks, and he acquainted them with secret White House documents containing the American assessment of the military-strategic balance in the world and the Carter administration's plans of action.[68] Special attention was paid to defining spheres of 'parallel interests' where, in the opinion of Brzezinski and the Chinese leaders, the Chinese and American interest basically coincided. In this respect, Brzezinski tried to prove to both American politicians and Chinese leaders that there were many regions in the world where 'the United States and China could make a contribution to the guarantee of peace', for example in a number of areas in Asia, in Southern Africa and in the Middle East.[69] Brzezinski did not conceal the fact that the formula of 'parallel' or 'coincident' interests meant in practice 'counteracting Soviet influence everywhere in the world'.[70] In summing up the results of his second visit, Brzezinski not only found it valuable for both sides, but he underlined in particular that the fundamental importance of the trip lay in its emphasis on the strategic nature of US–Chinese relations in the long term. He warned moreover that it would now be possible to use the Chinese factor from a strong rather than a weak position.[71]

Instead of the diplomatic expression 'the Chinese factor', in the world of the media and political commentary the idea of the 'China card' became firmly established at this time. Many articles and books were devoted to the use of the 'China card' in the great political game and especially in the 'game' against the Soviet Union.[72] In reality, observers ought also to have been talking about the 'America card' which China wanted to use in its new entry into the international arena.

On 16 December 1978 Washington and Peking simultaneously announced that diplomatic relations would be established on 1 January 1979, with the exchange of ambassadors on 1 March 1979. This decision was the result of prolonged secret talks and major concessions by both sides. Bearing in mind the statements and policies of the previous years, America's concessions were the greater. The United States agreed to break off diplomatic relations with Taiwan and from 1 January 1980 to renounce the US–Taiwan mutual defence treaty of 1955. It was agreed that US troops would be withdrawn from Taiwan and US military installations dismantled. The United States government promised to halt arms sales to Taiwan for a year and unambiguously recognized the jurisdiction of the People's Republic over Taiwan. For its part, the Chinese government accepted for all intents and purposes that the United States would continue to maintain 'unofficial' trade, cultural, scientific and other relations with Taiwan. The People's Republic took into consideration the American notification that in 1980 deliveries of US defence weapons to Taiwan would be resumed. An unofficial body, the American Institute in Taiwan, was established in order to maintain relations with the regime on the island, while for its part Taiwan renamed its embassy in Washington the Taiwan Coordinating Council for North American Affairs. Both these bodies in fact carried out the functions of embassies and within a year their officials had been granted diplomatic privileges.

The establishment of diplomatic relations between the United States and China evoked a variety of responses throughout the world, not least in the United States itself. A number of leading American politicians expressed their discontent above all with the change in the United States' relations with Taiwan, and under pressure from them Congress introduced some substantive amendments into the proposed legislation, chief among which was a declaration that the United States would maintain active, close and friendly relations with Taiwan, that it would preserve its ability to repel by military means any threat to Taiwan or to its social and economic system, and that it would regard any such threat emanating from Peking as a threat to the security of the Western Pacific, a cause of the most serious concern to the United States.[73] China objected to these formulations in the final legislation, but went no further than diplomatic and similar protests.

America's diplomatic recognition of the People's Republic was in the long term a rational and natural step to take, even if it was in effect merely following the example of the other major capitalist countries, albeit with a delay of 30 years. On the other hand, the United States had quite frequently delayed in recognizing political reality, as in the case of the Soviet Union for example, with which diplomatic relations had not been established until 15 years after the foundation of the state.

It would be wrong to underestimate the importance of America's formal diplomatic recognition of China, and Hua Guofeng was justified in describing the event as an 'historic turning-point'. The influential West German magazine *Der Spiegel* wrote that the union between America and China repre-

sented a classic shift in the system of alliances, a shift in the disposition of forces that had existed hitherto, comparable with the
end of hostility between the Habsburgs and the Bourbons in the
middle of the eighteenth, or the end of hostility between England
and Russia at the beginning of the twentieth century.[74]

America's diplomatic recognition of China was greeted by the
Soviet Union without enthusiasm. Replying to President Carter's
announcement of the United States' decision, L. I. Brezhnev
stated that the establishment of normal relations between two
sovereign states was the natural thing, and he went on: 'The
Soviet Union has always been and is now in favour of such
relations between countries. The basis on which such normalization takes place, and the aims of the two sides, is another question. This is also a natural question, in view of the entirely clear
direction of China's present course.'[75]

What was merely hinted at in Brezhnev's statement was
spelled out in detail by the journal *Problemy Dalnego Vostoka*
(*Problems of the Far East*), which wrote that

the normalization of Sino-American state contacts has a special
character, aimed as it is at smoothing out the differences between
one narrow group of countries, while sharpening relations
between others, between whole systems of countries, in order
both to encourage the hegemonist strivings of the Chinese
nationalists and to strengthen the position of imperialism in its
confrontation with world socialism.[76]

China and the United States were hardly a 'narrow group of
countries', however. The normalization of relations between the
two countries would undoubtedly help to dispel the inferiority
complex, or sense of inadequacy, which the Chinese leaders had
long felt and which had on several occasions incited them to take
precipitate action. The temporary and sometimes even the repre-
hensible motives and the long-term consequences of many
important political events frequently do not coincide.

After the normalization of Sino-American relations, both
sides hastened to consolidate the results they had achieved.
Those who are fond of citing statistics calculated that in 1979
around 30 Chinese delegations of all kinds visited the United
States every month, that is, four times more than in 1978.

One of the most important of these visits was that of Deng Xiaoping which took place from 29 January to 4 February 1979. Deng Xiaoping was not the formal head of either the state or the Chinese Communist Party. Hua Guofeng remained Chairman of the Central Committee of the Party and Prime Minister of the State Council. However, in the course of the complicated internal struggle which had taken place in China in 1978, and as the result of two plenums of the party Central Committee and a session of the National Assembly, both the composition of the State Council and, far more important, the composition of the Politburo of the Party Central Committee, had undergone important changes, all of which had greatly reduced the influence and power of Hua Guofeng. It was becoming more and move obvious that, as Deputy Chairman of the State Council and Deputy Chairman of the Central Committee, Deng Xiaoping was the leading figure in the People's Republic. He and his group were the initiators of all the chief economic and political reforms which were taking place in China with growing rapidity and energy. It was therefore not surprising that he should head the Chinese delegation to the United States. Hua Guofeng was entrusted with a visit to the main countries of Western Europe in the latter half of 1979.

Deng Xiaoping was received in the United States virtually as a head of state. The visit was compared, not unreasonably, with that of Khrushchev in the autumn of 1959. More than 1,100 journalists and all the main television stations covered Deng Xiaoping's visit, and it must be said that his manner, his informality and openness of style inevitably brought Khrushchev to mind. They were both reformers in major countries. Khrushchev had resolutely exposed the cult of Stalin and in effect undermined the foundations of the Stalinist regime in the Soviet Union. Deng Xiaoping had subjected the cult of Mao Zedong to no less a rigorous criticism and begun to set a course for the radical change of the existing Maoist regime. (The Soviet press constantly stresses the fact that Chinese criticism of Maoism is limited and inadequate. One may agree with that, but it should be added that, in the last five or six years, a far deeper criticism of Mao Zedong has been going on in China than the criticism of Stalinism and Stalin that has been or is being expressed in the Soviet Union. The Chinese Communist Party has carried out a more fundamental and extensive rehabilitation of the victims of Maoism than the Soviet Communist Party has of the victims of Stalinism, and Mao's regime has been subjected to far greater change than the Stalinist regime in the Soviet Union.) But if Khrushchev in 1959 frequently repeated, in front of American politicians and businessmen, that 'socialism will inevitably bury capitalism', and at the same time called for co-operation and peace, then Deng Xiaoping with no less frankness called on American politicians and businessmen not to trust the Soviet Union, not to go down the path of 'false *détente*', but to take 'effective, firm measures and real actions' in order to counteract 'Soviet hegemonism'. He signed a number of agreements with the United States on scientific, technical, cultural and economic co-operation. He gave many interviews in which he urgently and consistently called on the United States for joint containment of the Soviet Union. In one of these interviews he said:

If we really want to curb the white bear we must unite. It is the only realistic step. It is not enough to rely entirely on the might of the United States. It is also not enough to rely entirely on the might of Europe. We are an insignificant, poor country. But if we unite, our might will have to be reckoned with. .... The United States will undoubtedly gain benefits in helping China to carry out the Four Modernizations, but from the long-term point of view, such benefits will become even greater.[77]

The Chinese guest severely criticized the US–Soviet agreement on the reduction or limitation of strategic weapons, SALT 2, which both Carter and Brezhnev were preparing to sign. China's position did not prevent the signing of SALT 2 in Vienna later, but it had an obvious effect on the attitude of the United States Congress, where the opponents of the agreement were in the majority.

Deng Xiaoping's visit was of enormous importance in the history of Sino-American relations. The Soviet press remarked that

the visit was characterized by a rather high degree of mutual understanding and a common approach to the disposition of forces in the world. By applying the clause on 'countering hegemony' to the concrete context of the Indo-Chinese peninsula, the two sides reinforced the basis of joint co-ordination. Deng Xiaoping's talks with the American leaders created a precedent for Sino-American consultation on international problems, on the co-ordination of political positions to be taken in the United Nations, on inter-governmental exchange of opinion on questions of security and so on. Following Deng Xiaoping's trip, such consultations began to take place on a regular basis in Washington and Peking at ministerial and deputy ministerial levels and through diplomatic channels.[78]

Carter, Brzezinski and Deng Xiaoping were very pleased with the results of the visit, despite the fact that a number of liberal politicians were critical. Many conservatives were also very cool in their comments. Former head of the CIA and future Vice President George Bush remarked that the government representatives had spoken of 'playing the China card' as a means of securing strategic superiority over the Soviet Union, and they thought of normalizing relations with China as a way of forcing the Russians to make concessions. Unfortunately, he went on, the Russians were not scared, and in the end all America could hope for would be some minor trade benefits, while the manoeuvrings of the government over China would only serve to increase the alarm of America's friends and allies.[79]

Little was made of international problems in the final communiqué on the visit, although they had occupied an important place in the talks and negotiations. Certainly considerable time had been spent on the situation in Indo-China, during which Deng Xiaoping made it perfectly plain to his American hosts that China was firmly resolved to 'teach Vietnam a lesson'. These declarations were neither rebuffed nor condemned by American politicians. On the contrary, some of them greeted the news with satisfaction in the belief that any sharp conflict between China and Vietnam could only deepen the hostility between China and the Soviet Union.

Officially America declined to condemn the invasion of Vietnam by Chinese troops. China's military operations in Vietnam, which began immediately upon Deng Xiaoping's return from Washington, slowed down the development of contacts between the United States and China for a few months, but they did not cease altogether. The exchange of delegations continued, and on 1 March 1979 simultaneously in Washington and Peking the opening ceremonies of each country's embassies took place, with consulates set up in San Francisco and Houston and Shanghai and Guangzhou.

The collapse of China's military action in Vietnam did not arouse particular distress in the United States. Some politicians calculated that the weaker China turned out to be militarily the more she would need military and economic aid from America, and some influential American newspapers openly gloated that China had come out of the war with a damaged reputation and a bloody nose.[80]

Sino-American contacts were restored to a fairly high level in the summer of 1979 when the two countries signed an agreement settling the outstanding mutual financial claims of past decades, and on 7 July a trade agreement was signed in Peking which gave China most favourable conditions of trade and opened up wide opportunities for the credit-financing of Chinese imports from the United States.

Since Deng Xiaoping was not formal head of state, it was felt that a return visit by President Carter was inappropriate, and therefore it was Vice President Walter Mondale who undertook the mission. His visit, which lasted from 27 August to 1 September 1979, demonstrated very clearly the rapid rate at which Sino-American relations had been proceeding since the formal establishment of diplomatic relations nine months earlier. Mondale met Hua Guofeng and had two rounds of talks with Deng Xiaoping, with international problems forming the main topic. The further development of bilateral links between the two countries was of course not forgotten, especially since the official reason given for Mondale's visit had been to sign an agreement on American assistance in the development of China's hydro-electric industry and on credit for the Export-Import Bank to the tune of $2 billion.

Talks were held on a visit to the United States by Hua Guofeng in 1980 and a return visit to China by President Carter. Mondale was the first important Western leader to be televised throughout China and to be fully reported in the *People's Daily*. He spoke of America's readiness to give China all kinds of economic and military support, 'for both countries can co-operate in the development of the world community in the direction we both desire.' He went on: 'We shall consider that any country that tries to weaken you or seeks your isolation will have adopted a position that is in contradiction with America's interests. The power, security and modernization of China in the following decades will correspond to the interests of the United States.'[81] It was evidently no coincidence that Mondale's visit to China was timed to occur just before the opening of talks between China and the Soviet Union.

Soon after his return to the United States, Mondale said in an interview that, in their sincerity and maturity, Sino-American relations could be compared with America's relations with her European allies. Several members of the US government visited China in the second half of 1979, and it was announced that in January 1980 Defense Secretary Harold Brown would visit China to conduct talks on military and strategic co-operation between the two countries and American assistance in the modernization of China's army. In the course of 1979 in all 15 agreements on various aspects of bilateral links were signed, and, apart from a large number of business and political visits, some 40,000 American tourists visited China in that year.[82]

The rapid pace of *rapprochement* between the United States and China, based as it was to a large extent on an anti-Soviet posture, was evidently one of a number of reasons why the Soviet Union decided to send its troops into Afghanistan to save the pro-Soviet regime that was in a state of collapse. This decision, however, became an additional motive for still greater efforts by China and the United States to co-operate more closely, and not excluding the military and strategic sphere. Defense Secretary Brown's visit to China in January 1980 was a clear indication of this. He visited several important military sites, including tank and aviation divisions, a military academy, warships and ship-yards in the city of Wuhan. Accompanied by National Security Council aides and generals from the Pentagon, he held talks with senior Chinese state and military officials, their chief topic of discussion being American aid in the modernization of the Chinese army.

In getting to see something of the Chinese army, and even with their superficial knowledge of its recent 'punitive' expedition in Vietnam, the American specialists were convinced that it was not capable of carrying out a military action on the modern level. Furthermore, they concluded, China's nuclear forces were ineffectual, vulnerable and few in number. Reports in the Chinese press of tests of new intercontinental ballistic missiles with a range of 9,500 to 10,500 kilometres showed that China was making great efforts to develop her nuclear missile potential, but the new generation of offensive strategic weapons, several thousand units in number, would enter China's arsenal only during the late 1980s at best. Defense Secretary Brown assured the Chinese leaders in the agreement that the United States would sell China many manufactured goods with 'dual usage', for example computers that could be used for either peaceful or military purposes. China was also promised the sale of a special radio station that would receive information from the American space satellite *Landsat-D*, which could similarly be used for both peaceful and military purposes. Brown excluded the possibility of direct deliveries of US arms to China, however, as that would have required major amendments to United States legislation.

Brown's visit took place against a background of considerably heightened anti-Soviet propaganda and public opinion over events in Afghanistan, and inevitably Afghanistan formed one of the chief topics of his discussions with the Chinese leaders. According to the *New York Times*, Washington accorded great importance to the help China could give the Afghan rebels and was in no doubt at all that China would give such help.[83]

By substantially exaggerating the military aspect of the already considerably strengthened economic and political relations between the United States and China, the United States was attempting to exert pressure on the Soviet Union and making no secret of it. At a banquet at the House of the People's Assemblies in Peking, Brown stated that the very fact of his visit was of great significance, regardless of the details of the talks or understandings about subsequent steps.[84]

In the spring of 1980 several senior Chinese military officials visited the United States and held talks on the purchase of weapons. China, which had neither the funds for large purchases nor the possibility of acquiring large consignments of up-to-date weapons, managed to obtain consent to buy a number of different types of defence weapons. In May 1980 a Chinese military delegation visited the United States on a ten-day mission, this time led by Geng Biao, a member of the Politburo and Deputy Premier. Talks were held with President Carter, Secretary of State Edward Muskie – who had replaced the more moderate Cyrus Vance – and Secretary of Defense Harold Brown. During the talks the United States reaffirmed its intention to sell many kinds of 'non-offensive weapons' to China, although China repeatedly asked for the sale of basic varieties of offensive weapons as well. Before leaving for home, Geng Biao clearly expressed the wish that the United States would deal with China's requirements as she dealt with the requirements of other large buyers of American weapons, such as Israel for example. Since China was neither willing nor able to acquire large consignments of such extremely expensive weaponry, she tried everywhere, and above all in the United States, to buy models of modern weapons in an effort to facilitate the modernization of her army. According to Senator T. Stevens, there were officials even in the National Security Council who believed it to be both possible and desirable to effect the unlimited sale of weapons to China, but because of the objections of moderate officials in the State Department or, on the contrary, of those ultra-conservative politicians who were opposed to both Soviet and Chinese Communism, the National Security Council turned down proposals to sell offensive weapons to China. [85]

In July 1980 President Carter and Hua Guofeng met in Tokyo where, according to the Chinese News Agency, an exchange of views took place on a wide range of questions on the current international scene.[86] Meetings and talks continued at lower levels, but overhanging them all was a distinct sense of haste, uncertainty and publicity. It was election year in the United States, in addition to which the United States had recently suffered severe diplomatic and political defeat in Iran and Nicaragua. Carter needed to score some major achievements in foreign policy in order to ensure success in the pre-election debates. The *rapprochement* with China was therefore depicted as a most important step towards guaranteeing America's national interests. In justifying not only economic but also military co-operation with China, the *Christian Science Monitor* drew attention to several points: in deciding what America had to do to help China become a modern military power, it was vital to note that the greater the number of Soviet troops held down in the centre of Asia, the fewer there would be for other fronts; the moment US forces had left Vietnam, China's conventional forces ceased to be a threat to American interests; China did not have the possibility of using her conventional forces outside her own borders and, having no navy, she was no threat either to Taiwan or Japan; China was fully occupied by the containment of Soviet power in Asia, to the extent that it was possible, and the allies had much to gain from the improvement of China's defences.[87]

There were, however, many in the United States who were opposed to this approach, claiming that too close a collaboration with China, especially on the military plane, would not so much serve American national interests as subject Washington's activity to China's national interests and ambitions. One could find comments in the editorials of the *New York Times* of early 1980 to the effect that, to establish relations with the People's Republic was one thing, but for the American government to send the Secretary of Defense to Peking at a delicate moment was quite another, if it wanted to have realistic contacts with the Soviet Union; it was inept policy to bank only on the 'China card' while ignoring the 'Soviet card' altogether.[88] The same newspaper at the end of 1980 brought convincing arguments in favour of achieving a balanced policy *vis-à-vis* both China and the Soviet Union; the lack of such a balanced policy was being condemned in Western Europe and Japan and was not in the West's interest.[89]

To emphasize the importance of the *rapprochement* with China, President Carter also referred to the relatively rapid growth of Sino-American trade, which in overall turnover had increased almost 12 times – from $374 million in 1977 to $4 billion in 1980[90] – two and a half times more than the turnover in trade between the United States and the Soviet Union. Sino-American trade was, however, unbalanced, for China bought far more from the United States than vice versa. Carter's opponents, however, had another very weighty argument, namely the unstable nature of the Chinese leadership.

Indeed, during 1980 a complicated inner-party struggle was continuing and by the autumn would result in appreciable shifts among the leading figures on the Chinese political stage. From the purely practical point of view, Washington could perceive these changes as favourable to the development of Sino-American relations. The single most important event in the internal life of the Chinese Communist Party in 1980 was the Central Committee Plenum held in Peking on 23–9 February. The Plenum resolved to convene the Twelfth (Extraordinary) Congress of the Party, and to reinstate the Central Committee Secretariat that had been dispersed during the Cultural Revolution. All 11 members were appointed from among people who had either been considered as in opposition or had even been victims of the Cultural Revolution, some of them only recently having been rehabilitated. Hu Yaobang, who was appointed General Secretary and a member of the Permanent Committee of the Politburo, was, at 65, regarded as a loyal follower of Deng Xiaoping and generally seen as the most likely successor to the ageing leader. Another of Deng Xiaoping's supporters, the 62-year-old Zhao Ziyang, was similarly made a member of the Permanent Committee. Since the Plenum also decided to end the joint holding of responsible state and party posts, it soon became clear that Hua Guofeng, the current Chairman of the Party Central Committee, would have to give up the post of Premier and that this post would go to Zhao Ziyang. The Plenum removed four Politburo members who had until only recently been very influential, the chief among them being Wang Dongxing. All four had emerged as powerful during the Cultural Revolution, and while not belonging to the Gang of Four, had nevertheless been directly involved in the repression of party, state and army cadres in the 1960s. Their removal from the political scene greatly diminished the power base of Hua Guofeng and correspondingly strengthened the influence of Deng Xiaoping and his younger supporters. These changes in the leadership would be formally ratified a few months later at a session of the National Assembly.

The Plenum's most important decision was the complete rehabilitation of Liu Shaoqi, Mao Zedong's chief opponent at the end of the 1950s and beginning of the 1960s, and therefore the chief object of insult and attack during the Cultural Revolution. Inevitably, Liu Shaoqi's rehabilitation, and the publications and funeral ceremony in Peking associated with it, gave rise to even more profound criticism of the policies and practice of the Cultural Revolution.

In the autumn of 1980 the All-Chinese Assembly of the People's Representatives (or National Assembly) met in Peking. Many questions of the country's internal life were discussed, but most attention was given to relieving Hua Guofeng of the post of Premier of the State Council and appointing Zhao Ziyang in his place. The session officially acknowledged the ten-year plan for China's social and economic development (1976–1985) as incorrect and unreal.

3

Changes in the Strategic Triangle during the 1980s

China and the United States: signs of important changes

President Gerald Ford gained the Republican nomination over his rival, Ronald Reagan, in the 1976 American election campaign, but the result was a victory for the Democrats and the installation of Jimmy Carter in the White House. In 1980, however, the mood of the American electorate had changed. First, Ronald Reagan won his party's support in a contest against George Bush, and then in the national elections gained a large majority over Carter and became President. It was not only a new administration and a new party that came to power, but a new political grouping consisting of people who reflected the economic and political interests of elements of the American establishment other than those which had been reflected in the administrations of either Nixon, Ford and Kissinger, or Carter and Brzezinski. The new President and his entourage were distinguished by far greater conservatism and more sharply expressed anti-Communism than any American President of the past 50 years, and this circumstance would colour every aspect of America's foreign policy, including relations with China.

While still a candidate for the Presidency, Ronald Reagan had voiced extremely critical remarks about Jimmy Carter's Far East policy, declaring in particular that, should he be elected, he would restore official relations with Taiwan or, as he demonstratively called it, the 'Chinese Republic'. His remarks provoked a spate of abusive anti-Reagan articles and declarations in the Chinese media, to which some of Reagan's associates responded with comments on China's policies, such as those made by one of Reagan's chief consultants, Richard Kline, who called China an aggressive state and a threat to peace and stability in South-East Asia. Identifying the differences between various American conservative groupings, some observers concluded that those who had advanced and supported Reagan were anti-Communists who viewed the People's Republic above all as a Communist country and for that reason alone excluded any possibility of friendly relations. China was for them also a potential enemy and they therefore objected vigorously to Sino-American military co-operation and the supply of American military hardware to China. While emphasizing above all the ideological argument, these people also regarded the national interests of the two countries in the Pacific Basin as incompatible.

Once having become President, however, and representing the whole of America – at any rate, 'strong' America – rather than merely his own party or one faction, Ronald Reagan could not ignore the views and pressure of other political groups which continued to express their interest in the maintenance of good relations with China. The new administration could not, therefore, nor did it wish to revoke the agreements or alter the level of relations existing between the two countries. The two vast states had begun to move towards each other after 20 years of hostility and alienation and the movement continued, even if only through its own momentum. At most, the rate of *rapprochement* between these two superpowers slowed down perceptibly. The volume of trade, for example, rose between 1981 and 1982 by less than $200 million to $5.2 billion. Thousands of Chinese students, specialists and engineers continued their training in the United States, collaboration between institutions of higher learning went on, as did the broadening of exchanges and tourism. A number of prominent Republicans visited China at the beginning of 1981. Among them was former President Gerald Ford, who met Deng Xiaoping and conveyed messages from President Reagan which have never been published. The warm welcome shown to the American politicians was evidence that the Chinese leaders greatly valued Reagan's assurances of loyalty.

In June 1981 the new Secretary of State, Alexander Haig, paid an official visit to China and had meetings with the Foreign Minister Huang Hua, the Defence Minister Geng Biao, the Premier Zhao Ziyang and the Deputy Chairman of the Central

Committee Deng Xiaoping. Not only did Haig confirm the American agreement to sell 'dual usage' technology to China, but also promised to lift the embargo on the sale to China of many kinds of offensive weapon and to step up co-operation between the war departments of the two countries. A few months later, during a return visit to the United States by Huang Hua, it was announced that Peking intended buying Stinger missiles, regarded as the best in the Pentagon's arsenal, as well as guided anti-tank missiles.

Nevertheless, the general atmosphere of Sino-American relations gradually deteriorated during 1981–2, friction occurred more frequently, and the language of mutual reproach became harsher. Walter Mondale's optimistic belief that China's relations with America were comparable in their 'maturity' with those of the Western allies was proving to have been premature. Nor could the People's Republic see the United States as an 'ally' against the background of the 1980s. What was it that prevented the 'maturing' of the alliance, an alliance on which particular groups in both countries were counting?

The first problem which again became acute in the relations between China and the United States was that of Taiwan, in itself perhaps not of major importance, but a matter of great significance from the point of view of each country's prestige.

Before becoming President, Ronald Reagan had attacked President Carter for making too many important concessions to China when establishing diplomatic relations, concessions which allegedly were not in America's national interest, and Reagan had made it plain that in his view the greatest concession had been to break off 'official' ties with Taiwan. On becoming President, Reagan announced that he would abide by the special bill on relations with Taiwan passed by Congress in 1980, despite demands by the People's Republic that it be rescinded as contradictory to the establishment of diplomatic relations between itself and the United States. With Reagan's accession to power, America's military aid to Taiwan grew significantly, rising from $330 million in 1981 to $800 million in 1983.[1]

China's vigorous protests led to new talks and a joint communiqué of 17 August 1982 in which China promised to make every effort to achieve a peaceful solution of the Taiwan question, while the United States gave assurances of its willingness

gradually to run down and ultimately to cease weapons deliveries
to the Taiwan regime. This compromise turned out to be
unstable, as both Peking and Washington chose to interpret its
conditions in different ways. With his customary frankness,
Reagan at once announced that the United States would continue to arm Taiwan and that she would never refuse help to her
'old friends'. Military supplies to Taiwan were budgeted for
$780 million in the financial year 1984 and for $760 million for
1985. [2] China's protests and declarations were virtually ignored,
although some American political observers have asserted that
they were of a rather formal or even conciliatory nature, and
therefore practical measures were not to be expected in
response. This is an erroneous view. While the United States was
stepping up its military and economic aid to Taiwan, the People's
Republic was intensifying its efforts to 'bring Taiwan back peacefully into the bosom of the motherland' by announcing its willingness to start direct talks with the Nationalists (KMT) and
promising Taiwan considerable autonomy, the preservation of
the social and economic system on the island, and even offering
to give the Kuomintang a number of leading posts in the political
institutions of the whole, united country.

The Taiwan problem will continue to provoke differences and
arguments among American political observers for a long time to
come. Some of them agree with Solzhenitsyn, who spent some
time on Taiwan and found it to be a near-perfect anti-
Communist state, such as he had not found anywhere, either in
the West or the East. He called on the United States not only to
support Taiwan by all available means, but also to end the
rapprochement with China and to do nothing to promote the
development of the Communist regime. China, in his view, was
an empire of evil, in some respects even more dangerous than the
one in the Soviet Union, and he showered a hail of reproach
down on Nixon and Kissinger, and 'many American journalists
and influential capitulationist trends in American political
circles'. It was not very likely that leading American politicians
would follow his advice.

Among Western political observers and journalists, however,
the view has been expressed that Taiwan's strategic importance
to America's interests was insignificant by comparison, for
example, with that of either Israel or South Africa, in support of

which America accepted considerable criticism from those
wanting a policy of balance with the oil producers and Black
Africa. China, in this view, would continue to accept American
support against the Soviet Union, even without full diplomatic
relations, but America must recognize the danger of ignoring
China's feelings over an issue of national sovereignty, like
Taiwan. If China were to conclude that America was not a reliable partner, this would not lead to the restoration of China's
previous relations with the Soviet Union, but it could turn China
back to isolation. To give public support to a doubtfully democratic regime, which was not under direct threat and which
served no strategic purpose, against a totalitarian power of
decisive strategic importance for the West, and whose sovereignty over Taiwan America had anyway acknowledged, was
utterly foolish.[3] Such views were unlikely to convince leading
American politicians, however.

The second most important factor affecting the rate and scope
of the Sino-American *rapprochement* was the militant anti-
Communism inherent in the Reagan administration, which was
deeper, more intense and more active than in preceding administrations. Reagan is not inclined to divide Communism into
'bad' Soviet Communism and 'good' Chinese, Hungarian and
Yugoslav Communism. The spearhead of his anti-Communism
may be aimed against the Soviet Union, but in practice he has
pronounced a crusade against Communism throughout the
world, and China is no exception in this respect. United States
Far East policy is therefore contradictory, insincere and
unstable. Reagan and his entourage belong to that faction of the
American political and military élite whose views were formed
during the years of the Cold War of the 1950s and who have
never distinguished between the Soviet Union and China. In
their view, diplomats may make concessions to China, but it must
never be forgotten that China is a Communist country and is
therefore antagonistic to the American system of values, to
American ideals and American interests. And if many liberals
protested against the United States becoming 'the architect of a
great power which our grandsons may have to fight' and making
China 'more powerful than she would otherwise be in the normal
course of events',[4] then a large section of conservative opinion
was even more alarmed by the prospect.

It was not therefore surprising that, at the beginning of the 1980s, the voice of the Taiwan lobby and those who advocated the 'containment and isolation' of China should be heard sounding louder and louder in Washington. In any event, the question of alliance with China has been taken off the agenda as far as American politicians are concerned, despite the fact that Washington is ready in every possible way to welcome and support anti-Soviet tendencies in Chinese foreign policy.

The change of tone in Peking's foreign policy and the changes which took place in 1981–2 and which left the leadership in a more stable position, should also be noted. After losing the post of Premier, Hua Guofeng soon also lost that of Chairman of the Central Committee of the Party. The Twelfth Extraordinary Party Congress appointed a new Central Committee which was dominated entirely by Deng Xiaoping's supporters, all enemies of the Cultural Revolution. Hua Guofeng, although still a member of the Central Committee, was no longer a member of the Politburo. Deng Xiaoping became Chairman of the Central Committee's Military Council and also Chairman of a new party institution, the Central Commission of Advisers, which brought back the old guard.

The struggle for power and the instability of the Chinese leadership, accompanied as it had been by frequent and sharp zigzags in both foreign and domestic policy, had caused such colossal damage to the entire Chinese people and state that measures had now to be taken not only to create a stable and firm leadership, but also to create the conditions for the rational hand-over of power from generation to generation, that is to say a mechanism of succession for the government of the country and the party. These reforms of the structure and functioning of the highest organs of power would naturally entail a more precise definition of priorities in domestic and foreign policy. Chinese politics became calmer and more predictable.

Although the Chinese leaders began to realize more clearly than before just how far their country was lagging behind the more developed industrial nations, they nevertheless made no plans to obliterate the lag in some three or five years. The inferiority complex that had pushed previous leaders into many a precipitate act was beginning to evaporate. After Secretary of State Haig's unsuccessful visit, Deng Xiaoping said in an interview that the United States thought China was seeking America's favour:

> In fact, China is fundamentally independent: even if relations deteriorate to what they were before 1972, China would not perish. The Chinese people will never bow down and never beg or importune for help. Didn't the Chinese people learn enough lessons from the Opium Wars? I said as much to Secretary of State Haig when he came to China. If the United States wants to force China to act according to American wishes, China will never agree.[5]

The dominant theme of China's foreign policy in the 1980s is the assertion, first made in the 1970s, that China is a developing country which belongs to the Third World and which must defend the interests of the Third World against the exploitation, 'hegemonism' and claims of the First and, to some extent, the Second Worlds. As the largest and potentially most powerful country, China today claims to lead the Third World, and it is above all in the Third World that China seeks friends and allies. The Chinese division of the planet into three worlds, however, does not correspond in effect with either the Soviet or the American understanding of that division.

There are many ways to classify the world's 160 independent countries. In Soviet political terminology there are usually two categories which are applied. From the political point of view, the world is divided into, on the one hand, the socialist 'camp', to which belong the countries of 'developed' socialism as well as the less developed socialist countries, for example Vietnam, Laos, Yemen and so on, and, on the other hand, the imperialist 'camp', which includes all the main countries of developed capitalism and their allies among the less developed countries. Between these two 'camps' there is a block of non-aligned or neutral countries, including a number of socialist states, such as Yugoslavia and Cuba, and a number of capitalist states, such as Switzerland, Austria and Sweden, as well as some less developed countries. From the economic standpoint, the Soviet media divide the world into a group of industrial countries, a group of countries with moderately developed economies, and a group with either less developed or developing economies, and these are also often called countries of the Third World.

Top   Mao Zedong making a report to cadres in Yenan in 1942.

Bottom   Chinese leaving for the Front to fight the Japanese, carrying home-made rifles and spears.

Top   Women guerillas on parade.

Bottom   Poster proclaiming the friendship between the Chinese and Russian peoples.

Top   Soviet troops leaving Port Arthur in 1955 to return to the Soviet Union.

Bottom   Khrushchev and Mao Zedong meet in Peking in 1959. On the extreme left is Chairman Liu Shaoqi; on the far right is Mikhail Suslov, Chairman of the Foreign Affairs Committee of the Soviet Union.

| June | S | M | T | W | T | F | S | S | M | T | W | T | F | S | S | M | T | W | T | F | S | S | M | T | W | T | F | S | S | M |
| --- | 1 | 2 | 3 | 4 | 5 | 6 | 7 | 8 | 9 | 10 | 11 | 12 | 13 | 14 | 15 | 16 | 17 | 18 | 19 | 20 | 21 | 22 | 23 | 24 | 25 | 26 | 27 | 28 | 29 | 30 |

March courageously forward under the beacon of Mao Tse-tung's revolutionary line in literature and ar

Top Mao Zedong portrayed as The Rising Sun in 1969.

Bottom Mao Zedong's fourth wife, Jiang Qing, and her mother.

Top Demonstrators in Peking protest at American action in North Vietnam in 1964.

Bottom Cast of the Shanghai–Peking Opera salutes Zhou Enlai, Mao Zedong and Lin Biao on stage in 1967.

Top Alexei Kosygin on his way home from the funeral of Ho Chi-minh in 1969 stops briefly in Peking for a meeting with Zhou Enlai.

Bottom Mao Zedong and President Nixon in 1976.

Top Dr Henry Kissinger meets Mao Zedong and Zhou Enlai in 1973.

Bottom Poster showing caricature of the Gang of Four carried through the streets of Guangdong by demonstrators supporting the new Chairman Hua Guofeng.

Top Jiang Gai-shi aboard the USS *Wasp* off Formosa in 1954.

Bottom Ronald Reagan and Li Xiannian stand while the national anthems are played during the ceremony to welcome President Reagan at the Great Hall of the People, Peking, 26 April 1984.

Political scientists and politicians in the West generally apply a different interpretation. First, they speak of the 'free world', which means above all the developed capitalist countries. The second division of the world is composed of the 'totalitarian' countries, which means the Soviet Union and all the countries of Comecon and the Warsaw Pact, but includes China, a number of underdeveloped countries and, with reservations, an intermediate group of non-aligned countries. Economically, in the West they generally refer to the industrially developed countries of the North and the less developed countries of the South. There is also a decided political significance in the division of the world according to religious denominations – the Islamic countries, the Christian world, the areas of Buddhism and Judaism.

After several attempts – 'the world city' and the 'world village' – the Chinese developed a classification of their own. Repeating one of Mao's ideas, Deng Xiaoping said:

> The United States and the Soviet Union constitute the First World. The developing countries of Asia, Africa, Latin America and other areas constitute the Third World. The developed countries which find themselves between these two worlds are the Second World. China is a socialist country and at the same time a developing country. China belongs to the Third World.[6]

The doctrine of the three worlds was consolidated by being made the ideological basis of China's foreign policy at the CCP Eleventh Congress. The official interpretation, which was given in a seven-page editorial in the *People's Daily* of 1 November 1977, was also published as a separate pamphlet and translated into many languages.

Any one of the above classifications is open to the criticism that it is only partly true and that it contains contradictions and exceptions. The significance of the Chinese conception of the three worlds, however, is that it sets the First and Third Worlds in hostile opposition to each other. The Chinese claim to be the leader and protector of Third World interests. They can find allies and co-operation among the countries of the Second World. They can exploit the contradictions between the countries of the First World, that is, the United States and the Soviet Union, though they have to act with caution in relation to these two superpowers. This conception, which China persistently propagated in 1982–3, excludes all possibility of any kind of alliance with either the Soviet Union or the United States. When the issue is Afghanistan or Kampuchea, where each country feels its interests are affected, China can co-operate with the United States. But China cannot and will not support United States policy in Africa, Latin America and the Middle East, and American and Chinese interests will conflict in many countries and areas of Asia.

Another important factor which slowed down the development of relations between the United States and China at the beginning of the 1980s was China's decision, taken in 1979–80, to review the financial terms on which the country's economic development was to take place, that is loan periods, rates of repayment and sources of funding. The Chinese leaders decided not to go ahead with several large and ambitious industrial projects and they sharply reduced the scale of credits that had been requested, thus producing a decidedly dampening effect on the enthusiasm of Western business circles for developing economic co-operation with China. Originally, the plan for the Four Modernizations could have been carried out, but only assuming an investment of about $500 billion, including the import of equipment from developed capitalist countries to the tune of $100 billion up to 1985. This scale of investment, unrealistic as it was both for China and the Western countries, was the path not to modernization but bankruptcy. The vast projects turned out to have been badly designed from both the economic and technical points of view.

With the installation of a more stable leadership in China there also came greater clarity of understanding regarding the country's needs and possibilities. It became evident that neither the State Council nor the Party Central Committee had any precise notion of how to balance the proportions of even the most basic and relatively simple of the country's economic needs, let alone the complex relationship between the various social, economic, demographic and environmental elements. Although China had received many offers of credit in 1977–8, she had managed just in time to resist the dangerous temptation which has led Argentina, Mexico, Brazil, Yugoslavia and Poland, among others, into huge indebtedness to the West, indebtedness which has practically brought the economic development of those countries to a halt. China was more prudent, and many a Western corporation and bank found itself, not in receipt of profits and interest from China, but facing demands for damages incurred for not fulfilling previous contracts.

The Chinese leaders and economists began to look for other ways and other models for the economic development of their country. They recognized, for example, that the assertion 'steel is the decisive link' had been a mistake and that the plan to raise steel production to 60 million tonnes by 1985 had been Utopian. In fact, steel production in 1981 and 1982 remained at 12 million tonnes. This did not mean that China was repudiating the Four Modernizations and the plans for economic development and economic co-operation with the West. It merely meant that the forms of that co-operation were being looked at again. After 1980 China eschewed credits in favour of attracting direct foreign investment, that is the Open Doors policy which was ratified by the Twelfth Congress of the CCP. By the end of 1982 China had signed agreements for direct investments of $4.3 billion, although so far it has only amounted to $1.5 billion. China's external debt at the end of 1982 was only $4.7 to $5 billion, while its foreign currency reserves were standing at somewhere between $5 and $10 billion.[7] These are of course insignificant amounts for a country the size of China, but they are indicative of a more realistic economic course, rather than a climate of hasty deals and agreements, such as were made in China in 1978 and which were followed by an aftermath of confusion and uncertainty.

Finally, the state of Sino-Soviet relations has been another not insignificant factor in Sino-American relations, which were slowed down by American fears of a possible *rapprochement* between the Soviet Union and China, a fact which showed yet again that the desire to perpetuate the conflict between China and the Soviet Union has been the main stimulus for many American politicians in their attitude towards policy on China. Donald Zagoria, the eminent specialist on international relations, argued in the middle of the 1970s that the anti-Soviet trend in China's foreign policy – and its implicit pro-American obverse – was, as it were, the central link in America's security in the widest sense. A limited *rapprochement* between the Soviet

Union and China would, in Zagoria's analysis, run counter to American interests, as it would, first, weaken America's leverage in its talks with the Soviet Union, secondly, act as an incentive to both Chinese and Soviet militancy, thirdly, facilitate the radicalization of the Third World and, finally, reduce the freedom of action of the autonomous Communist parties.[8]

This seems to be the prevailing view among both American specialists on international relations and politicians, though there are, to be sure, other, more sober judgments. James Reston, for example, has commented that Russia and China needed to be drawn into the world structure which, although conceived in the United States, would never be stable without them.[9]

This is of course a correct argument, but will China and the Soviet Union help build a 'world structure' that has been conceived by the United States? It is plainly necessary not merely to involve them in such a structure, but also to include them in its design, for the ideas which the Soviet Union, China and the United States each have in mind for what they want as a world structure still remain essentially different. Professor Allen S. Whiting of the University of Michigan, who has expressed more precise ideas and more modest desires on the question, does not believe that a lessening of tension between China and the Soviet Union would automatically damage American interests. First of all, *détente* with the Soviet Union would be the sensible course for China, as it would reduce the threat of war, release colossal resources which are being swallowed up by military expenditure, improve the Chinese position in talks with the West, and increase flexibility in China's foreign policy. In Whiting's view, Sino-Soviet *détente* ought to be seen not only as a possible and probable event, but as the necessary and desirable condition for solving some of Asia's general problems.[10]

Even the most insignificant contacts between the Soviet Union and China tended to weaken the belief that an age-old geopolitical antagonism existed between the two countries which, in the struggle against Communism, the United States could and should exploit by supporting the weaker Communist state against the stronger and, in the American view, more 'dangerous'. Hence, during its first term the Reagan administration made it perfectly clear that it did not regard China as one of the superpowers with which good relations were vitally important for the organization of world order, not only in the twentieth but also in the twenty-first century. Instead the Reagan administration demonstrated that it saw China as a regional power which could only be a junior partner to the United States in the context of world politics. China, moreover, was to serve as a military-political counterweight to the Soviet Union in America's global strategy, deflecting onto itself part of the Soviet Union's military force. Many American politicians, moreover, were convinced that China was much more eager for co-operation with the United States than vice versa, and therefore, as far as they were concerned, the process of *rapprochement* could continue even without America particularly having to make concessions. This strategy did not suit China, however, especially in view of the fact that any demonstration of too close a partnership with the United States would manifestly damage China's reputation in the eyes of a number of Third World countries with which the Chinese leadership wished to remain on the best of terms. Such were the chief factors which in 1981–2 slowed down *rapprochement* between China and the United States.

The worsened state of relations was responsible for the breakdown of trade talks between the two countries. China could not agree to the American demand that she unilaterally reduce her exports to the United States, above all of textile goods, and responded to America's temporary breaking-off of the talks and her imposition of sanctions on the import of Chinese textiles by sharply reducing her own purchases of American agricultural produce from $950.8 million in the first six months of 1982 to $347.1 million for the first half of 1983. This reduced the overall volume of Sino-American trade and created a deficit for the United States in its trade with China where an active balance had existed previously.[11]

The Chinese stepped up their criticism of United States foreign policy significantly. Already at the Twelfth Congress China's total independence in foreign policy had been underlined and now, after a brief interval, once again the cry was the 'struggle against the two superpowers'. More and more distinctly the Chinese leaders proclaimed that China was 'equidistant' from both the United States and the Soviet Union. In a series of statements and interviews, Hu Yaobang declared that he saw little ground for optimism in Sino-American relations in the immediate future, and the Chinese Ambassador to the United States, Zhang Wenjin was saying the same thing to the National Committee for Sino-American Relations, a body which had been in existence in the United States for a long time. China's irritation and dissatisfaction with the situation was demonstrated over the fate of Hu Na, the woman tennis-player who, after competing in an international tournament, wanted to remain in the United States and requested political asylum. China's reaction, which was entirely out of proportion to what was essentially an insignificant episode, was to cancel the programme of cultural and sports exchanges with the United States which had been announced for 1983. The four-day visit to China by Secretary of State George Schultz did nothing to improve relations.

Some American politicians, political scientists and foreign policy experts, however, were entirely satisfied with the way things were going. In their view, the United States had already gone too far in its policy of *rapprochement* with China and the time had come to go into reverse. China was not yet 'ripe' for close relations with the United States and her utter backwardness and poverty made it obvious that an alliance would be extremely burdensome for the United States. Israel, with a population of four million, was one thing; China, with one billion, was quite another. In a study of China's global role, published in 1980, John Copper expressed the view that, by comparison with the superpowers, fundamental obstacles in every sphere hampered China's considerable possibilities for developing into one of the major participants in world politics. Her foreign policy had been perpetually characterized by bad relations with one or other of the superpowers, which showed that her diplomacy was based on the principle of trial and error and that her foreign policy was still in a state of formation.[12]

Many influential circles, however, were dissatisfied with the Reagan administration's attitude to China. Richard Nixon and Henry Kissinger, who had both been instrumental in making the first and most important change in Sino-American relations, criticized the new policy, as did former National Security Adviser to the Carter administration, Zbygniew Brzezinski, who had been involved in establishing diplomatic relations between the two countries. Brzezinski claimed that Sino-American friendship, broadly interpreted in the strategic context, could absorb specific bilateral disagreements which were not amenable to solution, and he cited Taiwan as an example. Since Reagan had come to power, Sino-American friendship had steadily narrowed and become more formal, while the Taiwan question had become dominant. China should be seen as a serious, global and strategic partner. Nor should the United States try to give the impression that Sino-American links were not influenced by the Soviet threat. On the contrary, Brzezinski went on, the common interest shared by China and the United States in opposing Soviet hegemony should be proclaimed to all the world. In certain circumstances this might entail supplying China with defence weapons, but the United States already supplied weapons to regimes of which she did not approve. A strong and well-defended China was in America's interest. Sixty-five years after the October Revolution and 32 years after the emergence of what had been perceived as the Sino-Soviet bloc, it was time the United States was able to distinguish between Soviet and Chinese Communism.[13]

The Reagan administration turned out to be extremely receptive to this criticism. In 1983 Reagan was already having to think about the forthcoming Presidential election and so far he had little to show in the way of success in his foreign policy. It was not therefore surprising that in the autumn of that year Sino-American relations took on a more active appearance and that a number of new features appeared. Most notably, two visits took place, one to China from 25 to 29 September 1983 by Defense Secretary Caspar Weinberger, and a similar four-day visit to the United States by Deng Xiaoping. Weinberger held talks with the Chinese Minister of Defence, Zhang Aiping, with Premier Zhao Ziyang and with Deng Xiaoping, who now occupied the new post of Chairman of the Central Commission of Advisers.

The central issue of Weinberger's talks with the Chinese leaders was the sale of American weapons and military technology. Earlier in the year, the American government had announced its decision to permit the sale to China of articles incorporating advanced technology which had hitherto been embargoed for sale to any Communist country. As US Secretary for Trade Malcolm Baldridge declared, trade with China should be carried on at the same level as that with all other friendly countries. China was thus accorded the status of a 'non-allied friendly power', and this permitted the sale to her of American computers, machinery for manufacturing semi-conductors and communications equipment. It was envisaged that these sales would increase the value of American exports to China by between $1 and $2 billion a year. Weinberger's announcement to the Chinese, with the President's approval, that the United States would be willing to sell China not only 'dual-usage' technology, but also several kinds of modern weapon, meant that President Reagan's government had gone further than any previous administration in the process of consolidating Sino-American relations.

It emerged, however, that selling arms to China was an extremely complex business in every sense – politically, diplomatically, technically and even administratively. The Chinese leaders stated clearly that they would not agree to allow the sale of a limited number of American weapons to the People's Republic to serve as a smokescreen for the delivery of unlimited quantities of modern weapons to Taiwan. A country the size of China could not arm its army with weapons bought over the counter, but needed instead to build its own defence industry. The Chinese therefore expressed interest in the purchase of up-to-date models of military technology with a view to organizing their manufacture in China itself, and sought assistance on the creation of an arms industry. The United States, however, was not prepared to perform a 'service' of this kind for a Communist country, even one with the status of a 'non-allied friendly power'. The Chinese, acutely sensitive to any hint of discrimination, also requested detailed information as to the kind of weapons they would be allowed to order from the United States without the risk of refusal. Washington, however, was not inclined to depart from customary procedure for China's sake. It proved to be a much easier matter to reach agreement on the exchange of military experts.

Arms sales to China became a topic of lively discussion and criticism among various political groups in the United States. Analysing the question, David Lampton, a political scientist at the University of Ohio, commented in an article that there was a dual aim at issue: one was to increase American influence on China and the other was to exercise restraint on the Soviet Union, aims which in Lampton's view were incompatible. Faced with Sino-American co-operation, the Soviet Union would become still more active on the international stage, while for their part the Chinese would object to the supply of weapons being linked to the Soviet Union's conduct on the international scene. Moreover, the insignificant sums involved would not make any appreciable impact on China's military strength, for the modernization of her army would require an expenditure of between $40 and $73 billion, and neither China, which was trying to reduce its military budget, nor the United States could contemplate such sums. Lampton rightly comments that the United States, in carrying out its *rapprochement* policy *vis-à-vis* China, must also take into account the reactions of its allies in the area – Singapore, Thailand, Indonesia, the Philippines, Taiwan and Japan – and should also be aware that friendship with China on a military level was pushing India nearer and nearer to military co-operation with the Soviet Union. The ASEAN (Association of South East Asian Nations) countries, with their large Chinese populations, Lampton goes on, feel threatened not by the Soviet Union, but precisely by China which gives support to the Communist parties of those countries. Apart from the territorial disputes which China has with a number of these countries – some of them over oil deposits – there was always the possibility that China would not remain moderate over Taiwan forever. All these were dangers the United States should not ignore, and instead of supplying arms to China, it would be prudent to reduce arms sales to Taiwan, increase the sale of 'dual-usage' technology to the People's Republic, and at the same time generally broaden the American domestic market to Chinese goods. The challenge to the United States lay in the fact that China's economic development would lead inevitably to the increase of her military might, and while America would lose more by remaining aloof, the Chinese people would do everything in their power to achieve their legitimate economic ambitions.[14]

During his visit, Weinberger elaborated the details of a visit to the United States by the Chinese Premier and a return visit to China by the American President, both to take place in 1984, a matter on which the Chinese had already taken a preliminary decision. The question had also been discussed by China's Foreign Minister, Wu Xiushang, during a visit to the United

States in October 1983. He had had talks with President Reagan, Vice President Bush, Secretary of State Schultz and many other American government officials, including the Director of the CIA, William Casey. These meetings indicated the range and depth of the questions discussed, although the only officially acknowledged result of Wu Xiushang's visit was the agreement to renew cultural exchanges, starting in 1984, which the Chinese side had broken off earlier.

The volume of trade between the United States and China fell from $5.2 billion in 1982 to $4.3 billion in 1983, while the range and number of cultural exchanges had similarly shrunk. In the autumn of 1983 both countries undertook a number of efforts to halt the estrangement which had been gathering momentum, and thus opened up, it would seem, new possibilities and trends in the attitudes of both sides. In January 1984 the visit took place of the Chinese Premier, Zhao Ziyang, the first visit to the United States by the (acting) head of state of the People's Republic.

Before the Chinese Premier arrived in Washington, a group of leading American specialists on China, members of a non-government organization called the Atlantic Council, drew up a report making recommendations to the White House on questions of Sino-American relations. The report noted that the Chinese leaders had carried out a measure of 'adjustment' to their foreign policy and were now approaching the development of their relations with the United States with 'some caution'. China had already gained and would continue to gain quite a few benefits from her relations with the United States, but she was hoping to gain still more from both the United States and the Soviet Union, if she could occupy an 'intermediate' position between the two. The report continued that, for the Chinese leadership, however, it was more important not to form a bloc with the United States in its confrontation with the Soviet Union, but to develop instead her links with the Third World. The widening of multilateral links between the United States and China was hampered by reason of ideology, yet, in matters of greatest importance to the United States, China stood closer at the present time to America than to the Soviet Union. China was defined in the report as a major, undeveloped, independent, non-aligned state which should be seen above all as a 'regional' power. In recognizing the chief element in Sino-American *rapproche-*

ment as the Soviet factor, the authors of the report remarked that it was precisely this resistance to Soviet hegemonism that made future co-operation between the United States and China possible in various ways.[15]

In many respects, Zhao Ziyang's visit confirmed the Atlantic Council's analysis, though not entirely. The Chinese leader above all categorically rejected the American attempt to view China as a 'regional' power and he persistently tried to gain American recognition of China's role as that of a great power which could and should participate on an equal footing with the United States in the solution of international problems, not only in the Far East and Pacific Basin, but throughout the world. As for the Pacific, Zhao Ziyang called on all countries in the area to support peace and stability in their region, to observe the principles of mutual respect, territorial integrity and sovereignty, mutual non-aggression, non-interference in each other's internal affairs, equality, mutual interest and peaceful coexistence, and the settlement of disputes by peaceful means without recourse to force or the threat of armed force. No country should seek hegemony in the region, or engage in an arms race, and competition in the race for nuclear weapons especially should cease altogether. All foreign military bases should be dismantled and foreign troops withdrawn. The Chinese Premier was not precise as to which country was most in violation of these principles at the given time, but everyone was aware that the United States had long ago created a ramified network of military bases in Hawaii, Japan, Australia, South Korea and the Philippines, and that a significant part of this system had as its main purpose the containment of Chinese Communism.

Zhao Ziyang gave no support to the American call for the renewal of an 'all-embracing strategic partnership' with the United States. While declaring China's condemnation of many aspects of Soviet policy, and agreement with the American assessment of the situation in Afghanistan and Kampuchea, he indicated that there were significant differences between China and the United States on many other questions, especially affecting the Third World. He felt compelled, for example, to condemn the American occupation of Grenada. He expressed himself in favour of an improvement in relations between China and the Soviet Union and, when asked bluntly by journalists on which side of the political conflict between the United States and the Soviet Union China stood, his answers, though evasive, were nevertheless sufficiently clear. He said that China pursued an independent foreign policy, but at the moment did not feel herself to be 'equidistant' from the United States and the Soviet Union. Observers concluded from these remarks that China saw the Soviet Union as the greater threat to her security and for the moment was more eager to improve her relations with the United States than with the Soviet Union.

The main aim of Zhao Ziyang's visit lay, however, not in foreign policy but economic relations. A new agreement on industry and technical equipment was signed and the agreement on co-operation in science and technology was renewed within a framework of 21 clauses covering specific issues. American assistance in the construction of nuclear power-stations in China formed an important part of the talks, with the building of eight such undertakings envisaged by the year 2000.

The problem of Taiwan also occupied an important place in the talks, with the Chinese Premier urging the United States, albeit without undue pressure, to halt its arms sales to the Nationalist regime. On her own part, China refused to give an undertaking not to use force against Taiwan, arguing that the demand that she should do so amounted to interference in an internal matter. Thus, both the United States and China assessed Zhao Ziyang's visit as an important step forward first and foremost in the sphere of economic relations.

The Soviet Union viewed the Chinese Premier's visit without the nervousness and rancour that had been characteristic of the 1970s. The journal *Mezhdunarodnaia Zhizn* (*International Life*) commented that, at the highest levels in the Soviet Union, it was accepted as obvious that the development of relations between two of the greatest states in the world – the United States and China – was a natural event.

Everyone recognizes the contemporary importance of meetings between government leaders, if they are aimed at the strengthening of peace and security, and not at the creation of new 'axes', 'triangles' or other geometric shapes, nor aimed at frustrating the interests of third powers. Time will tell where the present 'new phase' in the *rapprochement* between the United States and

China will lead and what international consequences will be evoked.[16]

Contacts between the United States and China continued through the spring of 1984, with economic and military co-operation as the main issues. Intensive preparations were being made in the United States for President Reagan's forthcoming visit to China, a visit which would have seemed impossible only a few years earlier and which was now seen as an important step in the development of Sino-American relations and no less as an important act in his election campaign. An article by former President Nixon, entitled 'The new map of China', published in the magazine *Newsweek*, and reflecting no doubt more than a personal view, made a number of interesting observations. Four truths, Nixon wrote, should be borne in mind in connection with Reagan's visit. First, although it was the Soviet threat that had brought China and the United States together, they would remain together as a result of their joint efforts to facilitate economic progress. Secondly, stronger economic ties were more important than stronger military ties. Thirdly, even without the Soviet threat, it was still vitally important that the world's richest country and the world's most populous country should continue to co-operate in the creation of a stable peace. And, finally, the United States should not be apprehensive, but rather welcome the efforts being made by the Soviet Union and China to reduce the tension between them. China, he went on, was a nerve point for the leaders in the Kremlin and it was incumbent on the United States not to give them any cause to launch a preventive strike against the Chinese forces. Nixon recalled that in his own talks with Mao Zedong and Zhou Enlai in the early 1970s they had barely touched on economic matters. Now, he urged, Sino-American relations should precisely be turned in that direction, for economic relations were natural relations. China was still a developing country and the United States could help her better than any other country in those areas most in need, namely agriculture and technology. A weak China was a target for potential aggression, but she could not become militarily strong before she had become economically developed, and if the West refused to give her help, she would inevitably turn to the Soviet Union. A strong China, moreover, would become a problem for the Soviet

Union long before she became one for the United States, and therefore America should be more alarmed by the prospect of a weak China than a strong one. The Sino-Soviet conflict would last for decades, and each side knew it, Nixon continued. It would be a fatal mistake for America to assume that a struggle between the two Communist giants would be in America's interest, for such a conflict would inevitably spill over into world war. In the same way, he concluded, the leaders in Peking must understand that a lessening of tension between the United States and the Soviet Union was also in America's interest.[17]

Not all of the assertions in Nixon's article were justified, but his main idea on the need to reduce tension between the three superpowers was both sane and fair. This was not the chief topic of the talks in Peking nor of the speeches made by Ronald Reagan during his visit, however.

Reagan's visit took place from 26 April to 1 May 1984 in circumstances of maximum publicity. It was covered by thousands of correspondents, hundreds of thousands of news reports were devoted to it, as well as countless analytical commentaries and predictions. Inevitably, electoral considerations provided merely a secondary backdrop for the trip, which was one of the most important events in the political calendar of 1984. Reagan and his entourage, whose pro-Taiwan attitudes had been so plainly in evidence as recently as 1980–1, now wanted to demonstrate their aptitude for a degree of political flexibility and compromise. Having proclaimed, on assuming the post of President, that his aim was 'a crusade against Communism' and that every form of Communism warranted destruction, Ronald Reagan now set out on a 'mission of goodwill and friendship' to one of the mightiest Communist countries in the world, whose leaders openly declared their main object still to be the building of socialism in China and the struggle against imperialism, including American imperialism.

Reagan was welcomed in China with great ceremony. In Peking, against a background of military bands and ovations, hundreds of thousands came out to greet him, while in Shanghai he was met by more than one million people, according to the reckoning of the Chinese press. He had talks with all the Chinese leaders, appeared on radio and television, and spoke in various auditoria. Meanwhile, the government officials and others who had accompanied him had talks with their Chinese opposite numbers, and it was in the realm of economic links that the visit achieved its main results. For example, agreements were signed abolishing double taxation on American companies operating in China, a measure which was manifestly intended to ease the penetration of American capital into China. Several other agreements were signed on scientific, technical and cultural co-operation, and on the exchange of information. An agreement was initialled on collaboration in the application of nuclear energy, on the basis of which American companies would have the right to participate in China's programme for the peaceful use of atomic power. Discussion was continued on the question of the sale of American weapons to China and the exchange of intelligence information. As expected, Reagan's visit brought no progress on the problem of Taiwan, and once again China and the United States took note of each other's opposing position.

Richard Nixon's advice to Ronald Reagan went unheeded and, indeed, whenever the opportunity arose to discuss the common interests of the United States and China and their common struggle against 'Soviet aggression', the President would raise the spectre of the Soviet threat in order to frighten his Chinese hosts. He frankly invited China to engage in all-round, open collaboration with the United States against 'Soviet hegemony' on all current issues, even including situations of conflict in the Third World.

Yet it was precisely in this area that the visit was to be reckoned a failure, for the Chinese leaders did not merely remain silent at those moments when the President was making especially sharp anti-Soviet remarks, they even had them taken out of his speeches when they were published in the Chinese press and omitted to have them translated into Chinese when the visit was being shown on Chinese television. They also excised his accusations against the Soviet Union over the shooting down of a South Korean civil airliner the previous September with the loss of all on board. China, in other words, was making it clear that she had no wish to become involved in quarrels between the United States and the Soviet Union. The Chinese media also excluded those places in the President's speeches where he indulged in unbridled praise of the virtues of capitalism and the market economy. The first occasion of such censorship prompted the spokesman for the White House, Larry Speakes, to express regret that some of the President's statements had not been included in the version published by the Chinese information organs, as they would have given the Chinese people a better understanding of America and the American people. Chinese officials justified their action by saying that 'it was inappropriate for the Chinese mass media to publish or broadcast remarks made by the President about third countries, as well as some of his other statements.'[18]

Once again China and the United States confirmed that their positions on Afghanistan and Kampuchea were in agreement. China, however, did not merely decline to enter into 'all-round' collaboration with the United States in the Third World, but declared her disagreement with American policy in a number of Third World territories, in particular in Central America and the Middle East.

In an effort to soften the hawkish image which many had of him, Reagan included in his speeches phrases such as 'the importance of reducing the danger of war', 'continuing our efforts at reducing the arms race', 'we must not allow nuclear war', and 'war is the greatest sin and a deplorable waste of resources', and these remarks were widely quoted in the Chinese media.

It is important to note, in assessing the results of Reagan's visit, that although it halted the divergence between the two countries which had been noticeable in 1981–2, the *rapprochement* was nevertheless now being conducted on a different basis from that of 1978–80. There was no talk now of a 'mature alliance', or of strategic co-operation in the struggle against the Soviet Union, or of a 'Washington–Peking axis'. The Western press were virtually united in their view that China evidently preferred to maintain her independence in foreign policy. The Chinese leadership which Reagan encountered was not the same as that which President Carter experienced in 1977–8. China and her leaders had at last acquired the stability that had been absent for more than 25 years, and this was the main factor with which the United States would henceforth have to come to terms.

Many in America were disappointed with the results of the trip, despite the fact that the administration, of course, depicted it as a great success. Robert Kaiser, deputy editor of the

Washington Post, an anti-Reagan newspaper, commented that, after three American Presidents in succession, from 1972 to 1979, had played the 'China card' against the Soviet Union to good effect, Reagan's trip to Peking marked a turning-point, for now it was the Chinese who were playing the America card and, while this new ploy might well suit Peking, it was questionable whether it was in America's interest.[19]

Not surprisingly, there were now voices heard in the United States calling for a change of policy and urging a 'cooling off'. The administration did not follow this advice and not only because it was attracted by the vast commercial market that China represented: co-operation with China would bring mutual benefits to both countries. During the Reagan visit, the well-known American China expert Arthur Barnett gave an interview for the journal *US News and World Report*. Asked to comment on the widespread American opinion that China was getting more out of the relationship than the United States, he replied that it might seem to the superficial observer as though America was making political and economic concessions, but since America was far stronger and far richer, she had far more to give, and America was not paying a high price for the strategic advantages that would follow. The United States would receive in exchange the opportunity to maintain a situation in the Far East in which China was not an enemy, and she could therefore avoid repeating the state of affairs that had existed for 25 years, during which she had spent billions of dollars and lost thousands of lives in the attempt to neutralize what she had perceived to be a threat from China. The price now being asked, he concluded, was negligible by comparison.[20]

This is a sensible point of view. For various reasons some people view with dissatisfaction China's efforts at maintaining some distance in her relations with the United States, conducting as she does a policy of 'equal distance' – though she has yet to achieve this – but it must be virtually certain that over the next 25-30 years China will above all consolidate her economic rather than military and strategic relations with the United States, although she will not decline the opportunity to exploit America's military experience and technical know-how, either. This much was confirmed in the summer and autumn of 1984, during an extended visit to the United States by the Chinese

Minister of Defence, Zhang Aiping, and the reciprocal visit to China by US Armed Forces Secretary, John Lehman.

As was to be expected, the Soviet commentaries on these visits, as on that of President Reagan, were sharply negative. It was significant, however, that the Soviet press directed the main thrust of its criticism, not against China and her leaders, but against America's plans, against Reagan and against his administration.

Ronald Reagan's victory in the presidential election of 1984, as many observers have pointed out, was not a victory for the Republican party over the Democrats, nor the victory of a particular grouping inside the Republican party. It was above all a personal victory for Reagan, who showed himself as a strong and decisive man who was able to win the sympathy of a large part of the American public, in particular the 'strong' American public. Reagan's personal power and his opportunities for 'making policy', both inside and outside the United States, grew after the November election. The important part played by the personal factor in the outcome of the election, however, makes it more difficult to predict American policy beyond the term of the newly elected President. Doubtless, Ronald Reagan acquired considerable experience of foreign policy during his first term in the White House, and his administration already appears less incompetent than it did to many observers, in East and West alike, four years ago. It has not, however, become less conservative. Reagan received a new mandate to continue a policy that has not made the world a safer or more secure place. He can carry out his policy with more assurance now, not only because he is himself more experienced, or because he can rely on more practised aides, but also because he does not have to worry about the Presidential election of 1988. Will President Reagan use his greater opportunities to bring about some major changes in foreign policy? It seems doubtful. In the first six months of 1985, nothing of substance altered Sino-American relations, nor have any memorable events taken place, and there appear to be no signs that major changes will occur over the next four years.

The statistics for 1984 showed that China had made a noticeable step forward in the development of its industrial and agricultural output. While the improvement was due in the main to internal factors, external factors also played an important part, including the widening of Sino-American economic co-operation. According to figures published in the Chinese press, the overall volume of trade between the United States and China for 1984 amounted to $6.1 billion, a considerable upward movement. Direct American investment in the Chinese economy also rose relatively fast, reaching $700 million in 1984. More rapid development of trade relations was hampered, however, on the one hand by the many restrictions retained by the US on the import of Chinese goods, notably textiles, while on the other hand the Chinese maintain a limit on the amount of profit Western businessmen may take out, which does little to encourage business circles in the United States. Significant and rapid changes in this connection are hard to expect, but gradual progress in the field of economic, scientific, technical and cultural co-operation will continue.

Far less progress is to be expected in the field of military co-operation. Discussion on the modernization of the Chinese armed forces, through bilateral Sino-American collaboration, hardly made any progress after Lehman's visit in 1984. A number of US generals and admirals visited China in early 1985 and their discussions were certain not to be about tourist trips, but such visits have generally been conducted in secrecy. There was, however, wide press coverage of the conflict that arose over US warships making calls at Chinese ports. A similar sort of demonstrative visit had been planned during talks the previous year, but then, in April 1985, both the Secretary General of the Central Committee and the Chinese Foreign Minister explained that what was at issue was an unofficial visit by ordinary US warships, whose exact time of entry into the Chinese ports was 'being co-ordinated', and that agreement had been reached that any ship entering Chinese ports would not be carrying nuclear weapons. Until now, US warships have been calling at ports all over the world, on the principle that they will neither confirm nor deny that they are carrying nuclear weapons, and the United States does not want to abandon that principle, even where the port in question is Chinese. Neither the United States nor China is willing to lose face over this problem, but its solution, however difficult, will determine in many respects the further development of Sino-American co-operation in the military field.

China and the Soviet Union: notable signs of change

The late 1970s was a time of extreme tension in relations between the Soviet Union and China. During China's ill-fated 'punitive expedition' into the northern provinces of Vietnam, a large number of Soviet divisions in the Far East and other sectors of the Sino-Soviet border were put on full alert. Hundreds of Soviet tanks were brought to within 200 or 300 metres of the border. According to the Western press, unpopulated areas of Chinese territory were shelled several times from the Soviet side and Soviet planes repeatedly overflew the Chinese border. Many Western observers expressed the view that the Soviet Union might undertake a similar sort of 'punitive expedition' in one of the regions of northern China. The Soviet Union, however, exercised restraint, as did Vietnam which resisted the temptation to use its battle-hardened and superbly armed regular forces to annihilate the badly trained and poorly equipped Chinese army.

The Sino-Soviet situation changed again in the early 1980s. While, with the advent of the new administration, relations between the United States and China began to undergo an understandable shift, by contrast the Sino-Soviet scene started gradually to improve. China virtually gave no response to the many offers to improve relations which were issued during 1981 by senior Soviet officials and contained in notes from the Soviet Foreign Ministry. The sharp polemics between the two countries continued in the press. The changes in the Chinese leadership which we have outlined above led to substantial changes in domestic policy but not in foreign policy. A special resolution passed at the Sixth Plenum of the Central Committee included condemnation of the Cultural Revolution, of Mao Zedong's repression of party cadres, and of his economic policy. Yet the entire blame for the worsening of Sino-Soviet relations was as before laid on the Soviet Union, and on Khrushchev and 'officials of the Khrushchev type' in particular.

Nevertheless, there was a general change in the climate. In the course of 1981, 17 groups of Chinese scientists and a substantial number of sportsmen visited the Soviet Union. China purchased half a million Soviet books and proposed an expansion of mutual trade, which in 1980 had amounted to no more than about 300 million roubles and was still falling in 1981. A number of Soviet scientists, specialists and sportsmen were able to visit China, and twice M. S. Kapitsa, head of the Far Eastern Section of the Soviet Foreign Ministry, visited China and had talks with Foreign Ministry officials.

This 'small steps' policy continued into the first half of 1982 with the exchange of specialist delegations. For example, a group of Chinese experts spent several months studying the work of Gosplan and Gosstroi (the Soviet state planning and construction agencies, respectively), as well as scientific institutes, enterprises and collective farms. Trade expanded between the north-eastern provinces of China and the neighbouring Soviet Siberian and Far Eastern regions, and exchanges in the fields of sport and culture increased. The Soviet press began carrying features showing various aspects of Chinese life and society in a positive light. A film on the Chinese people's creative achievements was shown on the central Soviet television network. Summing up the results of these changes, an editorial in *Pravda* commented that in a direct sense bilateral contacts between the two countries in the aftermath of the Cultural Revolution were being maintained at a certain level. Both countries' embassies were functioning as before. Trade was being carried on, although it could be much more. Regular airlines and rail-links and the posts and telegraph were working. An annual meeting of the joint commission on border river navigation still took place, as did that of the joint railway commission, and there were contacts between individual government departments over questions of mutual interest. Participants from both sides met at all kinds of international gatherings, conferences, symposia and sports competitions in both China and the Soviet Union.[21]

The Soviet Union proposed in 1982 that contacts in the scientific and technical fields be placed on a more regular basis and that an exchange of students take place. In a speech in Tashkent on 24 March, L. I. Brezhnev made a number of important remarks concerning the improvement of relations with China and he repeated them in Baku in September and again in Moscow in October on the occasion of a large meeting of Soviet military leaders. Meanwhile, at the Twelfth Chinese Communist Party Congress, Hu Yaobang declared that China was ready to develop further relations with the Soviet Union, but would judge the Soviet Union 'by its deeds' and from the point of view of China's security. The Twelfth Congress also announced China's readiness to develop contacts with other Communist and labour parties 'on the basis of Marxism and in accordance with the principle of independence'. China had, of course, long-established close ties with the Communist parties of Romania and North Korea, and more recently good relations had been established with the Yugoslav Communists, and there were constant contacts with the Communist parties of Italy and Spain. Even delegations from Communist parties usually described by the Western press as 'pro-Soviet' visited China in 1982, for example, a French delegation led by Georges Marchais.

The great changes which took place in China's foreign policy in the 1970s, and the no less significant changes in her domestic policies following the death of Mao Zedong, fundamentally altered the entire content of the Sino-Soviet ideological polemics. While relations between the Soviet Union and the United States were quickly worsening, those between China and the United States were rapidly improving and Chinese propaganda could therefore no longer accuse the Soviet Union of having 'made a deal' with the United States against China. In tackling fundamental reform of its own economic system within the framework of the Four Modernizations, China could no longer accuse the Soviet Union of 'capitalist regeneration' on the basis of the modest reforms in the Soviet economy that had been carried out in the late 1960s. Their condemnation of the Cultural Revolution and Mao Zedong's mass repression of the party cadres made it very difficult for China's new leaders to represent Stalin as a model Communist leader and Khrushchev and his successors as 'fascist renegades' who had rejected Marxism and socialism. The polemics between the two countries nevertheless continued in sharp form in the first half of 1982, as many articles in the Soviet press witness. If the position of Soviet specialists on China had not changed by early 1982, the same was true of Chinese specialists on the Soviet Union.

The American Sovietologist Robert Daniels was invited in the summer of 1982 to visit the Institute of the Peoples of the World of the Chinese Academy of Social Sciences. On his return home he wrote an interesting article on the atmosphere among Chinese social scientists and in particular among Sovietologists who, he found, were trying to echo the new ideas emanating from their leaders, but who took shelter in party clichés the moment they encountered a difficult question. For them, Khrushchev remained the villain of the piece, and Brezhnev merely represented Khrushchevism without Khrushchev. Their doubts about aspects of the pre-Khrushchev period, however, were raising questions about Stalin, who was still officially honoured and indeed whose portrait still hung in the Peking University Library alongside those of Marx, Engels and Lenin. Chinese social scientists, Daniels found, were not yet responding to the hints of *rapprochement* between the Soviet Union and China after 25 years of mutual recrimination nor were they yet incorporating them in their assessments of future Soviet intentions. They viewed the Soviet Union as an expansionist threat to the whole world and cited as evidence recent Soviet actions in the Horn of Africa, Afghanistan and Poland. The Russians had a government that was authoritarian, that cheated in both domestic and foreign policy, and that could decide to mobilize without a thought for the views of the people. They differed among themselves only as to whether the Soviet Union would make a nuclear strike first against the West or against China, or against both of them together, and then take over the Middle East and Africa, and they discussed these ominous possibilities quite seriously. Daniels also noted with interest that the Chinese used precisely the same vocabulary in their discussions of the Russian evil as the Russians have used over many years when depicting China's international aims. At the height of *détente*, he recalls, Soviet academics had viewed China as a greater threat to the Soviet Union than it could be to the United States, if only because it was closer, and Daniels concludes that each side is horrified by the mirror image of itself, and sees the other as a far greater mutual threat than any capitalist country.[22]

From the autumn of 1982 the Soviet press virtually ceased to publish any critical articles on Chinese policy. There is unfortunately no Soviet journal devoted solely to China. The journal *Problemy Dalnego Vostoka* (*Problems of the Far East*), which is published four times a year, tended in recent years to have its space taken up by critical material on China and the Chinese Communist Party, but the third and fourth issues for 1982 appeared without a single critical item on China. Instead it carried articles on medieval Chinese history, the initial phases of the Chinese revolution, the demographic and geographical problems of modern China, on changes in the national economy and criticism of American policy on Taiwan. The magazine *Opasnyi Kurs (Dangerous Course)*, which reproduced all the main anti-Chinese material from Soviet newspapers and periodicals, and which began to appear in 1969, came out with number 11 in 1981, and ceased publication thereafter.

The trends which had begun to develop in Sino-Soviet relations were not affected by the death of Leonid Brezhnev and the changes which ensued in the Soviet Communist Party leadership. A small Chinese delegation, led by foreign minister Huang Hua, attended Brezhnev's funeral, and the Western press did not fail to notice the brief meeting that he had with the new General Secretary of the Soviet Communist Party, Yu. V. Andropov, nor the talks that he had with the Soviet foreign minister Andrei Gromyko. On this occasion the discussion was over the renewal of Sino-Soviet trade. As he was leaving Moscow, Huang Hua not only praised the contribution Brezhnev had made to the improvement of Sino-Soviet relations, but also expressed his optimism about the talks that were soon to take place. At the same time, the editor of *Pravda*, V. G. Afanasyev, told a group of Japanese journalists that China and the Soviet Union could reach agreement on the mutual reduction of troops on their border. The world's press also noted that only a few days before the death of Brezhnev, Chinese diplomats from the Embassy in Moscow had attended the 7 November celebrations and had remained on the tribune during the parade of the Soviet Army.

On the other hand, even in 1982 it was still not possible to find any significant amount of information about China in the Soviet press. The materials of the various meetings of the Chinese Communist Party and National Assembly, relating to the very important decisions taken in 1981 and 1982, were published in the Soviet press only in extremely abbreviated form. As for Soviet magazines with mass circulation, the topic of China simply does not exist. One can readily read long articles on small African countries in such publications, but China, with its billion-plus population, does not figure. What critical material on China the Soviet press did publish in the autumn of 1982 and later tended to be reprinted from Vietnamese, Kampuchean or Mongolian newspapers.

Similar changes were taking place in China, if more slowly. The quantity of anti-Soviet material being published there – and meticulously registered in the Soviet Union – was much reduced and, although it did not cease altogether, its tone was somewhat less harsh. The content of Chinese textbooks, however, where the Soviet Union or Sino-Russian relations were mentioned, remained unchanged, a matter which prompted unfavourable commentaries in *Izvestiia*.[23] The study of the Russian language, which had totally ceased in the 1960s and 1970s, began again in 1981–2. Robert Daniels noticed in his meetings with Chinese social scientists that even those Chinese Sovietologists who had studied in the Soviet Union had practically forgotten their Russian, and therefore rarely referred to books published in the Soviet Union, although they eagerly read everything they could find on the Soviet Union that was published in the United States. On the other hand, Daniels thought it necessary to mention that many Chinese who had studied in the Soviet Union in the 1950s recalled their time with warmth.

In December 1982, on the occasion of the 60th anniversary of the Soviet Union, the Chinese leaders sent the following cable to Moscow:

China sincerely hopes for the gradual implementation of normalization and the establishment of good-neighbourly relations between our countries, for the development of friendship between the Chinese and Soviet peoples in the interests of peace in Asia and in the whole world. Both sides should take practical steps to remove the obstacles that lie in the path of consultation, applying their joint efforts to that end.[24]

The very slow process of *rapprochement* or normalization between the Soviet Union and China continued on into 1983. The Chinese deputy foreign minister, Zao Zecheng, arrived in Moscow at the end of February 1983 at the head of a delegation of advisers and experts, with the aim of reviving the bilateral consultation on various political problems which had begun in 1979 and been broken off at the time of the entry of Soviet troops into Afghanistan. The talks were conducted at deputy ministerial level. At the end of March Zao Zecheng had further talks with Andrei Gromyko and a short communiqué was issued stating that 'both sides had ascertained the positive importance of the fact that a political dialogue is taking place between the Soviet Union and China.'[25]

At the very beginning of 1983 the influential Moscow journalist and *Izvestiia* commentator, Alexander Bovin, made an extended trip to China. It is generally thought that Bovin had been Brezhnev's speechwriter in the period 1969–1972 and that even earlier he had been on close terms with Yu. V. Andropov, for whom he fulfilled the function of unofficial representative and adviser, but nothing appeared in print about his trip.

Although the Chinese press did not stop publishing critical articles about the Soviet Union, it virtually ceased using the term 'social imperialism' in that context. The Soviet Union is counted by the Chinese as one of the socialist countries, albeit with reservations. The Chinese press wrote about the corruption in the Soviet Union, but no longer asserted that the Soviet Union had 're-established capitalism'. On the other hand, in the Soviet press China similarly is included, albeit with reservations, among the socialist states.

The Association of Soviet Sinologists was formed in the summer of 1983, incorporating specialists from Sinology centres in Moscow, Leningrad, Alma-Ata, Tashkent, Vladivostok, Khabarovsk and elsewhere, and M. I. Sladkovskii, director of the Far East Institute, was appointed chairman. The revived Chinese Society of Sino-Soviet Friendship organized a meeting to celebrate the dual centenary of the death of I. S. Turgenev and the birth of Aleksei Tolstoy. A change was noticeable in the character of Chinese broadcasts to the Soviet Union. Addressing a press conference in Japan in July 1983, Hu Yaobang said: 'We hope for the normalization of relations with the Soviet Union. One cannot now say that they are normalized. I think that in the end they will go that way. Normalization will be to the advantage of both our peoples and to peace throughout the world.'[26]

For the first time in many years, an exchange of tourist groups between the Soviet Union and China took place in the autumn of 1983. The Soviet–Chinese Friendship Society sent a group to China, headed by Academician S. L. Tikhvinskii. The Soviet tourists visited several towns, factories and institutions, while the

Sino-Soviet Friendship Society in its turn sent their group in exchange, visiting Moscow, Leningrad, Baku and Tashkent, and collective farms, factories and educational establishments. As before, sports exchanges also took place, for example a group of Soviet chess-players and the Soviet 'Shakhter' football team visited China.

Trade between the two countries also grew, both in volume, exceeding 600 million roubles in 1983, and in the range of products. For the first time in many years a consignment of Soviet-made trucks passed through the town of Khorgos in the autonomous region of Xinjiang-Uighur and into China, where they were greeted by a Chinese welcoming ceremony. Since the mid-1960s, on the anniversary of the victory over Japan, Soviet diplomats had been prevented by the Chinese authorities from laying commemorative wreaths on the communal graves of Soviet troops who had fallen in battles against the Japanese in Manchuria. At the end of the 1970s these obstacles were no longer respected, although Chinese representatives did not take part in the ceremonies until 1983, when, for example, on 3 September the chairman of the Gianbei district in the province of Khebei laid a wreath bearing the inscription 'Eternal glory to the fallen heroes of the Soviet-Mongolian allied forces'.[27] The Chinese press, including the *People's Daily*, when the Chinese war against Japan was being discussed, again began to acknowledge the great contribution made by the Soviet Union to the victory over the Japanese occupiers.

The tragic episode over the Sea of Japan involving the loss of a South Korean airliner, which for two and a half hours had flown in Soviet airspace over strategically important Soviet military bases, and which was shot down by a Soviet fighter, provoked an explosion of authentic anti-Soviet hysteria in the United States, Japan and several other Western countries, even though the responsibility for the tragedy lay equally with the United States, South Korea and Japan. China, however, remained aloof from the well-orchestrated indignation. Chinese press comment on the matter was extremely restrained, and in the Security Council China abstained in the vote condemning the Soviet Union.

In the autumn of 1983 China took part for the first time in the Moscow International Book Fair and their pavilion enjoyed a great success. The American international relations expert,

Professor S. I. Levin wrote in 1983 that, while people had been thinking about the possibility of an improvement in Sino-Soviet relations, one could say that it had already happened without being noticed. The apocalyptic predictions of Sino-Soviet mutual destruction, which had been issued at regular intervals over the previous 25 years, had not come to pass. The Soviet and Chinese people had learned to live side by side in, if not friendly, at least peaceful co-existence in the highest degree. This had taken place without special visits and joint communiqués or other visible epoch-making events to attract public attention. It had been the result, Levin went on, of a slow accommodation which, nevertheless, was by no means irreversible, given the points of conflict between Moscow and Peking in global politics. Although the Soviets and the Chinese long ago stopped inviting each other to dinner, as Levin put it, they none the less had taken to exchanging opinions in the lobby and chatting over the fence. In Levin's view, this gradual development from hostility to a distrustful mutual tolerance, while it might disappoint some on both sides, was a positive step on the path to an international system, a mutual approach to global problems, rather than the sort of competition which could lead to destruction.[28]

In a congratulatory telegram to the Chinese leaders on the occasion of the 34th anniversary of the Chinese People's Republic, the Supreme Soviet and Council of Ministers of the Soviet Union again expressed the desire positively to develop Sino-Soviet relations and thus help to resolve the long-standing economic tasks which faced both countries.

It must be noted, however, that the Sino-Soviet normalization process again slowed down in 1984, in contrast to developments in Sino-American relations. To be sure, trade relations did grow between China and the Soviet Union. An agreement signed in Peking on 10 February 1984 on commodity circulation and payments envisaged a marked increase in trade between the two countries, both in volume and the range of goods delivered. The total sum of bilateral trade was expected to reach one billion roubles in 1984, that is 60 per cent higher than in 1983. From 12 to 16 March 1984 the fourth round of Sino-Soviet consultations took place in Moscow at deputy foreign ministerial level. Contacts between the two countries in the fields of science, culture and sport continued. No other new initiatives were taken in the first half of the year, however. On the other hand, factors which made relations more complicated appeared, notably the new worsening of relations between China and Vietnam and the renewal of armed clashes on the Sino-Vietnamese border. China set up its own administration on the islands of Huang Sha and Zhong Sha in the South China Sea, which she had seized in the last phases of the Vietnam war when they were under the control of the South Vietnamese authorities. This was, however, by no means an act of support for the forces of North Vietnam and guerrillas of South Vietnam: China was rather seeking to expand the potentially important area of its continental shelf.

Agreement had been reached as early as the spring of 1984 over the visit to China of the first deputy chairman of the Soviet Council of Ministers, I. V. Arkhipov, and, had it taken place, it would have significantly raised the level of relations between the two countries. However, shortly after President Reagan's visit to China and the worsening of relations between China and Vietnam, the Soviet Union postponed Arkhipov's visit without giving any explanation, although neither did it slam the door.

The 60th anniversary of Sino-Soviet diplomatic relations occurred at the end of May 1984, a date that was noted in all the main Soviet media. In particular, *Izvestiia* wrote: 'Normalization of Sino-Soviet relations is regarded in the Soviet Union as corresponding to the fundamental long-term interests of the peoples of both the Soviet Union and China, and to the interests of peace and security. As Comrade K. U. Chernenko has underlined, the Soviet Union is in favour of improving and restoring Sino-Soviet relations to health, although not, of course, at the expense of third countries. Progress in Sino-Soviet relations, and China's participation in the people's struggle to prevent war, would undoubtedly enhance the role of socialism in international affairs and the position of the forces of peace.'[29]

The summer of 1984, however, once again saw a considerable rise in the number of articles in the Chinese press criticizing the Soviet Union and its foreign policy. In addition to material of Chinese origin, the press, radio and television made abundant use of anti-Soviet commentaries culled from the Western mass media. The Soviet Union remarked on what was happening, but did not change the character of its own press comment.[30]

The 35th anniversary of the Chinese People's Republic fell in the autumn of 1984. The Soviet press announced that the Soviet Union was in favour of improving Sino-Soviet relations and against seeking out groundless reasons for slowing down the process. Chinese domestic policy, it was remarked, had in recent years undergone many positive shifts, and many phenomena of the past – such as the cult of personality, the Great Leap Forward, the Cultural Revolution, the communization of the village, the endless mass campaigns, disregard of the objective laws of economics, the levelling of distribution, the persecution of intellectuals – were now being more or less thoroughly criticized, and this represented an important prerequisite for the improvement of Sino-Soviet relations, despite the fact that new problems, new contradictions, new disproportions and new sources of possible social tension were arising in China.[31]

Deputy foreign ministerial consultations went on throughout the summer and autumn of 1984, a Chinese orchestra completed a successful tour in the Soviet Union and in reply a Soviet song and dance ensemble toured China in September. *Literaturnaia Gazeta* (*Literary Gazette*) and the journal *Inostrannaia Literatura* (*Foreign Literature*) both carried features on writers and literary life in China.

I. V. Arkhipov, whose visit to China took place in the last ten days of 1984, received a very warm reception at Peking airport, where he was met not only by Chinese officials, but also by the ambassadors of socialist countries, including Vietnam. The Chinese press, noting that he had led a large group of Soviet specialists working in China in 1957–8, wrote about Arkhipov as 'an old friend of China', and he had a reunion with economists and economic leaders who remembered him from the old days. The talks, which were the first to take place for many years at the level of deputy prime minister, rather than deputy foreign minister, and in which the Chinese Prime Minister, Zhao Ziyang, took part, did not touch on the main political and ideological issues dividing the two countries, but concentrated instead on co-operation in the economic, scientific and technical fields, and they were entirely successful. On 28 December 1984, I. V. Arkhipov and the Chinese deputy prime minister Yao Yilin signed three agreements: one on economic and technological co-operation, another on the creation of a Sino-Soviet commission on economic, trade, scientific and technical co-operation, and a third on scientific and technical co-operation.

As we have noted above, trade relations between the Soviet Union and China had been regulated in the 1970s by means of short-term agreements concluded annually. Agreement was now reached to sign a long-term agreement in the first half of 1985 on commodity circulation and payments for the period 1986–90, to co-ordinate plans for economic development in several different areas, and to increase substantially the volume of Sino-Soviet trade which, it was envisaged, would rise from 1 billion roubles in 1984 to 5 or 6 billion roubles by 1990, and thus reach the current level of China's trade with the United States.

The beginning of 1985 was marked by the appearance in Peking of a new journal, called *Soviet Literature*, the first issue of which was largely devoted to stories and tales on the Second World War by Soviet writers. Then, in February, a delegation of representatives of the Chinese People's Assembly paid a friendly visit to the Soviet Union. The Chinese Foreign Minister, Huang Hua, attended the funeral of L. I. Brezhnev, Deputy Prime Minister Wang Li came to Yu. V. Andropov's funeral, and in March 1985, Deputy Prime Minister Li Ben was present at the funeral of K. U. Chernenko. According to some reports in the Western press, Li Ben brought a personal message from the Chinese Party leader, Hu Yaobang, to the new General Secretary of the CPSU, M. S. Gorbachev, reports which have neither been confirmed nor denied in Moscow or Peking, and which, if true, would signify the first step for many years towards restoring inter-party relations between the CPSU and the CCP.

In his first speech to the Party Central Committee Plenum in March 1985, M. S. Gorbachev announced that the Soviet Union and the CPSU wished to have a serious improvement in relations with the Chinese People's Republic and that, given reciprocal intentions from the Chinese, they considered it entirely possible. Gorbachev later repeated this statement on several occasions.

China's relations with Vietnam remained bad, but it was noteworthy that China did not choose to increase the pressure on the Sino-Vietnamese border during the days and weeks when Vietnamese and Kampuchean forces were carrying out a successful attack to liquidate the last bases of the Khmer Rouge in the forest areas close to the Thailand border. After the operation, a part of the Vietnamese forces was withdrawn from Kampuchea.

The sixth round of Sino-Soviet political consultations took place in Moscow in April 1985, at the level of deputy foreign minister, and, according to the brief communiqué, they were conducted in a 'frank, calm and businesslike atmosphere'. The next round was scheduled to take place in Peking in October 1985.

Arkhipov's successful visit to China, and the widening of other contacts, are confirmation of the policy of 'equidistance' that the present Chinese leadership would seem to be trying to follow. In a majority of issues, of course, such 'equidistance' has not yet been achieved, and China's position is closer to that of the United States and the West than it is to that of the Soviet Union. What is often forgotten, however, is the general desire to build the just socialist society, as a factor that brings the Soviet Union and China closer together. It would be both naïve and wrong to reduce China's chief foreign policy motives to 'nationalism' and the Soviet Union's to 'expansionism', and to assume that Communist ideology and the drive to build the just socialist society is nothing more than an ideological smokescreen for 'hegemonism'. For all the deformations, distortions, personality cults, abuse of power and countless other lamentable deviations from the socialist ideal, both the Chinese and the Soviet peoples are far from abandoning that ideal in order to adopt some other system of values as the basis for their social life and activity. This circumstance constitutes the firm foundation, however cluttered up with garbage it might be, on which the development of Sino-Soviet co-operation will take place.

Factors and motives for Sino-Soviet rapprochement

What is it that compels the Soviet Union and China to seek the path of *rapprochement*? To answer this question, we must first of all discuss the disappearance, or at least the substantial reduction, in recent years of a number of factors and motives that in the past gave rise to alienation and hostility between the Chinese Communist Party and the Communist Party of the Soviet Union, between China and the Soviet Union.

It was not only Mao Zedong, but the entire generation of Communist party leaders of the 1920s and 1940s, who were raised in the firm conviction that the world Communist movement must have a guide, and that it should be the most experienced and authoritative of the Communist parties, as well as the most authoritative, most 'wise' of all the leaders of the Communist movement. As the inevitable consequence of a semi-religious system of cults, the line of Marx–Engels–Lenin–Stalin had to be continued. As the world leader died, so he became one of the 'gods' in whose name the new prophet on earth would lead the Communist movement, and the new prophet must be acknowledged as such by all Communist parties.

China could not deny that the most powerful force in the camp of Communist countries was the Soviet Union; but in the world of ideological movements, it is not a country's wealth or the strength of its army and its weapons that determines its authority. The strength of the Communist movement was understood to be inextricably linked with its unity, and this unity was impossible without the existence of generally recognized leaders and authorities. After the death of Stalin, however, the process of determining the new leader and prophet of the world Communist movement took an excessively long time. At the first postwar international conference of Communist and labour parties, held in Moscow in 1957, Mao Zedong resolutely declared that the world Communist movement must have its leader, and that this leader should be the Communist Party of the Soviet Union. Equally resolutely, N. S. Khrushchev in turn declared that the world Communist movement needed no such leader. Neither declaration was sincere.

In 1957, N. S. Khrushchev realized that he had neither the personal authority, nor as yet adequate achievements to his name, to justify taking upon himself the formal role of leader of the entire Communist movement. He was, however, fully convinced that only the Soviet Union and the CPSU were capable of leading the countries of the socialist camp and the world Communist movement. Therefore, in the complex situation that arose after the death of Stalin, without hesitation or preliminary consultation with other parties, Khrushchev initiated actions and took decisions that reflected on the position and authority of the entire Communist camp and on the personal lives of many Communist leaders. He thus took upon himself the role of leader of the entire Communist world inadvertently, as it were on the spur of the moment. He was convinced that his activity would soon allow him to become the generally recognized leader of the world Communist movement in the formal sense. This was clear from the kind of features of the Khrushchev cult that became most persistently embedded in Soviet propaganda after the Twentieth Party Congress. The majority of socialist countries and Communist parties were more or less compelled to accept the new order. Not, however, China, and not the Chinese Communist Party.

Mao Zedong for his part was convinced that with the death of Stalin there was no other Communist leader with greater claim to take upon himself the role of leader of the world Communist movement than he himself. He regarded himself as the sole surviving 'Marxist–Leninist classic' and he was deeply offended by the fact that his role as primary leader was not recognized by the rest of the Communist movement, and that Khrushchev did not even think it necessary to consult him before taking his most important decisions.

Posters were printed in China with the face of 'the great Chairman Mao' superimposed on silhouettes of Marx, Engels, Lenin and Stalin, although such posters could also be found in other countries than China. Nobody at that time in the Communist movement would deny Mao's great revolutionary and theoretical achievements, but only in his capacity as a regional leader. On the other hand, Mao himself was apt to exaggerate the importance of the Chinese experience and he did not fully understand the problems which time and circumstance had placed before other Communist parties.

The Great Leap Forward which was undertaken in 1958–9, though grandiose in scale, was adventurist in essence, and was dictated not only by the urge to overcome the country's backwardness as rapidly as possible, nor only by mistaken calculations or inadequate experience – it was also launched in order to satisfy Mao's passionate desire to prove to the whole world that he knew how to open up more effective and faster ways to build the socialist society. The collapse of that attempt, although it gave rise to doubts about Mao's 'wisdom' even in China itself, did nothing to diminish his ambitions or his vanity.

The fierce struggle for power which took place in China during the first half of the 1960s culminated in the Cultural Revolution and the deification of Mao Zedong. The creation of Maoist parties and groups in practically every country in the world was proof enough that Mao's claim to lead the world Communist movement and all the national-liberation movements had grown more inflated. These claims were, however, decisively repudiated by the new leaders of the CPSU and the majority of Communist parties alike. The Central Committee of the CPSU continued to insist that the world Communist movement did not need single leadership, and that what it required was co-ordinated action of the various socialist countries and Communist parties.

After the removal of Khrushchev, however, and the accession to the leadership of the CPSU by the relatively unknown 'apparatchik' L. I. Brezhnev, the ideological machinery of the Central Committee, under the guidance of M. A. Suslov, implemented its contacts and collaboration with other Communist parties on anything but an equal footing. Words were far from the same as deeds in this context, for the Soviet leaders were not merely convinced of their leading role in the socialist camp and the world Communist movement, but also that it was their proper function to direct it. The determination to assert this authority, and the readiness to employ armed force, dictated the Soviet occupation of Czechoslovakia, which in turn led to the creation of a Czech national and Communist party leadership that was subservient to Moscow, and to bitter criticism among Western Communist parties and in Maoist China, and resulted instead in a loss of authority for the Soviet Union and the new leadership of the CPSU.

In trying to explain the motives behind the Sino-Soviet conflict, some Western and Soviet specialists on China have tended to emphasize such factors as Chinese nationalism, Sino-centrism and even Confucian ethnopsychology, deriving from stereotypes which were formed 2,000 years ago. For example, M. S. Ukraintsev has written:

First among these sterotypes is an egocentrism which generates a number of postulates: China is the most cultured and powerful country; it is surrounded by vassals and tributaries; China must not allow powerful adjacent states to arise; links with other countries are permissible only if they are advantageous to China; barbarians must be subjugated by barbarous means; in conflict with the barbarians all means are justified, from plain deceit to war, and war in this context is called a punitive expedition, a lesson, or punishment. Armed with this attitude, Mao Zedong and his associates, striving to put the ancient to the service of the modern, in his words, felt themselves increasingly ill at ease in a world where, as it turned out, there were other powerful states. In 1959–62 they embarked on an offensive against India and began subversive operations against that country. They tried in every way to bring about a clash between the Soviet Union and the United States, to provoke a 'fight between the two tigers', while the 'wise monkey', i.e. China, sat on the hill and watched the encounter. Having failed to persuade the Soviet leaders to launch a nuclear attack against the United States, Peking moved to the left, accused the Soviet Union of a lack of 'revolutionariness', and ended up on the right, since when she has persistently tried to push the United States into war with the Soviet Union.[32]

Chinese nationalism, ethnopsychology and Sinocentrism undoubtedly played a role in the rise and development of the conflict between China and the Soviet Union. On the other hand, a precisely similar part was played by the Russian nationalism and remnants of great power chauvinism and 'Moscowcentrism' which could be readily found during the Khrushchev and Brezhnev periods, and were not an exclusive feature of the Stalin era. The biggest part in the rise and development of the conflict, however, was not played by hangovers and complexes from the past, but by the struggle for leadership of the world Communist movement, for influence in the national-liberation movements and for leadership of the socialist camp. These 'discordant factors' are now significantly diminished.

The concept of a world Communist movement as a united world party 'of the new type', requiring firm leadership and harsh discipline of all its 'national sections', was incorporated in the Comintern Statutes and plainly lost its force after the death of Stalin. Remnants of it, however, remained in the minds both of the new, post-Stalin Soviet leaders and of Mao Zedong. The departure of Khrushchev from the political scene, and the deaths of Mao and, in the 1980s, of Suslov and Brezhnev, effectively abolished the question of a leader or *vozhd* of the world Communist movement. The main Western Communist parties had long been solving their problems on their own, without special concern for the opinions of either Moscow or Peking. In this respect the new leaders in China differ greatly from Mao. They have stated publicly, and their actions support their claims, that they do not harbour any ambition to lead the world Communist movement.

As a result of the changes in China's domestic and foreign policy, most of the Maoist parties in different countries have either disintegrated or changed their image and loyalties. Even Albania repudiated its earlier friendship with China after the death of Mao, and now finds itself in total isolation from the rest of the world. China's political and economic experience over the last 25 years is too dismal and lacking in achievement to leave room for either the ambitious plans or the arrogance of earlier times. In any event, the position of the Chinese people is so hard that the leaders have to devote all their attention to solving their internal problems, and their main task is to try to create the conditions for a tolerable life in their own country. If one can speak today of China's foreign policy claims, then it is in the context of her desire to act on the world stage as the leader and protector of the Third World.

On the other hand, neither are the new leaders of the Soviet Union as ambitious as their predecessors in their desire to influence the world Communist movement and the socialist community. They accept the world as it is, and not as it was 25 or 30 years ago. And they, too, face many unresolved problems at home. For them, the issue of relations with China is not seen as one of subjugation, influence, leadership or a partnership of 'elder brother and younger brother'. It is a more a question of friendly relations between two neighbouring great powers which can and must collaborate. It is still not an easy question to resolve, but at least it does not seem insoluble.

The death of Mao Zedong and the emergence of a new leadership have led to fundamental changes in that vast country. In recent years, the activities of the Gang of Four have been condemned, many elements of Mao's political activity and his theoretical legacy have been acknowledged to have been mistaken, especially in the last 20 years of his life. In particular, the

Great Leap Forward, the Three Red Banners campaign, the Cultural Revolution, the political repressions of the 1960s and the many repressive campaigns against senior CCP officials in earlier periods, as well as several mass ideological campaigns of the 1960s and 1970s, and Mao's economic policies – they have all been severely condemned. It has been noted in the Soviet press that the Chinese criticism of Mao has been neither entirely consistent nor thoroughgoing – as if there has ever been a consistent and thoroughgoing criticism of Stalin's crimes and mistakes carried out in the Soviet Union! – but the repudiation of part of Mao's legacy has nevertheless removed one of the obstacles on the path to *rapprochement* between the Soviet Union and China. We have noted, however, that the area which has been subjected to the least revision by the Chinese leaders is the legacy of Mao's foreign policy.

Since Stalin had not allowed his enemies or opponents or the people he found personally uncongenial to remain alive, rehabilitation after the Twentieth CPSU Congress for all of the prominent Soviet state and party figures who had fallen victim to his arbitrary rule was posthumous. Generally, they were shot immediately after being sentenced. Moreover, 20 years elapsed between the mass repressions of 1937–8 and the mass rehabilitations of 1956–8. Hence, even those second echelon party and state officials who had somehow survived the appalling conditions of the concentration camps, were by then too sick, too old and too broken, both physically and mentally, to resume an active life in administration. Without doubt, the return 'home' of many millions of Stalin's concentration camp inmates had an appreciable effect on the social atmosphere in the country, but it was felt above all in the cultural sphere, in public opinion, in the activities of opposition trends, rather than in the composition and working practices of the highest institutions of party and state power.

In China, Mao Zedong had expelled nearly 80 per cent of the Central Committee which had been appointed at the Eighth Congress in 1956, but no more than 10 per cent of them died in prison or exile. Probably another 10 per cent died of natural causes since that time. The rest remained alive, and within ten to thirteen years after the Cultural Revolution were able to return to active life in the party and state apparatus, or to rejoin the

Central Committee and even the Politburo. Mao had tried to humiliate, disgrace, remove his political opponents from power, or send them to correction or labour camps in the remote countryside, but he did not attempt to liquidate them physically. They had to remain alive to witness his greatness and their own insignificance. This difference between Stalin and Mao in the application of terror was extremely important. Michael Reiman, a leading activist in the 'Prague Spring' and a former assistant to Alexander Dubcek, visited China in 1981 and has written:

> We should think seriously about this situation. If applied to the Soviet Union it could mean, for example, that after the Twentieth Congress in 1956 the power structures would have relied not on people who had come to the top and made their careers under the conditions of Stalinism, but on people who had suffered from Stalinism instead. It could have have meant that the first place in the centre of Soviet power would be occupied not by Khrushchev, but by Rykov or Bukharin or Tomsky and some of their collaborators, had they survived Stalin's torture-chambers by some miracle. At the very least, a faster and more decisive break with the past would have been the result.[33]

It is worth noting, moreover, that the mass rehabilitations of the victims of the Maoist repressions brought back to political activity a certain number of people who had grown up with an attitude of respect for the Soviet Union and for the traditions of Sino-Soviet friendship. Liquidating the effects of the Cultural Revolution has in general had the effect in recent years of resurrecting political and ideological values and structures in China that are similar to those of the Soviet Union.

The economic difficulties facing both countries are another factor pushing them towards normalization of relations. When both new leaderships are trying to effect the rapid development of peaceful branches of their economies and broaden the range of goods for public consumption, the military confrontation along a 7,000-kilometre border imposes too great a burden on each of them. At the beginning of the 1980s, China had already had to reduce her military budget and the size of her army, and significantly curtail the building of defence installations. Many arms factories in China are now employing a sizeable part of their workforce in the manufacture of consumer goods. As for the Soviet Union, while trying to develop peaceful branches of industry, once again it has to take account of a new round in the arms race being launched by the United States. In order to maintain existing parity with the United States in strategic weapons, and at the same time not to overload the Soviet economy with military demands, the Soviet Union needs to reduce its military expenditure in the east of the country by a substantial amount. For both China and the Soviet Union, direct economic co-operation could prove helpful. Occupying the position of 103rd in the world on a scale of per capita income, and counting on expanding its national income as fast as possible, China cannot afford to ignore the option of reducing its military expenditure and broadening its co-operation with all the countries in the world, including the Soviet Union.

The political and economic processes to which we have referred, and the changes of attitude of the Soviet and Chinese leaders, are proceeding at an exceedingly slow rate. Nevertheless, an awareness is gradually forming, and becoming firmer, that between Communist China, with all its current difficulties and deformations, and the Communist Soviet Union, with all its current deformations and difficulties, there are no economic, political or geopolitical contradictions that cannot be resolved.

Soviet fears and anxieties

The process of normalizing relations between the Soviet Union and China slowed down significantly from 1981 to 1983, virtually coming to a halt in the first half of 1984, and was revived only in December of that year. This is explained by the fact that, apart from the factors pushing both countries towards *rapprochement*, many doubts, both rational and irrational, remain. Regrettably, prejudice plays a considerable part in foreign policy and it is no simple matter to be rid of them. In politics it is not only reason that is instrumental, but also the emotions, both the emotions of ordinary people and those of the politicians themselves.

It is an established fact that all manner of disputes, wars, and persistent economic and political conflict have tended to occur most frequently between neighbouring countries, which have maintained bad relations as a result. This is true not only of relations between governments or ruling groups, but even between the ordinary folk of one nation in their attitude towards the ordinary folk of another nation. The widespread existence of national prejudice is self-evident. The French and Germans are hardly very sympathetic to one another. The Irish do not harbour warm feelings towards the English, or the Latin Americans towards the Americans, the Poles towards the Russians, or the Russians towards the Poles, the Georgians toward the Armenians, and the Armenians towards the Turks, to say nothing of anti-Semitism which is especially widely distributed.

However, no such hostile feelings were known to exist in past centuries between the Russians and the Chinese. In practice, they knew very little of each other before the seventeenth and eighteenth centuries, and could scarcely even be called neighbours. During the first period of their colonization of Siberia, the Russians came up against the resistance of relatively small nationalities, or ethnic groups, such as the Siberian Tartars, the Khanty, Mansi, and Trans-Urals Bashkir, all of whom were united under the authority of the Siberian khanate, or remnant of the Golden Horde. After the annexation of this khanate by Russia, the Russian state gradually also acquired the regions inhabited by the Buriat, Yakut, Khakas and others, but it was still a long way to China. The eastern regions of Siberia were sparsely populated and their indigenous population, consisting of the Koriak, Tungus and Chukchi, were unable to put up strong resistance to the Russian forces. Although Chinese did not inhabit the region, it was precisely in eastern Siberia that the Russian Empire first came up against the Chinese Empire, the clash coming not so much with the Chinese as with the inhabitants of Manchuria, whose warlike tribes had recently fought with the Chinese and formed a new imperial dynasty based on the Manchu nobility. They managed to halt the eastward march of the Russian Empire and to hold it back from the shores of the Sea of Japan for some 200 years.

Unfortunately, Russian expansion was not limited to the opening up of the virtually unpopulated territories of eastern Siberia and the Far East. The second half of the nineteenth century was a period of the most intensive colonial expansion by the European states and Russia had no intention of being left behind. As a result of a number of military expeditions, large areas of Central Asia were annexed to Russia, although the Amur and Ussuri regions and a number of other territories in the Far East were annexed by diplomatic means. The Russian imperial appetite, however, was whetted rather than slaked, and at the turn of the century Russian armies occupied a large part of Manchuria and Korea, a territory with a large Chinese and Korean population, which the tsarist government intended to colonize as an area which it cynically designated as 'Yellow Russia' (by analogy with White, Little and New Russia). The official press and propaganda of the time made virtually no mention of China's ancient history and culture, but tried instead to instil in the Russian people an attitude of contempt towards the Chinese as a backward and weak nation.

Direct confrontation between the Russian and Chinese nations was, however, not prolonged. Russian expansion in China and Korea clashed with the ambitions of young and thrusting Japanese capitalism. Russia's heavy defeat in the Russo-Japanese War forced the tsarist government to withdraw from Korea and a large part of Manchuria and to cede to Japan the southern part of Sakhalin. The political crisis which was sharpened as a result of the Russo-Japanese War was one of the chief causes of the revolution which took place in Russia in 1905–7, and it was precisely at this time that ruling circles and a part of the Russian intelligentsia began to talk of the 'yellow peril'. Official propaganda tried in every way to inflame hatred for the 'yellow race'. What was meant by the 'yellow peril', however, was the danger to Russia of, not Chinese, but Japanese expansion.

The Japanese remained the main danger even after the 1917 Revolution and the formation of the Soviet Union. Japanese troops were in fact, as late as 1922, the last of all the intervention forces to leave Soviet Russian territory. The Soviet state and Soviet propaganda depicted Japan in the 1920s and 1930s as an imperialistic and aggressive power, while they viewed the Chinese, on the contrary, as an oppressed nation struggling for independence. During that period the Russian people felt sympathy, not distrust, for the Chinese and their country. The development of the Chinese revolution, the formation of soviet zones and the struggle against Japanese aggression were all widely reported in the Soviet press. Throughout the war of 1941–5 – and not only in August 1945 – the Soviet people regarded China as an ally which was doing its best in the fight to smash world fascism.

The People's Liberation Army's victories in the civil war of 1946–9 and the formation of the Chinese People's Republic were greeted in the Soviet Union with unfeigned enthusiasm. Soviet youth sang the song 'Moscow–Peking' with genuine pleasure and warmly welcomed the Chinese students and specialists who came to study in the Soviet Union. The study of China and the Chinese language flourished. Friendly relations became especially strong in the 1950s. It is true there were examples of a different kind. It was at just that time that I was working as an agitator in workers' hostels and frequently, during conversations about the successful building of socialism in China, I encountered a more than cool attitude towards that country. Such attitudes, however, were widespread and were expressed about all the countries which the Soviet Union was helping rather generously at the time, for example Egypt, India, Burma, later on Cuba, Ghana and so on. One could easily understand workers feeling as they did, seeing the poor living conditions of their own hard lives, and many ordinary factory and office workers openly said that the Soviet government – or Khrushchev personally – was giving too much to other nations to the detriment of the interests and needs of the ordinary people of their own country. In the 1950s practically nobody knew of the hostility existing between Stalin, and later Khrushchev, and Mao Zedong.

Anti-Chinese feeling only began to be seen in the Soviet Union in the 1960s, in the context of the Sino-Soviet conflict, the Cultural Revolution, the manifest growth of blatant Chinese nationalism and various symptoms of Russian nationalism. These feelings grew in the 1970s but, from my own observations, they never reached the proportions of 'national enmity', as sometimes described by various Western writers.

Inevitably, the very fact that China, a country of one billion people and experiencing demographic difficulties, bordered on the vast, sparsely populated territories of Siberia, the Soviet Far East and Kazakhstan, with their natural resources, aroused anxieties among many Soviet leaders, as well as nationalistically inclined intellectuals, the same anxieties, in fact, that were being felt by the Russian borderland population. In 1970, the population of Siberia and the Far East, numbering 25 million, of whom 22 million were Russians, was growing only very slowly, and in some areas was even declining. It was not surprising that, in his unfortunate *Letter to the leaders of the Soviet Union*, Alexander Solzhenitsyn, without feeling any need to deny his own nationalism, advocated that the settlement of the Russian north-east be made a major national issue. In his view, the massive transfer of Russians, Ukrainians and Belorussians to Siberia and the Far East would both bring about the moral and religious regeneration of the Russian people, and serve to safeguard those regions from China's claims.

Every Soviet schoolboy knows about the sad consequences of the Mongol invasions of the thirteenth century suffered by Russia, the Caucasus and Central Asia, and about the 200 years of the Tartar yoke which Russia was forced to bear, and therefore the news that the Chinese People's Republic was commemorating Genghis Khan with honour, and that the Chinese had territorial claims against the Soviet Union, aroused further anxieties.

By the end of the 1950s, the Chinese leadership had lost its former stability and China's domestic and foreign policies had become harder to predict. As we have noted above, it was not accidental that the worsening of relations between the Soviet Union and China, the military operations on the Sino-Indian frontier and the onset of the bitter ideological polemics with the Communist Party of the Soviet Union, should coincide with the collapse of the Great Leap Forward. Vast areas of China were gripped by famine and economic chaos, and Mao Zedong tried to create the impression that the chief cause of the suffering was the 'crafty intrigues' of China's neighbours. Similarly, the armed clashes on the Sino-Soviet border coincided with the end of the Cultural Revolution which had deepened the economic and political chaos. In the early years following the death of Mao Zedong, China's domestic and foreign policies were extremely contradictory.

Since then, much has changed and both Chinese policy and the Chinese Communist Party leadership have acquired considerable stability, and they are applying more rational methods to achieve their goals. They have as yet not done enough, however, to allow their neighbours, including the Soviet Union, to regard their statements and policies with complete confidence. Stabilization of authority at all levels has not yet been accomplished, the attitude to Mao Zedong and his legacy has not been fully defined, and the tendency to falsify both Mao's image and many historical events has not been eradicated.

Soviet anxieties have also been aroused by the continuing support China is giving to the Khmer Rouge whose bloody deeds in Kampuchea only China, it seems, has not condemned. While some measures are being taken in the direction of liberalization, the political regime remains in general relatively harsh. Michael Reiman, whose article we have cited above, points to the dilemma facing China as analogous to that which in the Soviet Union gave rise to the emergence and victory of Stalinism, namely the need to effect a rapid growth of industry and transport, coupled with the lack of the means to do so. Stalinism, however, is not an inevitability in China, he claims, as she has more opportunities for getting foreign aid and credits than the Soviet Union had in its time. China also has the option of reducing the pressure of military expenditure, if it does not set itself the aim of becoming a superpower. The appalling effects of the Cultural Revolution, and not least the Soviet experience itself, may be acting as restraints on going too far, but in Reiman's view the danger of Stalinism in China remains. The plans for political democratization can only have limited application, while centralized power continues to compensate for the absence of other ties or forms of communication within the society.[34]

Finally, another cause for Soviet concern is the fact that Soviet politicians and academics know so little about contemporary China, and the wide reading public knows still less. Quite a few books on China have been published in the Soviet Union over the last ten years, but they present a limited and biased picture of the country. Soviet Sinologists have no opportunity to do their research in China itself and in close contact with Chinese academics. Their main sources are the press, including publications from Hong Kong and Taiwan, and to some extent Western works on China. Soviet journalists have no possibility of describing the everyday life or the problems facing the Chinese.

The Sino-Soviet border has ceased to be a troubled area and it is fair to assume that, among Soviet civil and military experts, nobody seriously thinks that there is someone somewhere in China plotting to conquer the vast unpopulated territories of Siberia and the Far East in order to alleviate their own problems. Nevertheless, many harbour a grain of doubt deep in their hearts.

China's fears and anxieties

The Soviet Union may have its various rational and irrational fears and anxieties about China, but the same is true in reverse. If the Russians still recall the Mongol invasions and are still proud of the struggle against the conquerors from the east in the fourteenth and fifteenth centuries, the Chinese remember Russia's eastwards expansion, the armed clashes between the Russian and Qing Empires in the seventeenth and eighteenth centuries, and the many unequal treaties which a weak China was forced to sign under Russian pressure in the nineteenth and early twentieth centuries. They remember Russia's participation in the fierce repression of the Boxer Rebellion, the Russian occupation of Manchuria and the Russo-Japanese War of 1904–5, which took place in the main on the hills of Manchuria, and which was mainly caused by the contest between Russia and Japan for subjugation of northern China.

We shall not undertake here to outline the long history of the territorial demarcation between Russia and China. The frontiers between large states in the past rarely emerged as the result of fair and reasonable talks, but more generally as the consequence of wars, threats and annexations. For example, much of the present-day US–Mexican border came about as the result of wars in the mid-nineteenth century between a powerful United States and a weak Mexico which had just been liberated from Spanish dominion. The unjust character of those wars was widely recognized by many Americans even while United States forces were seizing Mexican territory. And if Northern politicians protested against the annexation of California, New Mexico and Texas because they feared a strengthening of the slave-owning South, then on the occasion when, in 1847, the Mexican capital had been captured by American troops, Southern politicians came out in favour of annexing the whole of Mexico to the Union. The injustice of America's seizure of nearly one million square kilometres of Mexican territory is recognized not only by Mexicans, but by the majority of American historians. Nevertheless, Mexico does not demand the return of her lost territories.

In its eastwards march, the Russian Empire occupied a good deal of land over which the Qing Dynasty claimed sovereignty. The population of these lands, while not Chinese, was both varied in ethnic composition and extremely insignificant in size. China, however, was not a nation state at that time, but, like Russia, an empire, and its imperial rulers regarded as 'theirs' not only the land which was inhabited by the preponderant nationality of the empire, but also all the other lands which it had annexed. It comes as no surprise, therefore, to find that Chinese historians have a quite different version of the struggle for control over Siberia from that of their Soviet counterparts. It is important to distinguish between theoretical disputes over historical events and a concrete territorial claim. In an interview with the German weekly magazine *Der Spiegel*, Huang Hiyang, director of the Peking Institute of Foreign Affairs and an adviser to the Chinese premier, stated that China would not demand the return of the Soviet Far Eastern provinces, but insisted on recognition of the fact that these regions had been seized from China by means of the unequal treaties. [35]

Although the more than 20-year history of Sino-Soviet talks has not been especially well publicized in the Soviet press, from what has been published in both the Soviet Union and China one can nevertheless gather that the main argument is over the definition of precisely which treaties are to be regarded as 'unequal'. The Soviet side acknowledges as unequal the treaty of 1896 on the building of the Chinese Eastern Railway, the Boxer Protocol of 1901, imposed on China after the Boxer Rebellion, and all the treaties between Japan and Russia, concluded between 1907 and 1916, in so far as they affect China. All earlier treaties, and in particular Aigun (1858), Peking (1860), Chuguchak (1864), St Petersburg (1881), as well as the other treaties on which the territorial demarcation of Russia and China was based, are not regarded by the Soviet Union as meriting inclusion in the category of 'unequal'. For their part, the Chinese side considers as unequal virtually all the treaties that were made by the Qing Dynasty with Russia and other states after its defeat in the Opium Wars.

There can doubtless be little question at the present time of substantive changes being made to the historically determined border between China and the Soviet Union, although individual adjustments to the line could and should be carried out. The Soviet law of 1960 on the state frontier lays down that the border of the Soviet Union on navigable frontier rivers is located in the centre of the main fairway or river bed, and in non-navigable rivers in the centre of the river or the centre of its main branch.[36] The same article with some qualifications was included in the new law on the state border passed in the autumn of 1982. Moreover, as we have noted above, the Sino-Soviet border on the River Ussuri passes not through the fairway, but along the Chinese shore, which is manifestly unfair. An alteration of that situation would undoubtedly be to the benefit of both sides. The same applies to the general assessment of the treaties on territorial demarcation listed above. Until the emergence of the Sino-Soviet conflict, Soviet historiography regarded as unjust, not only the treaties concluded in the 1890s and at the turn of the century, but also many of the earlier ones. From the strictly historical point of view, therefore, the current Soviet position does not look particularly convincing. For example, the first edition of the *Bolshaia Sovetskaia Entsiklopediia* (*Great Soviet Encyclopaedia*) has this to say about the Treaty of Aigun:

The Treaty of Aigun between Russia and China was signed on 16/28 May 1858. It was the first decisive step by Imperial Russia in the seizure of Chinese territory. This seizure was dictated by the growth of commercial capitalism in Russia which needed also to be able to penetrate into China, and to the shores of the Great (Pacific) Ocean even more so. His troops having seized the left bank of the Amur, Governor-General of Eastern Siberia Muraviev forced the Chinese to sign the Treaty of Aigun, according to which the left bank of the Amur from the River Aigun to the sea was recognized as a Russian 'possession', while the right bank downstream to the River Ussuri was recognized as a Chinese possession. Russia's acquisitions under the Treaty of Aigun were finally consolidated by the Treaty of Peking in 1860. By this latter treaty, Russia acquired both the River Ussuri and the southern ports on the shore of the Great Ocean.[37]

Current research yields quite different assessments, however, as, for example, A. Prokhorov's book, *K voprosu o sovetsko-kitaiskoi granitse* (*On the question of the Sino-Soviet border*), where we read:

> The Treaty of Aigun represents an important act in treaty law accomplished by Russian diplomacy.... Under this treaty, Russia received a substantial part of the land seized from her by the Qing Dynasty under the terms of the Treaty of Nerchinsk. The left bank of the Amur ... was recognized as a Russian possession [and] Russia's position in the Far East was [thus] significantly strengthened. However, Russia did not receive the lands on the right bank ... which had gone to the Qing Dynasty ... under the Treaty of Nerchinsk. Russian plenipotentiaries were unable to secure the maritime territories from the Ussuri to the sea which they had insisted on at the outset of the talks. The real success of Russian diplomacy was the virtual opening up of the Amur lands by the peoples of Russia, whereas the Chinese did not inhabit these lands and the Qing Dynasty did not exercise control over them, nor have any practical tie with them. It follows that the Treaty of Aigun did not cause any damage to the Qing Dynasty, neither in the territorial nor the material sense. In fact, it was a friendly act of alliance ... directed against the expansionism of the Western capitalist powers and as such it formed a barrier which prevented them from taking over the Amur region.... If the treaty was at all unequal, then it was in relation to the Russian side, inasmuch as its first clause permitted Chinese jurisdiction to operate for the small Chinese population on [that part of the] left bank which belonged to Russia.[38]

As for the Treaty of Peking, which was concluded two years later, A. Prokhorov asserts that, together with its protocols, it

> represented an important step towards fixing a firm and permanent border between the Russian and Chinese states ... and consolidating Russia's position on the Pacific Ocean. The securing of Russia's position forever on the Ussuri, and earlier on the Amur, made possible the settlement of these territories by Russian peasants and Cossacks and the development of their productive strength, which in turn facilitated the growth of the economic and military might of the Russian state. The Treaty of Peking was a significant achievement of Russian diplomacy. The

unification of the Amur and southern Ussuri regions with Russia
. . . was the central event in Russia's Far Eastern policy in the nineteenth century.[39]

One would not expect to find similar interpretations of the
Aigun and Peking treaties in the works of contemporary Chinese
scholars. From the materials published in Prokhorov and in any
other book on nineteenth-century Chinese history, one dis-
covers that the Treaty of Aigun was concluded at the height of
the famous Taiping Uprising, a great and protracted peasant war,
in the course of which the insurgent armies not only occupied
many major cities in China, but even formed their own state with
its capital at Nanjing.[40] The Manchu Dynasty could not cope
with the Taiping rebels and was on the verge of collapse. Exploiting the situation, England and France launched the second
Opium War against China and, after winning a number of victories over the weak forces of the Qing Dynasty, imposed the
humiliating and enslaving treaties on China.

Russia did not take part in the war against China on that
occasion, having herself only just suffered a humiliating defeat
at the hands of England and France in the Crimean War of
1853–4. In the course of the Crimean War, the English and
French Fleets had appeared in the Sea of Okhotsk, and the small
Russian garrisons on Kamchatka and the shore of the Sea of
Okhotsk found themselves in a critical situation. The Russian
government sent reinforcements by the Amur, after informing
the Chinese government. The latter, however, preoccupied as it
was with the Taiping Uprising, did not even reply to the Russian
message, despite the fact that the local Chinese authorities on
the right bank of the Amur, far from hampering the progress of
the Russian units, actually gave them assistance. In 1854–5,
small Russian settlements and naval posts were set up on the
estuary and left bank of the Amur. The new emperor, Alexander
II, had a natural desire to consolidate the areas of the right bank
of the Amur for Russia, and with that aim Russia began to exert
heavy pressure on China. The Chinese authorities plainly did
not want to yield the right bank of the Amur to Russia. Weng
Xiang, the most influential member of the war council in Peking,
declared: 'We definitely cannot permit the building of Russian
fortifications on the banks of the Amur, but it is equally im-

possible to enter into open enmity with Russia over this circumstance.'[41]

The talks between the Governor-General of Eastern Siberia, N. N. Muraviev, and the Qing Emperor's emissary, I-shan, were conducted as anything but talks between friendly powers. The Chinese side tried to show that they received tribute from the right-bank regions of the Amur and had guards there who were capable of defending the left-bank territory. Muraviev retorted that the Chinese were collecting tribute illegally, that their guards had no guns and were not capable of holding the Amur region against the Russian army. This was open duress. Even the Soviet historian, A. Prokhorov, provides evidence that the Chinese side at first categorically refused to sign the treaty on the grounds that it would virtually amount to treason for them to do so. Nevertheless, on 16 May 1858, after six days of talks, Muraviev and I-shan signed the Treaty of Aigun. It was ratified on 2 June 1858 by decree of the Qing Emperor. The Great Khan, Xian Feng, in announcing that everything that had been included in the talks had been ratified, thereupon appealed to the Russian authorities 'to use their efforts to appeal to the consciences of the English and French to put a limit to their unjust demands'. When Alexander II read the translated decree, he wrote in the margin: 'We could not have wished for better.'[42]

The Qing emperor soon died, and when in 1859, under the new emperor, Xian Feng, Chinese forces scored a number of victories over the Anglo-French fleet, the Chinese announced that all the previous negotiations and agreements concluded with foreign governments were null and void.

China's victories were, however, shortlived. Preoccupied with the Taiping struggle, the imperial forces could not prevent a new Anglo-French intervention – the third Opium War. Anglo-French forces captured Tianjin and many other cities and were advancing on Peking. The Chinese emperor fled to the Manchurian province of Chengde, leaving his younger brother, Prince Gong, in Peking with the task of negotiating with the European powers. At that moment, the Russian envoy, Major-General N. I. Ignatiev, arrived in Peking. He agreed to act as intermediary between the Qing authorities and the Anglo-French command, but only on condition that the Chinese government ratify the Treaty of Aigun in accordance with the Great Khan's decree of

2 June 1858, and that it settle the outstanding question of the territory from the Ussuri to the sea which had been left hanging in the previous negotiations. Faced with no other choice, Prince Gong gave in to Ignatiev's demands. The Russian general's mediation proved successful and, after the evacuation of the Anglo-French forces, Ignatiev and Prince Gong signed a new Sino-Russian Treaty of Peking, according to which the Ussuri region was henceforth Russian territory.

Russian diplomacy had indeed 'scored a great success', having been able to exploit the hopeless situation facing the Manchu imperial dynasty in China. This gave no cause, however, to regard the treaties that had been achieved in this way as 'equal', 'just' or even 'friendly'. It is noteworthy that in recent years the Soviet press has acknowledged that many of the clauses in these treaties were unjust. Thus, for example, in an article entitled 'What precisely constitutes the difficulties in the Sino-Soviet border talks?', P. Dalnev writes:

> The Soviet side has never set out to defend the truly unequal treaties or the unequal clauses in the treaties and agreements, nor the aggressive policy pursued by Russian tsarism. Nobody would deny that in a series of Sino-Russian treaties dealing with the border . . . there were unequal clauses which gave Russia consular jurisdiction, and the unilateral right to most favoured status, to free and customs-free trade, and which compelled China to agree tariffs with Russia and so on.[43]

In other words, even though a substantial number of its clauses were blatantly unfair, the treaty itself was on the whole fair. The logic in such arguments is not very apparent. As is well known, Marx and Engels paid close attention in the 1850s and 1860s to the colonial expansion of the European countries in Asia, especially in China. One can therefore readily find quotations from their letters and articles in which their assessments of Russia's Far East policy, and the treaties she concluded there, differ greatly from the current Soviet view. Let me cite just one article of Engels, 'Russia's successes in the Far East'. At the end of October 1858, Engels wrote:

> Indeed, Russia's position emerged as unusually favourable. . . .
> While the English wrangled with petty Chinese clerks in Canton,

the Russians were taking over the territory to the north of the Amur and most of the Manchurian coastline to the south of the river; they consolidated themselves there, carried out surveys for a railway line and chose sites for future towns and harbours. When England finally decided to go to war on Peking and France joined her in the hope of snatching something for herself, Russia, while at that very moment she was taking away territory from China equal in size to France and Germany put together, and a river the length of the Danube, contrived to emerge in the role of the disinterested protector of weak China, and virtually to play the part of mediator at the peace talks; and if one compares the various treaties concluded at those talks, it is impossible not to see what is obvious to everyone, namely, that the war was advantageous not to England and France, but to Russia.[44]

To cite the Treaty of Nerchinsk, as A. Prokhorov and other authors do, as allegedly having led to the detachment of the Maritime Province and the Amur region from Russia, is utterly unconvincing. In Prokhorov's exposition, the argument is advanced that the Treaty of Nerchinsk is an historic injustice that the Treaties of Aigun and Peking put right. No Chinese historian would agree with such a reading of Nerchinsk. It was concluded nearly 200 years before Aigun and Peking. The first small Cossack detachments only began to appear in the Amur region in the middle of the seventeenth century, and while they managed to establish a few stockades and small settlements, they were quite unable to secure these vast territories for Russia because China opposed them with armies many thousands strong. The frontier wars went on with interruptions for several decades and ended with the Treaty of Nerchinsk which fixed the border between Russia and China which had not existed at all hitherto, and established free trade relations between the two countries. There are no grounds for interpreting the Treaty of Nerchinsk as China's taking territory that legally belonged to Russia. In the middle of the seventeenth century, the Amur region was neither a Russian nor a Chinese possession, but was inhabited by various ethnic tribes, not united by any sort of union or state formation. As Prokhorov cautiously writes:

It should be noted that during their progress through Siberia, the Russian military sometimes came up against resistance from the local population. ... The policy of the tsarist government in the Amur region in the seventeenth century reflected the character of the Russian state of the time and was constructed on the basis of class principles and economic opportunities.[45]

The local population in the Amur region at the time the Treaty of Nerchinsk was concluded amounted to about 40,000, while the Russians numbered about 2,000.[46]

In order to get a clearer idea of the different interpretations of these events to be found in Soviet historical writing from before and after the outbreak of the Sino-Soviet conflict, let me cite from two Soviet encyclopaedias. In the third (1973) edition of the *Bolshaia Sovetskaia Entsiklopediia* (*Great Soviet Encyclopaedia*), we read of the first stage of Sino-Russian relations:

As early as the rule of the Ming Dynasty, Russia made contact with China and attempted to form diplomatic relations and set up trade. ... After the Qing Dynasty came to power in China, Russia continued these efforts ... but they did not achieve positive results. Pursuing an aggressive policy in the 1650s, the Qing Dynasty attempted by military means to seize Russian possessions in the Amur Basin, where Russian frontiersmen had opened up a wide area of territory on both banks of the river, which had hitherto been subject to nobody. The Qing Dynasty's attempts, and those of the 1670s and 1680s, were not successful. In 1689, however, by means of the open threat of war, the Qing government forced the Russian government to sign the Treaty of Nerchinsk, according to which Russia ceded to the Qing Empire her possessions on the right bank of the Argun and part of the left and right banks of the Amur. ... The border between Russia and China was finally established by the Treaties of Aigun (1858) and Peking (1860)[47]

Let me now cite what the *first* edition of the same encyclopaedia wrote on the same subject in 1938.

Manchuria first entered into relations with Russia in the early seventeenth century. In 1643, the Cossack Vasili Poiarkov and his 'hunting party' travelled the length of the Amur as far as its mouth. In 1649, the enterprising adventurer Yerofey Khabarov established a fort at Albazin. The Russian newcomers, in search of easy gain, robbed the Daur, Gogul and Diucher who were forced to abandon their lands and seek refuge in the valleys of the rivers Nonni and Mudang-tsian. In 1652, Stepanov, the official representative of the Muscovite tsar, arrived in Amur with a detachment of Cossacks and attempted to make his way up the river Sungari, but met resistance from Manchu-Chinese forces. Border conflicts between Russian and Manchu forces continued up until the conclusion of the Treaty of Nerchinsk of 1689, by which the border between the state of Muscovy and Manchuria was established along the Argun and Shilka rivers. . . . The whole of the Amur region remained in Chinese hands. The fort at Albazin had to be removed. The Russians were kept away from the Manchurian frontier for a long period. A fundamental alteration of the frontier occurred in the second half of the nineteenth century as a result of Russia's successful progress to the Far East. In the 1840s Russians again appeared on the banks of the Amur. . . . Chinese weakness as a result of the Opium War and the Taiping Rebellion eased Russia's expansion in the Far East. The Treaty of Aigun (1858) gave Russia the entire area of the left bank of the Amur, from the Argun to the mouth of the Amur, while the area on the right bank to the River Ussuri remained a Chinese possession. Under the Treaty of Peking (1860) Russia also received the Maritime Province.[48]

The later edition is extremely vague about Russian expansion in China in the nineteenth and twentieth centuries. Nothing is said, for example, of Russia's annexation of Manchuria and other similar facts. Indeed, it contains no separate entry on Manchuria at all, despite the fact that Manchu and Manchurian history are not the same thing as the history of China and the Chinese. Russia's occupation of Manchuria is mentioned only during the account of the Russo-Japanese war of 1904–5. The first edition, moreover, goes on:

At the end of the nineteenth century, Russian aggression was compounded by Japanese aggression in Manchuria. Despite Japan's victory in the Sino-Japanese war of 1894–5, her attempts to take the Liaodong peninsula failed as a result of the energetic resistance of Russia, Germany and France. Russia advanced a loan to China to pay off the indemnity to Japan and received in exchange the concession to build the Chinese Eastern Railway, and in 1898 also a 25 year lease on the Liaodong peninsula. The railway gave Russia the opportunity to establish firm control over the territory and natural resources of Manchuria. In 1901, on the pretext of putting down the Boxer Rebellion, Russia sent in troops and occupied Manchuria. ... The Russo-Japanese war, which ended in defeat for Russia, halted the further advance of tsarism in Manchuria.... Under the Treaty of Portsmouth, Russia ceded the southern sector of the Chinese Eastern Railway to Japan, together with all the leased territory of the Liaodong peninsula. Manchuria was thus divided into two spheres of influence, with Russia in control of the northern part, and Japan in control of the southern. The practical effects of this division were repeatedly formulated in secret agreements.[49]

We have cited at length from various books and encyclopaedias in order to show the many causes for China's anxieties. For 150 years, China was the object of imperialist expansion on the part of many countries, most notably of England and France, then by Russia and Japan, and later by Japan and the United States. The fear which the Chinese had of their northern neighbour more than 100 years ago was easily revived, and if we declare Chinese authors as lacking objectivity over Russo-Chinese relations, then we must also recognize that in China many Soviet publications on the same themes will similarly be accused of lacking objectivity. Without infringing historical truth, or its own dignity, the Soviet Union could acknowledge as unequal and unjust many of the treaties which served as the basis of territorial divisions between China and Russia in the last century, without at all implying that any territory should be 'handed back' to China. There are hundreds and thousands of such unequal treaties in history whose consequences are irreversible.

Chinese fears are fed by the experience they have of Stalin's China policy, and by his attempt to extend his authority over the Chinese Communist Party. Equally their anxieties were later intensified by Khrushchev's China policy, by the inadequacies and contradictions to which we referred above.

Undoubtedly, China was informed of the Soviet debate over whether or not to make a preventive nuclear strike against her with the aim of averting the creation of powerful nuclear weapons complexes. If Kissinger's memoirs are to be believed, L. I. Brezhnev discussed the problem with him on more than one occasion and attempted to ascertain how the United States would react to such a step. If such soundings took place, one can be sure the Americans did not fail to let the Chinese government know, but while the situation on the Sino-Soviet border was alarming, and the leadership of Mao and the Gang of Four did not inspire confidence, Brezhnev's fears were nevertheless exaggerated. The Sino-Soviet border needed to be reinforced, but the deployment of a vast army which, together with its rear and auxiliary units, and reserve and second echelons, amounts in all probability to not less than 100 divisions, is an entirely inappropriate response to the scale of the threat, if it is only a question of a defence response. The reduction of this army and its gradual redeployment to areas further from the border – probably already under way – should help to reduce Chinese fears and anxieties.

Whatever reasons the Soviet Union advanced for sending its troops into Afghanistan, they were bound not to be understood by the West and China alike. And if the United States and the West are alarmed at the narrowing of the distance between the zone of Soviet military presence and the Persian Gulf area, then China is alarmed at her territory being surrounded on the north, west and east by unfriendly countries.

We have referred above to the fact that both Soviet leaders and specialists know very little about contemporary China, and that the same is true in reverse. Both the Soviet and Chinese leaderships have, however, changed markedly in the last two or three years, and while the Soviet side has shown less anxiety and more willingness to establish good-neighbour relations with China, it has done very little so far to give the Chinese cause to feel more confident. For this to happen, new initiatives, and not merely time, are needed.

4

The USSR, the USA and China:
prognoses and perspectives

What the West and the USA can give China,
and what China can give in return

We have already noted that at the end of the 1970s China revised
her earlier plans for extremely rapid economic development.
The Four Modernizations programme was retained rather as a
slogan, while the real state of the national economy called for a
more modest programme of 'adjustment'. This was first outlined
in 1979–81 and made the basis of the sixth Five Year Plan for
1981–5 which was ratified in December 1982.

The new Chinese Five Year Plan envisaged an increase in
gross output from both industry and agriculture of roughly 22
per cent at an annual rate of 4 per cent, well below the rate of
development that had been set for 1976–80. The plan for
1981–5 included the construction of about 900 large and
medium industrial and agricultural plants, no less than 400 of
them to be completed by the end of 1985. These were not exorbi-
tant targets for a country the size of China, and from figures available at the beginning of 1985 it appears that China's sixth Five
Year Plan is not only well under way, but significantly over-
fulfilled. In 1983 and 1984 the annual rate of growth in gross
output was not 4 per cent, but nearer 10 per cent, and the average
for the years 1981–4 was closer to 7.5 per cent. In many
branches of industry and agriculture, the targets for the end of
the Plan were already achieved in 1983–4. The average family
income for factory and office workers rose in 1982–4 by 6–7 per
cent, and for peasants by 13–14 per cent, a substantial success
which Chinese leaders are hoping to sustain over the next 15 to
20 years at an annual average of 7–8 per cent.

In 1977–8 the Chinese had announced their intention of

increasing gross national output fourfold by 1990, an unrealistic objective. Now they speak of a fourfold increase to be achieved over the period 1981–2000, which, though an attainable goal, nevertheless demands the maintenance of a high rate of growth and gigantic efforts in all fields of national construction.

One important measure being taken to achieve this goal is the revision by the Chinese of many of the principles governing their economic policy and their system of management and leadership. They are implementing significant economic reforms which envisage the creation of a mixed economy, or a pluralistic structure, to last for an extended period. What they have in mind is the introduction of a Chinese variant of the New Economic Policy which was applied in Soviet Russia in 1921–2 and was then artificially broken off in 1929–30. Without going into the Chinese economic reforms in detail, we can nevertheless say that their general direction is decidedly the right one. The tendentious assessments which predominated in the Soviet press in 1982 were wrong, and they have now been replaced by a more cautious approach. China's only mistake was not to introduce the reforms much earlier.

Some time before the formation of the Chinese People's Republic, during the civil war, the Chinese Communist Party had not only elaborated various plans and principles for the country's future economic development, but had actually put many of them into practice in the areas which it had liberated either from the KMT or the Japanese. The CCP's economic principles changed at different stages of both the civil war and the war for national liberation, but they invariably included various types of pluralism, or mixed economy. It was proposed that even after the unification and liberation of China, there would be a relatively liberal economic policy for many years, with a strong state sector in industry and agriculture, the preservation of small and medium industries in the hands of the patriotically minded bourgeoisie, the establishment of joint stock companies, and even access to the Chinese economy for foreign capital on certain conditions. It was a realistic programme for a country that was both so extremely backward and so ruined by endless wars.

In the 1950s, however, the CCP declined to introduce this Chinese version of the New Economic Policy (NEP). In the countryside they rushed through collectivization, while in the cities all industry was taken by the state out of the hands of the national bourgeoisie, who were supposed to be given a certain amount of compensation and submit themselves to 're-education'. There is no doubt that the new regime was rushing its fences and that many other mistakes, both economic and political, were made in the process, as a result of which the progress of the Chinese economy between 1960 and 1980 was slow, uneven and unbalanced. Given the substantial increase in the size of the population, China was heading for catastrophe.

Even today, China remains a poor, underdeveloped country, whose population, moreover, is not moved by the sort of enthusiasm which in the 1950s made it relatively easy to mobilize hundreds of millions of people to carry out this or that political or economic campaign. For this reason, the decision to revise the fundamental principles of economic policy, and to take the course of a mixed economy, is undoubtedly the right thing to do, however long delayed.

An important part of China's NEP is allocated to co-operation with the advanced Western capitalist countries. Up to now this has meant credit for China and mutually advantageous trade, and these arrangements have begun to widen in scope. Foreign firms have received various concessions in China, for example in the field of oil exploration, and joint stock companies have sprung up with the participation of foreign capital. In recent years China has granted permission for the creation of wholly foreign-owned firms and of zones of 'free economic development'.

The policy seems in general to be the right one. The Soviet press in recent years has criticized many aspects of the Chinese NEP, for the most part unjustly. When the New Economic Policy was introduced in Soviet Russia in 1921, Lenin was counting not only on increased trade with the capitalist countries of the West, but also on attracting the investment of foreign capital. The Soviet government offered many Western firms concessions on favourable terms, especially in Siberia and the Far East. If the policy did not prosper especially, that was rather because Western capital was extremely reluctant to participate in direct investment in the Soviet Union.

The attitude of Western capital to China is different. As early as 1979, the Japanese Foreign Minister, S. Sonoda, declared:

'The Western countries must approach the question of aid to China in a positive fashion ... in order to exclude any likelihood of a Sino-Soviet handshake.'[1] It would, however, be a mistake to assume that such considerations are the only motivation for co-operation of the West with China. This co-operation is and will continue to be determined above all by economic advantage. Capitalist firms are not willing to carry losses simply in order to hamper Sino-Soviet *rapprochement*.

In a country as vast as China, everything has manifold causes and complex solutions. China's backwardness and poverty are still so great that they create many problems both for the countries that today are expressing their willingness to help develop the Chinese economy and for China herself. We shall make a few general observations below on the problems of economic relations between China and the West.

The chief element in the system of economic relations between China and the United States and the other Western countries has up to now been foreign trade. In the last few years, of China's overall trade turnover, the socialist countries accounted for no more than 6–8 per cent, the developing countries 12–15 per cent and the developed capitalist countries almost 80 per cent. China's chief trading partner is Japan, and a substantial volume of trade is accounted for in Western Europe, while the United States accounts for roughly 10–12 per cent; China's trade with Hong Kong is significant. China's overall turnover in foreign trade rose from $14.8 billion in 1975 to $37.8 billion in 1980, and $43.13 billion in 1981, but it fell in 1982 to $40.88 billion,[2] and preliminary figures suggest that 1983 did not provide an increase in the volume of China's trade with the West.

By 1982, China's small trade deficit with the West had virtually disappeared. In 1981, her exports were equal to her imports – $21.56 billion to $21.57 billion. In 1982, exports increased to $21.94 billion, while imports fell to $18.94 billion.

Overseas trade at a level of $40 billion for a country the size of China is still extremely small. In per capita terms, China annually imports and exports goods to the value of $20 per head of the population! By comparison, Japan, with a population of 120 million, has an annual overseas trade turnover of roughly $300 billion, while West Germany, which has a population of 60 million, has an even greater turnover. Pride of place in the capitalist world in terms of volume of foreign trade goes to the United States, which has an annual average of $450 billion. Thus, we can see that the developed countries have an annual import and export of goods per head of the population worth roughly $1,000 – with West Germany as high as $2,000 – which is 50 or even 100 times greater than the level in China at present.

With foreign trade, before deciding what is to be imported, the question of what a country can export has to be resolved, and China's possibilities in this regard are still very limited. American economists who in 1980 tried to predict China's foreign trade activity for the period 1981–5, calculated that her exports would double to $35 billion by 1985, while her imports, taking account of credits and other resources, would cost $41.4 billion dollars.[3] These predictions have not been borne out in practice, and even now it is clear that China's imports for 1985 will not reach $30 billion, let alone $40 billion.

It is not the case, however, that China produces no goods whatever of interest to the West, rather that they are very few in number. Inevitably, the developed capitalist countries need energy and raw materials above all, and exploration for such products in China has not been sufficiently developed. Even the current levels of mineral and energy production are not sufficient for her own needs. At the moment, China produces 100 million tonnes of oil and more than 700 million tonnes of coal. At the beginning of the 1980s, fuel accounted for about 25 per cent of China's exports from the sale not of surpluses, as in the case of other oil- and coal-producing countries, but of the fuel that she needs urgently for her own use, and that she was selling in order to pay for goods that she needs even more desperately.

Apart from fireworks, which China has made for centuries and at a rather high level of perfection, the only industry which manu-factures export goods of any importance is the textile industry, predominantly in the manufacture of silk products. Taking fabrics as a whole, China produces about 12 billion metres a year – compared to the Soviet Union's 11 billion – and this is not enough for her one billion people. Nor is the quality high enough for her to compete on Western markets. In recent years, there-fore, China has tried to suppress domestic demand and increase the export of textiles to the United States and Western Europe. The West, however, is not suffering from a shortage but a surplus of its own mass-produced goods, and the import of Chinese goods has caused blatant ill feeling. In the United States, for example, protests by business forced President Carter to impose substantial limits on the import of textile goods from China, and the conflict grew sharper with the new administration, which is less well disposed towards China than Carter had been. In any event, China's request for the import of her textiles to the United States to be increased by 6 per cent a year was turned down, with the result that China responded by reducing her own imports from the United States and, as we have seen, causing a fall in the overall level of trade between the two countries in 1983.

Given China's limited ability to import, she has to approach the selection of goods which she acquires from the West with great care. It goes without saying, for example, that China's grain purchases in the United States are in general not an economic bargain for her, just as, incidentally, the Soviet Union's grain purchases in the United States and other capitalist countries have not been economically advantageous.

For the giant astronomical observatory which she is building in Tibet, China naturally has to go to the United States, West Germany or Japan for all the basic equipment, as it makes no sense, given the present state of Chinese industry, for her to create the capacity needed to build large telescopes. Similarly, having no ability to create her own nuclear industry, China has also signed an agreement with the United States for the supply of nuclear power engineering. The production of cameras for popular use, however, and film and related products, China must set up at home for herself.

With an area of 10 million square kilometres and a population of over one billion, China cannot approach its economic problems in the same way as Cuba or Taiwan, South Korea or Pakistan, West Germany or even Japan. China must create an economy with a certain minimum degree of self-sufficiency, and to that end foreign trade above all must be made subservient. China has to set up for herself the production of all important manufactures for mass consumption, regardless of whether such products are for the population or the use of industry. China cannot base her agriculture on the purchase overseas of tractors and combines, but must develop her own agricultural engineering industry. China cannot guarantee her population Japanese television sets, radios and tape-recorders, nor can she equip her army with fighters, tanks and rockets bought in the United States or England. However difficult it may be, China has to learn to do all this for herself. In order to build airplanes, agricultural machinery or television sets, special factories have to be built, and it is difficult to do this quickly without foreign help, but even here the basic work and the basic equipment should be Chinese, and not bought in Japan or the United States. In other words, China has to create a national engineering industry in all its chief branches.

China, of course, already buys a number of high quality consumer goods in Western countries for state institutions, for the Chinese 'Nepmen' and for some of the elite. In recent years, China has also had to buy from abroad such goods as grain, sugar, fats, cotton, wool, pig-iron, rolled iron, paper, wood products, chemical fertilizer and so on. This was done to satisfy some acute current needs, rather than long-term economic requirements. The main items of China's imports should be various forms of Western technology and know-how, licences, payment for the services of foreign specialists, in other words anything that will facilitate the most rapid construction of China's own industry, and the modernization of her agriculture, transport and armed forces. China must have hard currency in order to broaden the education and training programmes for her students and graduates overseas. There are, of course, other economically oriented plans. For example, China needs to attract Western firms to come and create a network of modern hotels and other tourist services as fast as possible, since the Chinese foreign tourist industry is developing rapidly, and foreign investment in this area will bring further gain to China. China also has to buy complete enterprises, if they constitute an essential link in the development of modern industry and the Chinese lack the necessary materials, equipment or experience to do the job themselves. In the same way, Italian firms helped build the Togliatti automobile works in the Soviet Union, German and American firms helped build the Kama truck plant, and French firms aided the reconstruction of the Moscow small-car factory.

Widening the range of such imports is good both for China and for the countries of the West. In some respects, and for a certain period of time, this economic co-operation will increase China's dependence on the West, but in the final analysis, with proper planning and a sensible technical policy, it will hasten the development of China's maximum economic independence.

Both Western analysts and Chinese experts have often declared that it is better for China to buy expertise and technology from the West rather than from the Soviet Union, since the Soviet Union has not yet caught up with the developed countries of the West in technological terms. For the most part, this is a natural, realistic and well-founded position to take, dictated as it is by the desire to achieve a higher technical level without going through all the intermediate stages. The American journalist Michael Parks visited the north-eastern provinces of China in 1982 and acknowledged that the scale of Soviet help to China in the 1950s had been vast. The main plants now operating there were built with Soviet help. Parks saw it as one of the greatest development projects ever undertaken in a Third World country. Both the population and the leaders in the north-eastern provinces know perfectly well the origin of those factories and plants, but because of their hostility to Khrushchev, they associate Soviet aid with the name of Stalin. Parks found that when Chinese officials acquaint the locals with the steelworks and tractor factories, the petrochemical plants, the coalmines and other industrial facilities built or modernized during the 1950s, they readily announce that they were built with the help of the Soviet Union under Comrade Stalin. They recognize that, as most places in Manchuria have boulevards and parks named after Stalin, the region must be the only place outside his birthplace where Stalin is so highly respected. When the future industrial development of Manchuria is mentioned, however, according to Parks, the local leaders are unwilling to turn to the Soviet Union for help. Contrary to Western opinion, Parks claims, the managers and engineers in these factories, which were built by the Soviet Union, see no point in refurbishing them with more recent Soviet equipment when they can buy American, Japanese or West European technology. The deputy manager of the great port of Luda (Dairen), which the Soviet Union enlarged and equipped in 1950, told Parks that if they were to buy their equipment in Moscow, they would be tying themselves down with old technology. They could always go there for spares, but their best suppliers were in Japan and Scandinavia. And he was also told by the people who were responsible for planning in the province that, in their efforts to attract foreign capital investment, they would not be looking for any in the Soviet Union.[4]

One can understand this. After all, many Soviet engineers would also like to buy the machinery for their enterprises in Japan or West Germany. The majority of Soviet consumers are very happy if they can get hold of imported clothes, or shoes, or radio equipment. It is, however, one thing to wish for and another thing to achieve the real possibility of co-operation and trade, and Chinese co-operation with the West is today facing a number of difficulties.

It is well known that engineering and technology develop in different ways. Sometimes highly efficient new machinery is developed at the expense of simpler, more reliable and cheaper schemes, technological processes or equipment. It is natural that a country embarking today on the path of industrialization can and should skip two or three rungs on the ladder of technological advancement. Thus, China is not going to build factories today in order to manufacture radio valves or expensive and cumbersome first-generation computers.

In most cases, however, scientific and technical progress is accompanied today by the creation of, not only more efficient, but also more complex and expensive equipment, and by the displacement of less-skilled manual labour. What is needed is greater numbers of the most highly skilled and qualified workers, technicians and engineers. How can an underdeveloped country make effective use of such equipment if it lacks the sort of workforce and technical personnel who know how to handle the latest technology? In this situation, China can expect to pass straight through several stages of technical development more rapidly than other countries were able to do in the past, but she cannot expect to go straight to the top of the ladder at once.

Contemporary Western engineering and technology require not only the availability of highly qualified workers and technicians, but also a highly developed manufacturing infrastructure, including roads, supplies, improved storage facilities, a system of scientific and technical information, automated systems of control for large industrial complexes, a developed service industry, and so on, in short a great deal of what China still lacks.

If substantially more developed countries than China, like Poland, Yugoslavia or Argentina, found they were unable to establish efficient and profitable industries during the 1970s on the basis of plant and factories bought from the West, then China is bound to find it even more difficult to do so. Even in the 1950s, when Soviet plans for the building of large factories, power stations and similar projects were being examined, Chinese officials would insert considerable modifications and simplifications, all with the aim of trying to ensure that, wherever possible, expensive machinery be replaced by the cheap (in China) manual labour of workers and peasants. This aspect of Chinese economic reality has not changed significantly over the last 25 years. It is of course important for China to have a certain number of hyper-modern enterprises of the Western type, but it would be rash to plan for the restructuring of the whole of industry and the national economy using Western models and Western technology within a historically short period.

The same considerations apply in the case of Western credits, in so far as they are used in part by the less developed countries to buy the latest technology. Few countries have succeeded over the last 15 or 20 years in developing their economies with the help of credit from the United States, Japan or Western Europe. It is therefore difficult to imagine that China will succeed where significantly more developed countries have failed. Even now some of these countries have not escaped the danger of economic and political bankruptcy, thanks to the inexperience, thoughtlessness and even greed with which they asked for and got credits from their wealthier neighbours in the capitalist world. Some of the debtor nations are even finding it hard to pay the interest on the loans, and the whole of their income from foreign trade goes on repayments.

The financial aid which the developed capitalist countries give to the less developed countries is not based on altruism, but on the well-established rules of capitalist business. In offering credit, the private Western banks, which represent the main source of commercial credit, have a right to expect an even bigger return on their capital than they would get from investing in their own or in other developed countries. It could hardly be otherwise, given the competition that exists in the world of big industry and finance capital. If a private bank were to reduce its demands from one of its credit clients, it would risk losing both its profit and its investors.

China, however, is not in a position to guarantee the rapid repayment of large Western investments and credits, and for this reason in 1979–80 she pulled out of many contracts and credit arrangements that had already been agreed. Instead of loans from private banks and corporations, China opted for cheaper and longer-term state credits and aid from the International Monetary Fund, which also gave her access to the International Bank of Reconstruction and Development.

In the late 1970s, a number of economists were predicting a relatively rapid increase in China's overseas economic indebtedness, and a figure of $25 billion was envisaged by 1985, rising further during the late 1980s.[5] This has not happened. China has been able to escape becoming a debt-slave of the developed West, and has kept her indebtedness within reasonable bounds, not exceeding her gold reserve, itself very great. At the end of 1983, this amounted to 12.67 million ounces, while her hard currency reserves came to $14.342 billion, but her foreign debt was only $3.02 billion.[6]

Attempts to transfer elements of Western industrial culture to China too hastily have often done more harm than good. Western countries can deliver their engineering and technology to China, and send in a limited number of specialists, but the fundamental work of building and commissioning the new enterprises has to be done by Chinese workers, engineers and technicians, the very categories which, as we have already pointed out, China lacks, especially those able to handle the new Western technology. Moreover, the building industry in China is one of the most backward sectors of the economy and the one which China can develop least of all by means of imports. On all the main construction sites, the basic building materials, the labour and the building technology are neither American nor Japanese, but have remained Chinese.

The political upheavals, the instability of the governmental and economic leadership, the destruction of the educational system and other disorders of the 1960s and 1970s, all caused great delays in the completion of large projects. According to Chinese statistics, the time taken in the 1950s to commission large and medium schemes was an average of five years. Between

1960 and 1980, this became 11 years, with 30 per cent of projects in the process of construction for anything from 10 to 20 years, and 10 per cent for more than 20 years.[7] In the area of capital construction, China suffered not only from a severe lack of skilled engineering workers, but also an even greater lack of scientific and technical personnel, and all this creates great difficulties when it comes to planning the construction and commissioning of entire complexes. The value of machinery and equipment exported to China by the West has grown consistently over the last 10 years, but when at the end of the 1970s China began buying a greater quantity of complex foreign equipment, the additional financial cost of learning to use it was often five or seven times greater than the total value of the equipment itself.[8]

Financial burdens on this scale exceeded the state's capacities, and the inevitable result of such incompatibility was the disruption of established completion schedules. But even after large projects have been commissioned, equipped as they are with foreign technology, effective work on them has been held up by inadequate infrastructure, the lack of raw materials and energy, but above all by the lack of skilled workers. According to the Chinese press, more than half the Japanese and West German steel-rolling machinery which was bought for the Wuhan metallurgical plant stood idle for a long period. The majority of oil pipelines have not reached even 50 per cent of their planned flow-capacity, and only five out of the total of 28 pipelines are at 80 per cent of capacity.[9] According to the available figures, out of a total investment sum of 600 billion yuans between 1952 and 1980, only 250 billion have proved to have been effectively invested. In the early 1980s, the Lanzhou oil refinery, the Nanjing chemical combine, and many artificial fibre factories using equipment bought abroad were all working below capacity.[10]

To be sure, the industrial sites which China constructed in the 1950s with Soviet help were equipped with less advanced technology than what the West can offer today, but, according to figures issued by the Chinese Ministry of Mechanical Engineering, the time required to pay for large and medium projects built during the first Five Year Plan was on average 3.5 years, while not one of the similar projects built in the 1970s had yet been paid for by 1980. Thus, the economic efficiency of capital investment at the end of the 1970s was half what it had been during the 1950s.[11]

It should be noted that both efficiency and capital recovery dropped during the period 1960–80 in the Soviet Union as well, if on a smaller scale, and perhaps the large purchases of expensive Western technology that were made in the 1970s were similarly involved. One could find plenty of evidence in the Soviet press to show that in the Soviet Union imported equipment is handled and put to use in anything but the best way. It was precisely recognition of the difficulty of mastering Western technology that led the Chinese in 1980–1 significantly to reduce joint schemes that had been planned earlier, and to pull out of contracts and even temporarily to close down projects that had already been started.

Since the Chinese market is potentially vast and its capacity and demand can only grow with time, and since the Western capitalist system is very flexible, then in many cases Western entrepreneurs could organize the manufacture of machinery and equipment specifically for Chinese use only, as it were, that is to say models that would be cheaper and easier to manage. The organization of such a scheme would, however, take many years and much more experience of relations with China than the West has yet accumulated.

Lacking surpluses of raw materials and other scarce goods, China does, however, possess vast surpluses of unskilled labour, and therefore a few years ago the authorities announced the formation of a special organization which, relying on the undemanding nature and 'cheapness' of the Chinese labourer, would accept orders for the 'delivery' of Chinese workers to countries abroad. Wages would be paid in part to the workers themselves, and the rest would go into the state treasury. A number of such agreements were made with Japanese and Italian construction companies, but the assumption that it would be possible to send up to one million Chinese workers to advanced countries was never realized. The West has unemployment, and it is still rising, and some countries are today more concerned with reducing the number of foreign workers they already have, rather than bringing in still more. The organized and unorganized export of labour, moreover, has long been supplied by many underdeveloped and less developed countries, like Turkey,

Yugoslavia, Algeria, Mexico, Morocco, Pakistan and others. Hence, even in this area China faces stiff competition, and at the end of 1983 there were only 40,000 Chinese workers abroad on these special agreements.[12] Far greater remittances of money come to China from the millions of relatives permanently living abroad, whether elsewhere in Asia, such as in Hong Kong, or Indonesia, or in the United States.

One of the most effective ways of attracting foreign currency into the country has been the development of foreign tourism. It goes without saying that a country like China, with its ancient civilization, is highly attractive to Western tour operators. Already in 1981 China received about 7 million foreign tourists and more than $700 million income from this source.[13] It is not surprising, therefore, that a substantial part of foreign capital investment at the beginning of the 1980s went into the building of hotels, restaurants and Western-style cafés and similar tourist projects.

As a result of their many failures to master foreign technology, but also in order to accelerate economic development and co-operation with advanced capitalist countries, as well as to use their experience, the Chinese decided not only to permit but also to encourage direct foreign investment in China. Article 18 of the Constitution, passed at the fifth session of the Fifth People's Assembly, reads: 'The Chinese People's Republic permits foreign firms and other economic organizations or individuals to invest capital in China in accordance with the regulations laid down by Chinese law, and to engage in economic collaboration with Chinese enterprises or other economic organizations of various kinds.'[14]

For a socialist country like China, lagging substantially behind many developed countries, as it does not only in the economic sense, but also in the legislative field, coming to terms with foreign capital investment is an extremely complex affair, from the political, juridical and economic points of view. In contrast to the risky economic 'experiments' of their predecessors, however, China's new leaders have approached the question of foreign investment with sensible caution. To gather experience and to prepare the necessary legislation, they announced in 1979 the creation of several 'open' or 'free' zones, where a separate and special economic and financial regime would operate, and where it would be possible to open mixed companies based on jointly held Chinese and foreign capital, as well as wholly foreign-owned companies. The scheme first involved separating off small enclaves, or enclosed economic zones in areas adjacent to China, that is Hong Kong, Macao and the airports, where foreign companies can, freely and without paying customs duties, bring in industrial raw materials and half-finished products for completion in China and for unhindered re-export to overseas markets. Companies have gradually been formed which produce goods for sale in China itself. There were four such zones at first, in the vicinity of Shengzhan, Zhouhai, Shangdu in the province of Guangdong, and Xiamen in the province of Fujian.

Foreign investors were quick to take advantage of China's new initiative. The first to respond were, not surprisingly, entre-preneurs from the Chinese business communities of Hong Kong, Macao, Singapore and elsewhere. They supplied up to two-thirds of foreign investment and also acted as agents for other companies. The scale of foreign investment was still not very great, amounting in 1983 to no more than $1 billion, or 1.3 per cent of the total sum of capital investment in the Chinese national economy.[15]

Foreign companies had, of course, had the opportunity to make large capital investments in China earlier, but only in a number of specialized fields and areas, for example in offshore oil-exploration and prospecting for minerals. There now opened up before them the opportunity for direct participation in pro-duction. Both sides exercised caution. Fearful of becoming too dependent on foreign capital, the Chinese authorities legislated regulatory acts for foreign enterprises, limiting their activity to 20 years and allowing for their eventual transfer, on payment of compensation, into Chinese ownership. By 1983, China had passed 40 such acts in connection with bringing in the invest-ments of foreign entrepreneurs. Between 1980 and 1983, several mixed companies of various kinds had arisen in which foreign capital owned between 20 per cent and 49 per cent of the equity. Apart from overseas Chinese businesses, investments started to come from Japan, West Germany, the United States, France and Switzerland. For example, one of the biggest European lift manufacturers, based in Switzerland, formed a company in China in which it owned 25 per cent of the capital.

The Swiss firm guaranteed the necessary equipment, the documentation and a small team of technical personnel. At the end of 1982, there were 2,200 Chinese working at the factory and, instead of the 620 lifts planned for production in that year, they produced 930. Despite the success of the operation, however, various misunderstandings occurred which in Europe would have been settled easily, but which in China called for considerable effort. The Chinese personnel, for example, were shocked by the fact that the deputy manager, when he arrived from Switzerland, was receiving a salary equal to the wages of 100 Chinese, wages which, though commonplace in Europe, are simply unimaginable in China.[16]

Most of the joint companies established in China up to 1983 have been assembly plants, or firms involved in the servicing of foreign trade or tourism. In 1983–4, however, the Chinese began to encourage the establishment of wholly foreign-owned companies, and special seminars were held in order to help foreign businessmen understand the Chinese better. In early 1983, *Newsweek* magazine reported that the Chinese were considering an approach by the 3-Ms company of Minnesota which wanted to form a wholly American company in China, and which would be the first private foreign commercial company to exist in Communist China. The firm proposed to pack insulating tape imported in bulk. The relatively small production would be done entirely by Chinese labour and the company would not bring in high-efficiency machinery or technology. In seeking to broaden its relations with Western companies, China, *Newsweek* predicted, will one day be thinking about increasing their investments.[17]

Newsweek's prediction soon came true. In 1983, China announced the formation of a 'free' zone in Shanghai, followed by the decision to create wholly foreign-owned enterprises throughout the province of Fujian and Guangdong (Canton), in Peking, Shanghai and Tianjin. In the spring of 1984, the government decided to open fourteen cities on the coast and the island of Hainan to foreign capital. Speaking at the second session of the Sixth Peoples' Assembly, Prime Minister Zhao Ziyang said:

> We must increase our ability to examine and approve requests to use foreign capital and advanced foreign technology, we must

simplify the entry and exit procedures for foreign entrepreneurs. We must also allow foreign entrepreneurs to establish companies wholly with their own resources and we should correspondingly lengthen the period of common ownership of joint enterprises which operate with Chinese and foreign investment. The ports named above and the four special zones which are joined by the coast into a single line, constitute a forward region which we have opened up to the outside world.[18]

The statistics for the number of foreign companies and the size of foreign investment change rapidly. It was reported in 1981 that foreign investment in China amounted to $1.8 billion, at the end of 1982 the total amount was given as $2.9 billion, and by the beginning of 1984 the total sum of foreign capital invested in more than 2,100 enterprises in China, judging by contracts signed, was of the order of $6.5 billion, plus $2.7 billion of realized assets.[19] According to the Chinese press, the global sum of foreign investment attracted into China by all forms of co-operation, amounts to $15 billion,[20] not a vast amount for a country like China. The Chinese leadership is counting on increasing this amount substantially. Predictions have been published claiming that China can realistically expect to increase the amount of foreign investment to $40–50 billion by 1990, and to $200 billion by the year 2000.[21] But both the Chinese authorities and the foreign investors are showing caution on this question. American investment analysts, whose job it is to assess the perspectives and opportunities for American investment, and who give commercial and financial advice to owners of capital, do not accord China a very high place in terms of the favourability of its internal situation. The Soviet press has noted with satisfaction that the American analysts put China only in ninth place out of 13 countries which they assessed in the Asian–Pacific region, and rated the economic wisdom of investing in China even lower.[22] These evaluations, however, were made on the basis of material published in the American press in early 1982. Since then the position for foreign investors in China has improved noticeably, and the practical experience of companies where foreign capital is involved was characterized in 1981–4 by extremely fast rates of completion and repayment, with a high level of labour productivity, good organization and effective production.[23] Hence, one sees a rapid growth in the rate of foreign investment in China.

The co-operation of the Chinese national economy with foreign capital should be seen as a positive experience in general, although certain dangers do exist, of an ideological rather than economic kind. The Soviet press up to now has written with hostility and even condemnation of the 'intrusion of foreign capital' into China. We have already noted that, in the early 1920s, Lenin was counting on the investment of foreign capital under his New Economic Policy as a means of rehabilitating and developing the economy of Russia, and that he failed because foreign investors were reluctant to trust the Soviet Union, despite the attractive concessions that were on offer. Even in the 1960s and 1970s, the Soviet Union held talks with several Western entrepreneurs, not only on credits, but also on the possibility of sharing in the building and profits of various enterprises. Building the Kama motor works was discussed with Gerald Ford, and several other schemes, including the building of foreign hotels in Moscow, were also tabled. Most of them were rejected, not by Moscow, however, but by Washington.

The experience of China's economic development up to the present is still not very great, and in many respects it still bears the stamp of an experiment. However, it deserves the sort of careful and self-interested study that so far has not been undertaken in the Soviet Union, though it is being done in many Chinese studies centres in the West, but is pursued most intensively in China itself.

In the first half of 1985, both China's leaders and the population have been able to take stock of the country's development for 1983–4 with satisfaction. According to a number of important indicators, for example in grain production, China has managed to reach the level set in the 1977–8 'modernization' plans for 1985, which the Chinese leaders themselves had abandoned as unrealistic. Economic progress over the last two or three years has been made in rapid strides, on a healthy economic basis, and without the aid of loud mass campaigns. The Open Door policy, which was first introduced only for a few small zones, and then extended to 14 coastal cities, is now being proposed for the entire coastal strip, with its population of 200 million. A substantial increase of investment in infrastructure in the coastal regions is planned for 1985, in particular to extend the rail and road network, to improve the standard of existing roads and to strengthen the energy base of the maritime provinces.

The new economic policy is not to be limited to the attraction of foreign capital into the country's coastal regions only, but also to extend the opportunities for private and personal economic initiative throughout the entire country. Chinese periodicals have begun to speak of the 'third economy' or 'third industry', by which they mean the sphere of trade, services and small production, where private initiative is beginning to play an increasingly active part. Figures up to the end of 1984 show that 2.7 million people are engaged in the private sector in the cities, and 8.4 million are privately engaged in small production and trade in the countryside, excluding agriculture. The figure for peasants operating as individual farmers grew five times in 1982–4. According to the Chinese press, there are 120,000 privately owned trucks and more than 2.5 million tractors, mostly obsolete and low-powered machines. Up to 11 per cent of the retail trade is now in private hands.

While reporting these facts very sparingly, the Soviet press customarily underlines the negative aspects of the development of private production and trade, and the increase in foreign investment. Despite all the possible negative features of the new policy, however, its positive overall results for the Chinese economy and society are obvious. The production of consumer goods is growing rapidly, unemployment, which became a serious social problem in the late 1970s, is falling substantially, the countryside has very quickly been able to secure sufficient food supplies for the population, and they in turn support the new policy.

Although we have referred above to the 'Chinese NEP', the economic situation in the Soviet Union of the mid-1920s, and that of China in the mid-1980s, are radically different. In the Soviet Union, NEP preceded mass industrialization and was introduced only in order to restore the economy which had been ruined by the First World War and the civil war. With the onset of industrialization and collectivization, NEP was artificially terminated, before exhausting all its possibilities. China's New Economic Policy is being brought in together with industrialization, and with the re-organization of industry on a new scientific and technological basis. China's NEP, with its small production and trade, is accompanied by the scientific and technological revolution, and it is happening in the country with the world's largest population. The economic, environmental and technical problems are more complex than those facing the Soviet Union 60 years ago. The rate of industrial and agricultural development can be increased, but there are limitations, for the average technical, productive and educational level of the Chinese working class and peasantry cannot be raised very rapidly.

For both foreign investors and the Chinese people, there is the very important question of the solidity and stability of the new economic policy, especially as Chinese policy over the last 30 years has been extremely unstable, and only very recently was put on a new footing. In this connection, one may recall the sudden, savage and harsh methods used to terminate the New Economic Policy in the Soviet Union at the end of the 1920s. An unequivocal answer to this question cannot be readily given, for it is not only the success of the policy itself that is at issue, but also the stability of China's new political leadership. The Third Plenum of the CCP Central Committee of October 1984, and all subsequent sessions of the leading institutions of party and state, have dwelt at length on both the problems of stability and of the succession, the preparation of young cadres who will in time replace the current leaders, and who will essentially continue this policy. Whether all their efforts are to be crowned with success, only time will show.

What the Soviet Union and China can give each other

We have asserted above that the fundamental differences between the Soviet Union and China over the last 25 years have been in the realm of ideology and politics, and in the last ten that of foreign policy. Analysing these differences, many American commentators have tended to regard them as irreconcilable, at least during the period under review. For example, Harold Hinton, reviewing several books on the subject published in the United States between 1974 and 1978, was extremely dubious about any positive outcome from negotiations between China and the Soviet Union. As the weaker power, China, according to Hinton, resented the Soviet Union's bullying behaviour since 1969, and feared that any reconciliation would be on Moscow's terms, with the status of semi-satellite being thrust upon China, an outcome wholly unacceptable to Peking. Moscow, meanwhile, according to Hinton, so distrusts Peking, and is so infected with 'great nation chauvinism', as the Chinese would say, that only if China is indeed cast in the role of semi-satellite will Moscow be satisfied. Without it, Moscow is certain to maintain her threatening and humiliating (from China's point of view) military presence on the Sino-Soviet border, and it was therefore no surprise when the talks were broken off by Peking in January 1980 on the pretext of the Soviet invasion of Afghanistan.[24]

Three years later, in the same journal, *Problems of Communism*, William E. Griffith wrote in far less categorical terms, since it was precisely during the period 1981 to 1983 that relations between the United States and China had worsened noticeably, while those between China and the Soviet Union had somewhat improved. Griffith suggested that Sino-Soviet *rapprochement* was possible only within a very narrow circle of issues, and that a serious compromise or co-operation between the two countries was not to be expected.[25] There can be no doubt that any talks between the Soviet Union and China will not compel the Soviet Union to change the character of its relations with Mongolia or the countries of Indo-China. The Soviet Union is not about to withdraw its military support for the regime in Afghanistan, or to return to the sort of disposition of its forces in the Far East that existed there during the Khrushchev era – although the redeployment of these forces, or part of them, away from the Chinese border to more northerly positions, and the reduction of their numbers, are also distinct possibilities. Nevertheless, a significant improvement in relations between the Soviet Union and China increasingly becomes a more real possibility as the difficulties of rapid economic development become China's main national problem.

Are there really no longer any political and ideological contradictions between the United States and China, or between China and Japan, or between the countries of Western Europe? Is there really not the slightest hope that the United States will change its attitude on the Taiwan question during the period under review, and that a solution to this problem will be found, in the same way as one was found recently to the Hong Kong question? The leading American expert on China and former director of the Harvard East Asian Research Center, John K. Fairbank, commented in his recently published memoirs that Taiwan's security had become for the United States the nub of the China problem. Taiwan was the symbol of the civil war in which the United States lost everything except Taiwan. Taiwan was an island base of 18 million people, there for the grabbing by a billion Chinese. It was an economic miracle, the United States's sixth largest trading partner, a flourishing language school, an accessible repository of art objects and archives brought out of Peking. It was the last treaty port with big possibilities. It was America's unaggressive, deserving and necessary ex-ally, and much more.[26] In Fairbank's view, even despite Taiwan's annoying shortcomings, America cannot pull out, even if it should mean losing China again. Fairbank believes that the Taiwan problem will be solved in time, and Reagan's visit to China in 1984 would seem to have vindicated this view to a considerable degree. However, as far as China is concerned, time must also help to settle the Mongolian and Vietnam questions, both, moreover, involving independent, sovereign countries, rather than a province that was torn by force from the mainland.

It is certain that relations between the Soviet Union and China will improve, however slowly, especially as the Soviet Union has not set itself the task ascribed to it by Harold Hinton – either at this time or even in recent years – namely to turn China into a semi-satellite of Moscow. Nothing is being said today even of renewing the allies' relations that existed between the Soviet Union and China in the 1950s. As for normal or more friendly relations, along the lines, say, of the friendship that has long existed between the Soviet Union and India, they would be perfectly possible, and a start should be made in that direction by stepping up Sino-Soviet economic relations.

To be sure, the Soviet Union today possesses less economic potential than the United States, and it has not overcome its technological backwardness in relation to many Western countries. Nevertheless, there is much room for wide and deep economic co-operation between the Soviet Union and China which would benefit both countries. China's needs are too great for her to count solely on co-operation with the developed capitalist countries, and she should rather concentrate on developing multilateral relations with the socialist countries which share her socio-economic structure, as well as with the countries of the Third World which are closer to her own level of economic development. Only in this way can China accelerate her own economic development.

The experience of 1953–8 demonstrated the value of Sino-Soviet relations to China. Most of the enterprises that were built then with Soviet aid are still functioning today and indeed constitute an important part of the Chinese economy. It is true that, from China's point of view, not everything was a success in her relations with the Soviet Union in the 1950s. Nor was it from the Soviet point of view either. During that period, the main issue was the one-sided aid being given to China by the Soviet Union in the form of credits on terms that were advantageous to China, but it should be noted that even after the break in both economic and political relations, China paid off all her debts and interest to the Soviet Union, in strict accordance with the terms of the credit agreements.

The Soviet Union has by now accumulated a considerable store of experience of economic co-operation with the less developed countries, in addition to which its industrial power has at least quadrupled since the middle of the 1950s.

In most branches of industry, Soviet engineering and technology are less efficient than those of America or Japan. On the other hand, the machinery and vehicles that the Soviet Union produces for export are simpler to use and cheaper than similar products made by Western firms. In the 1960s and 1970s, the Soviet Union built enterprises neither in China nor in the capitalist countries, but during this time it did help to build and equip with its own machinery hundreds of large and medium enterprises in various Third World countries. Some of these enterprises are working more efficiently than similar ones established in the Third World by developed capitalist countries. The Soviet Union has considerable experience in building metallurgical plants, power stations and some kinds of engineering factories in the Third World. Certain machines and equipment made in the Soviet Union are readily imported by capitalist countries. Even in the most advanced country, there are always factories which have jobs requiring simpler, cheaper machinery, rather than expensive automatic or computer-controlled equipment.

It is well known that since the late 1920s the Soviet Union has given priority to the development of heavy industry, and the capacity of this industry is now very great, even if the quality of the machines and equipment it turns out is not as high as that of the United States, West Germany, or Japan. Nevertheless, Soviet engineering plants of today have considerable unused capacity, a fact that is demonstrated by the patterns of shiftwork and employment of equipment. At the present time, but for the fact that it lacks marketing experience, the Soviet Union could now, much to its own economic benefit, be producing substantial numbers of machines and equipment for export. Apart from Eastern Europe, Cuba, Vietnam and India, the Soviet Union sells machinery to quite a few countries, chiefly in Asia and Africa, countries which do not have sufficient resources to buy large consignments.

In this respect, China is a potentially important sales market for the Soviet mechanical engineering and instrument-making industries. The purchase of such Soviet equipment could also be advantageous and important for China. It is not merely that using Soviet technology would be a good intermediate step towards mastering more complex technology. China is too large to restrict itself to buying goods and technology only from the West. There are many projects that either already exist, or are in the building or planning stage, where Soviet engineering and technology could be used effectively. It is hardly surprising that after 25 years of using the Soviet equipment that was installed in the huge port of Dairen in the 1950s, there is now a demand that it should be replaced by machinery from Japan or Sweden. The Soviet Union itself has also approached Japan for help in the supply of equipment for a number of ports in the Far East. China, however, has neither the possibility nor the need to supply all its factories with the latest Western machinery. Not so long ago, the United Nations Organization on Industrial Development (UNIDO) held an international symposium in Tbilisi on 'Contemporary Technology and Development'. Scientific and government representatives from 23 countries took part. The main object of the symposium was to study and draw conclusions on the influence of the scientific and technical revolution on the developing countries of the Third World. It was remarked that all the latest achievements, for example in biotechnology, micro-processors, new materials and new sources of energy, should not be the monopoly and privilege of the industrially advanced countries, but should also serve the aim of developing the recently independent countries. It was also remarked, however, that taking into account real conditions as they are, the develop-ing countries cannot orientate themselves towards using only the latest achievements of science and technology, but must exploit the whole gamut of existing technical resources and processes, the latest as well as the traditional, emerging out of the concrete conditions of the country concerned.[27]

This conclusion can be fully applied to the case of China. At the moment, China has about 240 million people over the age of twelve who can neither read nor write, and probably there are many more young and middle-aged people who have had only the most basic primary education. It will take decades to correct this situation. Meanwhile, all the Chinese have to be given work that they are capable of doing.

In order to deal with the employment problem, China embarked in the 1970s on a programme of maximum develop-ment of small, low-capital, labour-intensive industries, and as a result today has far more small factories than the Soviet Union. In 1978 China had 350,000 small industries employing 80 per cent of the entire industrial labour force of the country.[28] In 1980 the number rose to 377,300, and by 1982 the number had risen again to 388,600. Large industries numbered 1,600 in 1982 and there were 3,800 medium-sized industries.[29] In seeking to avoid the mistakes of the Great Leap Forward, the Chinese authorities have created numerous both medium and small coal-mines, and a large number of small hydro-electric power stations, with a capacity which increased in the period from 1978 to 1983 from 5.3 million kilowatts to 8.5 million kilowatts. Small power stations today produce half the electricity needed in the country-side. This is a rational course, although naturally the technical level of small industry is lower than that of large industry. During the modernization of factories which were built in the 1950s, the Chinese authorities sold off in provincial markets the equipment and machinery that it would be unwise to use in the modern factories of Shanghai or Harbin, but which can still be of great use in small industries and workshops. When factories in the heavy industrial centres of the Soviet Union are being reconstructed, a substantial part of the machinery is not melted down, but instead it is hived off to smaller factories with a lower level of technical requirement. The Soviet Union could take part in such markets in China and sell both the products of its modern engineering works and equipment that had become obsolete for Soviet factories of the 1980s, but that was still in good condition and could run for many more years under the sort of conditions that prevail in the Chinese provinces. It could be sold at very low prices, and the trade would be good for both countries, as it would help the Soviet Union to renew its machine stock and stimulate technical progress at the same time. In addition, the Soviet Union could give China many kinds of tried and tested documentation and drawings, virtually free, as was done in the 1950s. Meanwhile, the West gains considerably from the sale of licences, technical drawings and so on. The payment of Soviet advisers and specialists would be incomparably cheaper for China than what it is paying to specialists from the United States and Japan.

The Soviet Union cannot offer China the sort of large credits that the West can offer, but the Soviet financial system, not being based on private ownership, can therefore offer credit on longer terms and at more moderate rates of interest. In view of the resources to be found in its eastern regions, the Soviet Union could also sell China some of the raw materials that are in extremely short supply in China's more developed northern provinces.

At present, the volume of Sino-Soviet trade is insignificant. For the two years 1970–1 the total value of Soviet exports to China amounted to 170 million roubles, while China's exports to the Soviet Union were worth 179 million roubles. Ten years later, in 1980–1, Soviet exports to China amounted to 252 million roubles, and China's to the Soviet Union 241 million roubles.[30] It is edifying to compare these figures with those of Soviet trade with India. In 1970–1, Soviet exports to India amounted to 255 million roubles, while imports from India were worth 568 million roubles. Ten years later, in 1980–1, Soviet exports to India had risen to 1.925 billion roubles, and imports from India to 2.212 billion roubles.

Even if trade between the Soviet Union and China were to grow in the coming years to the present level of Soviet trade with India, it would increase tenfold, and China not only has a much bigger population than India, it also has better means of communication with the Soviet Union. As in the 1950s, China would be able to organize the mass training of its cadres in the Soviet Union, which would be substantially cheaper than putting them through training in the West.

What else can China and the Soviet Union give each other within the framework of economic co-operation? First of all, it must be said that a reduction of the military confrontation would of itself remove a large burden from the Soviet economy. China would also benefit, but the main relief would be felt by the Soviet Union, for it is invariably the more developed side that loses most in a military confrontation: nobody would dispute that the war in Vietnam cost the United States dozens of times more than it cost North Vietnam.

On the other hand, the purely economic aspects of normalizing Sino-Soviet relations should not be ignored. Given that the disproportionate Soviet concentration on heavy industry has caused light industry to fall seriously behind, there is an extreme shortage of very many consumer goods, while consumers' purchasing power considerably exceeds the supply of high-quality goods. While continuing to develop its own light industry, the Soviet Union could, with benefit to itself, offer China a substantial slice of its domestic market for a range of goods, such as textiles, stationery, craftwork, bristles, bamboo products, fruit, and raw silk, all goods which China can export, and which it would be easier to sell on the poorly supplied, but centrally controlled Soviet market, than on the domestic markets of the industrialized West.

Up to now, the Soviet Union has shown no interest in the idea of forming joint stock companies on Chinese territory. There may, however, be considerable interest in the Soviet Union in the possibility of using Chinese manual labour on large building projects in the Far East and Siberia, where there is an acute shortage of labour. Chinese workers could also be taken on under contract in many of the industrial enterprises in the region. At the moment, tens of thousands of Vietnamese are working in the Soviet Union under an arrangement that satisfies the Soviet Union, Vietnam and the Vietnamese workers alike.

We have been discussing economic relations, but there is much more that can be done by mean of cultural, scientific and sports links, and by the exchange of tourists between the Soviet Union and China. Certainly, the widening of economic and cultural links requires an improvement in the political climate, but, similarly, mutual exchange can itself enhance the political climate, and it should not take many decades to effect such improvements.

Conclusion

In the introduction to his book *The Dragon and the Bear*, written in 1980 or 1981, Philip Short asserts that the 1980s would be critical for the future of the West. The decisions taken in Washington and the other NATO capitals, and in Peking and Moscow during this decade, will either lay the basis for a triangular understanding that will permit a more stable peace to be established than ever before, or they will launch the slide towards war such as occurred in the 1930s. In this context, he continues, what happens in China, what kind of country it becomes, and what happens in the Soviet Union after the death of Brezhnev, will affect everyone's life. From the West's point of view, Short goes on, the key indicator of internal change in China and the Soviet Union is how far they can match the West's conception of democracy and how they deal with dissent, how far their values differ from the West's, and how much they coincide. But to avoid a one-sided, superficial picture of the likely evolution of Sino-Soviet society, this should all be put into the perspective of how one and a quarter billion people live and think.[1]

Half of the decade has already elapsed since Short wrote his book, but China, the United States and the Soviet Union are still a long way from establishing the 'basis of a triangular understanding', and there is not much hope of it coming into being before the end of the decade. It would be good if the elements of such an understanding could be found by the year 2000. It is hard to agree with Short's prescription, that the criteria for the triangular understanding depend on how closely the Soviet Union and China approximate to what Washington and the NATO powers regard as their own values. There is no denying that both China and the Soviet Union need democratization and a completely different attitude to dissidence from that which now exists, but equally they have their own values, and these do not coincide with those of the capitalist West, nor are they prepared to repudiate them, neither in the 1980s nor the 1990s. This difference in national values, however, should not prevent peaceful coexistence and peaceful co-operation, whether within the framework of a USA–USSR–China triangle, or within a wider framework, including Western Europe, Japan, India, Asia, Africa and Latin America. The three countries which form the subject of this book, however, can make a decisive contribution to the realization of this prospect, the alternative to which could be the destruction of mankind.

China and the United States accuse the Soviet Union of 'hegemonism', the Soviet Union accuses the United States and China of 'hegemonism', and both accusations have a grain of truth. It is a natural desire of the superpowers to try to increase their influence among other countries, many of which as a consequence try to unite and co-operate as a defence against one or other superpower. Everything depends on the means that are employed in forming these alliances and exerting this influence.

What is certain is that China will never again become the sort of military and political ally of the Soviet Union that she was in the 1950s. But it is equally certain that she will not become America's military and political ally either, something which some influential American politicians have reckoned on. China will not become the junior partner in any military and political alliance, but will defend the independence which she has won with such effort. From this position China, as she grows in economic, political and military power, can become a stabilizing influence in world politics. If, however, China does not overcome her own backwardness, and if convulsions like the Cultural Revolution should recur, then China can also become a powerfully destabilizing force in world politics. It appears that China's new leaders are wise enough to use their growing influence to reduce rather than increase international tension, and to define the 'Chinese road' to socialism, and to avoid the mistakes of both the Soviet and recent Chinese past. The Chinese people will be the first to benefit from this.

Notes

Notes to Chapter 1 - The USSR and China

1 *Pravda*, 26 August 1919. This declaration was first made at a meeting in Moscow on 25 August 1919 in the presence of Chinese who had taken part in the Russian revolution.

2 M. I. Sladkovskii, *Istoriia torgovo-ekonomicheskikh otnoshenii SSSR s Kitaem, 1917–1974 gg.* (*The history of Sino-Soviet trade and economic relations, 1917–1974*), Moscow, 1977, pp. 31–7.

3 Sun Yat-sen, *Izbrannye proizvedeniia* (*Selected Works*), Moscow, 1964, pp. 556-7.

4 Otto Braun, *Kitaiskie zapiski (1932–39)* (*Chinese Notes (1932–39)*), Moscow, 1974; Van Min (Wang Meng), *Polveka KPK i predatelstvo Mao Tze-duna* (*Half a century of the CCP and the treachery of Mao Zedong*), Moscow, 1975; Zhang Guodao, *My reminiscences* (in Chinese), Hong Kong, 1966-71; *History of the modern Chinese revolution* (in Chinese), Peking, 1958; *Ocherki istorii Kitaia v noveishee vremia* (*The modern history of China*), Moscow, 1959.

5 A. S. Titov, *Iz istorii borby i raskola v rukovodstve KPK* (*The struggle and split in the leadership of the CCP*), Moscow, 1979; F. Burlatskii, *Mao Tzedun i ego nasledniki* (*Mao Zedong and his heirs*), Moscow, 1979.

6 V. I. Chuikov, 'Missiia v Kitae (Mission in China)' in *Novyi Mir*, 1980, nos. 11 and 12; *Na kitaiskoi zemle: vospominaniia sovetskikh dobrovoltsev, 1925–45* (*On the land of China: reminiscences of Soviet volunteers, 1925–45*), Moscow, 1977.

7 P. P. Vladimirov, *Osobyi raion Kitaia, 1942–45* (*A Chinese special zone, 1942–45*), Moscow, 1973.

8 *Istoriia sovremennoi kitaiskoi revoliutsii* (*The history of the modern Chinese revolution*) (transl. from Chinese), Moscow, 1959, pp. 488, 499.

9 *Materialy VIII-go Vsekitaiskogo s'ezda KPK* (*Materials of the VIII All-China Congress of the CCP*), Moscow, 1956, p. 198.

10 Emi Xiao, *Mao Tzedun. Chzhu De* (*Mao Zedong. Zhou De*), Moscow, 1939, pp. 46–7.

11 David Floyd, 'Mao against Khrushchev', in *Stalin against Mao*, London, 1964.

12 *Pravda*, 18 February 1950.

13 *Pravda*, 9 February 1953.

14 *Ocherki istorii Kitaia v noveishee vremia* (*The modern history of China*), Moscow, 1959, p. 598.

15 Ibid. p. 600.

16 Ibid. pp. 603-4.

17 *Leninskaia politika SSSR v otnoshenii Kitaiia* (*Soviet Leninist policy towards China*), Moscow, 1968, p. 166.

18 O. B. Borisov and B. T. Koloskov, *Sovetsko-kitaiskie otnosheniia* (*Soviet-Chinese relations*), Moscow, 1977.

19 *Leninskaia politika SSSR v otnoshenii Kitaiia*, p. 203. A more detailed account of Soviet–Chinese economic collaboration can be found in M. I. Sladkovskii, *Istoriia*; *Bolshaia sovetskaia entsiklopediia* (*Great Soviet Encyclopaedia*), 2nd edition (*BSE* hereafter).

20 *Ocherki istorii Kitaia*, and *BSE*, 2nd edition.

21 Liu Shaoqi, *About the Party* (in English), Peking, 1951.

22 *Materialy VIII s'ezda*, p. 98.

23 *Pravda*, 22 September 1963.

24 *People's Daily*, 10 December 1960.

25 *Leninskaia politika*, p. 197.

26 *Izvestiia*, 4 August 1963.

27 See for example *Russkaia Mysl* (*Russian Thought*), 23 February 1978, p. 7.

28 *People's Daily*, 8 March 1963.

29 Karl Grobe, *Chinas Weg nach Westen* (*China's path to the West*), Frankfurt-on-Main, 1980, p. 15.

30 Edgar Snow, *The Long Revolution: China between tradition and the future* (German translation), Stuttgart, 1973, p. 234.

31 According to the Chinese account, even before 2 March Soviet border guards had chased a number of fishermen off Damansky Island, killing and wounding some of them.

32 *Pravda*, 11 September 1969.

33 *People's Daily*, 7–8 October 1969.

34 Andrei Amalrik, *SSSR i Zapad v odnoi lodke* (*The USSR and the West Are in the Same Boat*), London, 1958, pp. 55–7.

35 *Pismo vozhdiam Sovetskogo Soiuza* (*A Letter to the Soviet Leaders*). Solzhenitsyn's document was circulated in 1974 both as a small pamphlet, published in the West, and in typed copies.

36 From *Chto zhdet Sovetskii Soiuz* (*What awaits the Soviet Union*), compiled in *samizdat* by M. Agurskii, 1974, p. 6.
37 Ibid. p. 106.
38 *Der Spiegel*, 1974, no. 37, p. 105.
39 *Vneshniaia torgovlia SSSR v 1975g. Statisticheskii sbornik* (*Soviet foreign trade in 1975. Statistical handbook*), Moscow, 1976, pp. 239–41.
40 *Pravda*, 28 December 1975.
41 *People's Daily*, 23 August 1977.
42 *Die Welt*, 27 September 1977.
43 *Istoriia mezhdunarodnykh otnoshenii na Dalnem Vostoke* (*History of international relations in the Far East*), Khabarovsk, 1978, p. 439.
44 *Pravda*, 21 March 1978.
45 *Pravda*, 5 April 1979.
46 *People's Daily*, 25 December 1978.

Notes to Chapter 2 – The USA and China

1 Alan Nevins and Henry Steele Commager, *A history of the United States* (in Russian), New York, 1961, pp. 412–13.
2 C. Crow, *400 Million Customers*, New York, 1937.
3 Herbert Hoover, *Memoirs: the Cabinet and the Presidency, 1920–33*, New York, 1952, p. 369.
4 S. R. Smith, *The Manchurian Crisis, 1931–32*, New York, 1948, pp. 149–50. The Washington Agreement was signed by nine powers who resolved in 1921–2 to establish 'equal opportunities' for themselves in China, at the same time restricting Japan's ambitions.
5 *Statistical Abstract of the United States*, Washington, 1948.
6 F. R. Dulles, *China and America*, Princeton, 1946, p. 209.
7 *Pravda*, 3 August 1940.
8 *Pravda*, 9 November 1940.
9 Joseph Stilwell, *The Stilwell Papers*, New York, 1948, p. 190.
10 Department of State, *Foreign Relations of the United States. The Conference at Malta and Yalta, 1945*, Washington, 1955, p. 544.
11 *Vneshniaia politika Sovetskogo Soiuza v period Velikoi Otechestvennoi voiny* (*Soviet foreign policy during the Great Fatherland War*), Moscow, 1947, vol. 3, p. iii.
12 B. Cochran, *Harry Truman and the Crisis Presidency*, New York, 1973, p. 173.
13 *Mezhdunarodnye otnosheniia na Dalnem Vostoke* (*International relations in the Far East*), Moscow, 1956, pp. 638–9.

14 G. Yefimov, *Ocherki novoi i noveishei istorii Kitaia* (*The modern and recent history of China*), Moscow, 1951, p. 389.

15 *Ocherki istorii Kitaia v noveishee vremia* (*The recent history of China*), Moscow, 1959, pp. 385–6.

16 *The Memoirs of Harry S. Truman*, vol. 1, *Years of Decisions*, 1955, p. 310.

17 Ibid. vol. 2. *Years of Trial and Hope, 1946–53*, p. 66.

18 *Jiefang Zhibao* (*Liberation Daily*), 12 October 1945.

19 *United States Relations with China, with Special Reference to the Period 1944-49.* Department of State Publication 3573, Washington, 1949.

20 *New York Times*, 26 June 1948.

21 *Congressional Record*, 28 July 1948, p. 4908.

22 *United States Relations with China*, pp. 1053–4.

23 Ibid. pp. xv-xvi.

24 B. I. Bukharov, *Politika SShA v otnoshenii KNR (1949–1953)* (*US policy towards the Chinese People's Republic (1949–54)*), Moscow, 1958, p. 12.

25 *Sovremennaia vneshniaia politika SSha* (*Contemporary US Foreign Policy*), vol. 2, Moscow, 1984, p. 309.

26 Nevins and Commager, *A history of the United States*, p. 572.

27 J. C. Thompson, P. W. Stanley and J. C. Perry, *Sentimental Imperialists. The American Experience in East Asia*, New York, 1981, pp. 234, 256.

28 'China and U.S. Foreign Policy', Washington, *Congressional Quarterly*, 1971, pp. 21–2.

29 *Sovremennaia vneshniaia politika SSha*, vol. 2, p. 313.

30 *American Foreign Policy, 1950–5. Basic Documents*, Department of State Publication 6446, Washington, 1957, vol. 2, pp. 2484–5.

31 M.S. Kapitsa, *KNR. Tri desiatiletiia – tri politika* (*The CPR. Three decades, three policies*), Moscow, 1979, p. 205.

32 *People's Daily*, 4 September 1958.

33 A. G. Budanov, *Amerikanskaia agressiia vo Vietname* (*American aggression in Vietnam*), Moscow, 1967, p. 5.

34 *Nezavimost i mir vietnamskomu narodu* (*Independence and peace for the people of Vietnam*), Hanoi, 1967, p. 13.

35 *Keesing's Contemporary Archives, 1961–62*, p. 17925.

36 *The Pentagon Papers*, as published by the *New York Times*, New York, 1971, p. 45.

37 *Department of State Bulletin*, 31 July 1961, p. 179.

38 *China and the Great Powers*, New York, 1974, p. 51.

39 Ye. P. Bazhanov, *Dvizhushchie sily politiki SShA v otnoshenii Kitaia* (*The motive forces of US policy on China*), Moscow, 1982, p. 91.

40 M. S. Kapitsa, *KNR*, p. 277.
41 *US policy with respect to Mainland China,* Hearings before the Committee on Foreign Relations, US Senate, 89th Congress, Washington, 1966, pp. 45–78.
42 *Mainland China in the World Economy.* Report of the Joint Economic Committee, Washington, 1967, pp. 7–8.
43 Richard Nixon, 'Asia after Vietnam', in *Foreign Affairs,* October, 1967, pp.119–23.
44 *The New Republic,* 1 May 1971.
45 B. V. Vorontsov, *Kitai i SShA: 60-70-e gody (China and the USA: the 60s and 70s),* Moscow, 1979, p. 35.
46 *Hearings before the Sub-committee on Asian and Pacific Affairs of the Committee on Foreign Affairs,* House of Representatives, 91st Congress, 2nd Session, Washington, 1970, pp. 285–7.
47 O. Borisov and M. Ilyin, 'Maoistskaia kulturnaia revoliutsiia' (The Maoist cultural revolution), *Voprosy Istorii,* 1973, no. 12, pp. 78–100.
48 Henry Kissinger, *The White House Years,* Boston, 1979, p. 701.
49 Edgar Snow, *The Long Revolution,* New York, 1972, pp. 171–2.
50 *Washington Post,* 15 April 1971.
51 *New York Times,* 16 July 1971.
52 Ibid. 12 January 1972.
53 Stanislaw Pawliak, *Politika SShA po otnosheniiu k Kitaiu (US policy towards China)* (transl. from Polish), Moscow, 1976, p. 283.
54 *BSE. Ezhegodnik (BSE. Yearbook),* Moscow, 1971, p. 434.
55 V. V. Kuzmin, *Kitai v strategii amerikanskogo imperializma (China in the strategy of American imperialism),* Moscow, 1978, p. 172.
56 *Time,* 8 November 1971, p. 16.
57 *Newsweek,* 14 February 1972, p. 46.
58 *Direction of Trade,* 1976, no. 11, pp. 3–4; ibid. 1977, no. 6, pp. 3–4.
59 Department of State press release, 24 December 1975.
60 *New York Times,* 5 September 1977.
61 *Newsweek,* 12 September 1977.
62 *The China Business,* September–October 1978, p. 27.
63 George Kennan, *Cloud of Danger,* Boston, 1977, cited in the journal *SShA. Ekonomika. Politika. Ideologiia (The USA. Economy. Politics. Ideology),* Moscow, 1979, no. 10, p. 85.
64 *Newsweek,* 12 September 1977, p. 27.
65 Allen S. Whiting and Robert F. Dernberger, *China's Future. Foreign Policy and Economic Development in the Post-Mao Era,* New York, 1977, pp. 2–3.
66 *People's Daily,* 23 August 1977.

67 *Washington Post*, 5 December 1978.
68 *Foreign Affairs*, January 1979, p. 599.
69 *New York Times*, 26 May 1978.
70 Ibid. 28 May 1978.
71 Ibid. 26 May 1978.
72 Teo Sommer, *Die chinesische Karte* (*The China Card*), Munich, Zurich, 1979.
73 *Washington Post*, 14 March 1979.
74 *Der Spiegel*, 25 December 1978, p. 80.
75 *Mezhdunarodnaia Zhizn* (*International Life*), 1980, no. 3, p. 34.
76 *Problemy Dalnego Vostoka* (*Problems of the Far East*), 1979, no. 1, p. 28.
77 *Time*, 5 February 1979.
78 *Sovremennaia vneshniaia politika SShA* (*Contemporary US foreign policy*), vol. 2, Moscow, 1984, p. 331.
79 *New York Post*, 1 February 1979.
80 *Wall Street Journal*, 8 March 1979.
81 *People's Daily*, 28 August 1979.
82 *Washington Post*, 21 January 1980.
83 *New York Times*, 9 January 1980.
84 Ibid. 11 January 1980.
85 *Washington Post*, 5 January 1980.
86 Report of the China News Agency, 10 July 1980.
87 *Christian Science Monitor*, 4 June 1980.
88 *New York Times*, 27 March 1980.
89 Ibid. 5 November 1980.
90 Ibid. 29 July 1981.

Notes to Chapter 3 – Changes in the Strategic Triangle

1 *Mezhdunarodnaia Zhizn* (*International Life*), 1984, no. 5, p. 39.
2 Ibid. pp. 39–40.
3 Philip Short, *The Dragon and the Bear*, London, 1982, pp. 488–9.
4 *Commentary*, October 1978, p. 68.
5 *Ming-bao* (*Daily Information*), Hong Kong, 25 August 1981.
6 *Kommunist*, 1978, no. 5, pp. 90–1.
7 *BSE Yearbook*, Moscow, 1983, pp. 283–4.
8 *The United States – The Soviet Union – China: the Big Triangle.* Washington, 1976, p. 121.
9 *Washington Post*, 2 December 1976.
10 Allen Whiting, *The United States – China Relations: the Process of Normalization,* Washington, 1976, p. 154.

11 *SShA. Politika. Ekonomika. Ideologiia*, 1984, no. 1, p. 74.

12 John F. Copper, *China's Global Role*, Hoover Institution, Stanford, California, 1980, pp. 99, 132.

13 *International Herald Tribune*, 23 November 1982, p. 4.

14 David Lampton, 'Misreading China', *Foreign Policy*, no. 45, Winter 1981–2, pp. 103–14.

15 In *China Policy for the Next Decade*, Washington, 1983.

16 *Mezhdunarodnaia Zhizn*, 1984, no. 3, p. 75.

17 *Newsweek*, 30 April 1984, pp. 32–3.

18 *SShA. Politika, Ekonomika, Ideologiia*, 1984, no. 8, p. 21.

19 *Washington Post*, 8 May 1984.

20 *US News and World Report*, 7 May 1984.

21 *Pravda*, 20 May 1982.

22 *Washington Post*, 3 September 1982.

23 *Izvestiia*, 20 April 1983.

24 *Pravda*, 26 December 1982.

25 *Pravda*, 22 March 1983.

26 *Pravda*, 18 July 1983.

27 *Pravda*, 5 September 1983.

28 *Obozrenie (Survey)*, an analytical journal published by the Paris Russian-language newspaper *Russkaia Mysl (Russian Thought)*, no. 3, February 1983, p. 5.

29 *Izvestiia*, 30 May 1984.

30 O. Petrov, 'Vrazhdebnaia kampaniia' (Hostile campaign), in *Pravda*, 19 July 1984.

31 *Mezhdunarodnaia Zhizn*, 1984, no. 11, p. 37.

32 *Problemy Dalnego Vostoka (Problems of the Far East)*, Moscow, 1982, no. 2, pp. 16–17.

33 *Sintaksis*, Paris, 1982, no. 10, p. 48.

34 Ibid. pp. 63–4.

35 *Der Spiegel*, 1983, no. 52, pp. 93–7.

36 *Vedomosti Verkhovnogo Soveta SSSR (USSR Supreme Soviet Gazette)*, no. 34, 30 August 1960.

37 *BSE*, 1st edn., vol. 1, 1929, pp. 756–7.

38 A. Prokhorov, *K voprosy o sovetsko-kitaiskoi granitse (The question of the Sino-Soviet border)*, Moscow, 1975, pp. 118-19.

39 Ibid. pp. 131–3.

40 See G. S. Kara-Murza, *Taipiny (The Taipings)*, Moscow, 1957.

41 A. Prokhorov, *K voprosu*, p. 113; see also *Russkii Arkhiv*, 1914, book 10, p. 177.

42 M. I. Sladkovskii, *Kitai. Osnovnye problemy istorii, ekonomiki, ideologii (China. Fundamental problems of history, economy, ideology)*, Moscow, 1978, p. 204.

43 *Mezhdunarodnaia Zhizn*, 1981, no. 10, p. 81.
44 Marx and Engels, *Sochineniia* (*Works*), 2nd edition, vol. 12, p. 638.
45 A. Prokhorov, *K voprosu*, p. 31.
46 V. A. Aleksandrov, *Rossiia na dalnevostochnykh rubezhakh* (*On Russia's Far Eastern borders*), Moscow, 1969, pp. 21–34.
47 *BSE*, 3rd edition, vol. 12, Moscow, 1973, pp. 209–10.
48 Ibid. 1st edition, Moscow, 1938, vol. 38, pp. 79–80.
49 Ibid. p. 80.

Notes to Chapter 4 – The USSR, the USA and China

1 *Problemy Dalnego Vostoka*, 1982, no. 4, p. 31.
2 *Ekonomicheskaia Gazeta* (*Economic Gazette*), 1983, no. 31, p. 21.
3 *Business America*, 11 August 1980.
4 *International Herald Tribune*, 24 November 1982, p. 7.
5 *Beyond Normalization*, Report of the UNA–USA National Policy Panel to study USA–China Relations, New York, 1979, p. 20.
6 *BSE Yearbook*, Moscow, 1984, p. 283.
7 *Jingji yanjiu* (*Economic Reearch*), No 6; *People's Daily*, 17 March 1980.
8 *People's Daily*, 10 January 1981.
9 *Struktura ekonomiki Kitaia* (*China's economic structure*) (an abridged translation from Chinese), Moscow, 1984, p. 295.
10 *People's Daily*, 5 and 6 September 1980.
11 *People's Daily*, 21 January 1980.
12 *BSE Yearbook*, 1984, p. 282.
13 Ibid. 1982, p. 290.
14 *People's Daily*, 5 December 1982.
15 *People's Daily*, 30 April 1984.
16 *Der Spiegel*, 1983, no. 13, pp. 168–171.
17 *Newsweek*, 14 March 1983.
18 *People's Daily*, 2 June 1984.
19 *People's Daily*, 30 April 1984; *Beijing Review*, 1982, no. 14, p. 21; *China Daily*, 8 February and 26 March 1984; *Guoji maoyi* (*International Trade*), 1983, no. 7.
20 *Pravda*, 21 July 1984.
21 *Shijie jingji* (*World Economy*); *Jingji wenti tansuo* (*Enquiry into Economic Questions*).
22 *Problemy Dalnego Vostoka*, 1984, no. 4, p. 40.
23 *People's Daily*, 6 May 1983.

24 *Problems of Communism*, New York, 1980, May–June, p. 73.

25 Ibid. 1983, March–April, pp. 20–28.

26 John K. Fairbank, *Chinabound: a Fifty-Year Memoir*, New York, 1982, pp. 409, 434.

27 *Pravda*, 3 May 1983.

28 *People's Daily*, 7 December 1979; *Hongji* (*Red Flag*), 1980, no. 11, p. 22.

29 *Statisticheskii ezhegodnik Kitaia* (*Chinese Statistical Yearbook for 1983*), Peking, 1983, pp. 213, 220.

30 All data on foreign trade are taken from the statistical handbooks, *Vneshniaia torgovlia SSSR* (*Soviet foreign trade*), published annually by the USSR Ministry of Foreign Trade, Moscow, Finance and Statistics Publishing House.

Note to Conclusion

31 Philip Short, *The Dragon and the Bear*, London, 1982, pp. 13-14.

Index

As in the text, Chinese names are given here in Pinyin with appropriate cross-references.

Index by Joyce Kerr